Hearing Ourselves Think

SOCIAL AND COGNITIVE STUDIES IN WRITING AND LITERACY
Linda Flower, Series Editor

Oxford University Press and
The Center for the Study of Writing
at Berkeley and Carnegie Mellon

A series devoted to books that bridge research, theory, and practice, exploring social and cognitive processes in writing and expanding our knowledge of literacy as an active construction process—as students move from high school to college and the community.

The Center for the Study of Writing (CSW), with the support of the Office of Educational Research and Improvement, conducts research on the development of writers and on writing and literacy as these are taught and learned in the home, in elementary and secondary school, in college, in the workplace, and in the community. In conjunction with schools and teachers, CSW develops projects that link writing research to classroom practice. A list of publications is available from CSW at the University of California, Berkeley, 5513 Tolman Hall, Berkeley, CA 94720

Reading-to-Write: Exploring a Cognitive and Social Process
   Linda Flower, Victoria Stein, John Ackerman, Margaret J. Kantz,
   Kathleen McCormick, Wayne C. Peck

Hearing Ourselves Think: Cognitive Research
in the College Writing Classroom
   Edited by Ann M. Penrose, Barbara M. Sitko

Hearing Ourselves Think

Cognitive Research in the College Writing Classroom

Edited by

ANN M. PENROSE

BARBARA M. SITKO

New York   Oxford

OXFORD UNIVERSITY PRESS

1993

Oxford University Press

Oxford New York Toronto
Delhi Bombay Calcutta Madras Karachi
Kuala Lumpur Singapore Hong Kong Tokyo
Nairobi Dar es Salaam Cape Town
Melbourne Auckland Madrid

and associated companies in
Berlin Ibadan

Much of the work reported here was initially performed pursuant to
a grant from the Office of Educational Research and Improvement/
Department of Education (OERI/ED) for the Center for the Study
of Writing. However, the opinions expressed herein do not necessarily reflect the position or policy of the OERI/ED and no official
endorsement by the OERI/ED should be inferred.

Library of Congress Cataloging-in-Publication Data
Hearing ourselves think : cognitive research in the college writing
classroom / edited by Ann M. Penrose, Barbara M. Sitko.
p. cm. — (Social and cognitive studies in writing and
literacy)
Includes bibliographical references and index.
ISBN 0-19-507833-0
1. English language—Rhetoric—Study and teaching.
2. English language—Rhetoric—Research. 3. Cognition—Research.
I. Penrose, Ann M. II. Sitko, Barbara M. III. Series.
PE1404.H395 1993
808'.042'07—dc20   92-23469

9 8 7 6 5 4 3 2 1

Printed in the United States of America
on acid-free paper

Foreword

This volume marks a significant coming of age in a number of ways. It is edited and written by a group of promising young researchers, who have already received a handful of well-deserved honors and awards for their work. And, as the book will show, it is written by equally talented and dedicated teachers, who see these two commitments going hand in hand.

These writers are challenging some of the old boundaries that have separated teaching and research — boundaries that reflect not only patterns of power and status in English departments and education, but ones that reflect old assumptions and stereotypes — that theory is impractical, that research is irrelevant, and that good teaching keeps a savvy distance from both.

These writers are not only challenging the wisdom of that boundary, but arguing that it needs to be reconceived as a two-way street. That is, theory-guided, research-sensitive thinking can make us better teachers. And by the same token, the practice of observation-based theory building, situated in our teaching, can make us better researchers.

The close collaboration on the agenda that marks this book began in 1986 with the founding of the Center for the Study of Writing at University of California, Berkeley and Carnegie Mellon. Ann Penrose, and later Barbara Sitko, worked with the other authors of this volume to develop the traveling Research-For-Teaching Seminar Series at Carnegie Mellon. The designers and presenters of this series, who met with faculty from high schools, writing projects, colleges, and universities around the country, set a goal that was not always easy to meet. They wanted each seminar *to present* new research on issues, such as writing and learning, reading and writing connections, and at the same time convincingly *to demonstrate* ways research-based thinking could be woven into better teaching. If we began with the idea of research designed *for* teaching, as the work and as this book matured, the other lane of the two-way street began to widen, as classrooms became sites for inquiry by teachers and students alike.

There is nothing new about the desire to translate research into good practice. What is most exciting about this book is its attempt to blaze a new trail by which teachers and students can become more acute observers of teaching, learning, thinking, and writing.

This book also helps mark a coming of age in the field more generally of cognitive rhetoric and social/cognitive theory. Cognitive rhetoric envisions writers and readers as rhetors, social beings standing within the circle of other people, their discourse, and their culture. And at the same time it reveals them as individual agents and thinkers, engaged in personal/public acts of interpreting and constructing meaning. As part of the larger community of social/cognitive research, it is asking how these twin dimensions of meaning making co-construct not only written meaning but one another. Answering questions like these takes a boundary-crossing frame of mind that bridges traditional perspectives. SOCIAL AND COGNITIVE STUDIES IN WRITING AND LITERACY, of which this book is a part, was initiated by Oxford University Press and The Center for the Study of Writing to encourage just such bridge building. *Hearing Ourselves Think* is a model of what is possible when some exceptional younger scholars try to create portraits out of their own practice, in which teaching, research, and theory become interconnected roads to understanding.

Linda Flower

Preface

This project began at Carnegie Mellon University in 1986 with the establishment of the Center for the Study of Writing at UC–Berkeley and at Carnegie Mellon. Sponsored by the Office of Educational Research and Improvement (U.S. Department of Education), and recently renewed as The Center for the Study of Writing and Literacy, the Center is a collaborative research initiative that brings together teachers and researchers from the fields of English, rhetoric, linguistics, computer science, psychology, anthropology, and education.

The Center's dual goal has been to foster "research-sensitive practice" and "practice-sensitive research," a goal that can only be achieved through collaborative interaction between teachers and researchers. The contributors to this volume were part of an early dissemination project for the Center, the Research-for-Teaching Seminar Series at Carnegie Mellon, through which they developed and conducted seminars at local and national writing conferences, state teachers meetings, and at individual colleges and universities nationwide. They currently teach at a variety of universities across the country, where they continue to study writing and reading in new institutional settings, with varied student populations, and in the company of faculty colleagues of diverse interests and backgrounds. They have continued to develop and test their ideas and activities in these new contexts, as well as in print and at national conferences.

The topics and concerns of the seminar series reflected Carnegie Mellon's emphasis on cognitive research on reading and writing processes. In developing this collection, we asked former seminar leaders to reflect on this research from their perspective as teachers — to examine their own courses and describe the principles and practices that govern their teaching. In short, we wanted them to try to articulate the insights gained through their research experiences and to show us how these insights have influenced their writing classrooms. This occasion for reflection and articulation has been an invaluable opportunity for all of us.

Many people helped bring this project to completion. We are indebted to our Center colleagues, especially Patricia Combies, Alexander Friedlander, Margaret Kantz, and Joseph Petraglia, whose valued commentary helped shape the work presented here. We have benefited also from interaction with the many teachers and researchers in our seminar audiences; their lively response and suggestions energized the seminars and helped our ideas develop.

Our special gratitude goes to Linda Flower and John R. Hayes, who first introduced this line of inquiry and who have inspired and nurtured much of the research that followed, including that represented in this volume.

Raleigh, N.C.   A.M.P.
Pullman, Wash.   B.M.S.
August 1992

Contents

Hearing Ourselves Think

1

Introduction: Studying Cognitive Processes in the Classroom

ANN M. PENROSE AND BARBARA M. SITKO

Directions: Your task is to read the attached article on hurricanes and to write a paper on that topic. Your paper should be an informative essay, focused around the key issues or concepts that you think someone should know from the reading.

Alan is speaking aloud into a tape recorder as he reads his task directions and begins to work. He hesitates not a bit in responding to this assignment. He reads the three-page article from beginning to end, pausing for comment after each sentence or two: "ah, it seems like the key clue" . . . "underline that" . . . "key dates." Then he rereads the task directions, decides there are "two key issues here . . . the definition of a hurricane, the history," and proceeds to write his paper by stringing together the facts he'd highlighted under these two headings. Alan churns this one out easily, pausing during the writing process only to complain about the tedium of the task and the poor quality of his own text: "this is a terrible intro" . . . "this is bad" . . . "this paper is not making too much sense" . . . "this is so trivial . . . I hate this . . . nothing to it."

Across the hall, another college freshman in this writing study is stuck. Rob has read through the text twice, noting important facts on the first pass, much like Alan, and taking a second pass to decide what sub-topics he should include in his own paper. Rob's comments in this second pass reveal a pervasive concern with audience, occasionally echoing the task directions which note that he should focus on concepts "someone should know" from the source text: "hmm . . . that's important . . . someone should know that." At this point Rob is "trying to figure out how to start this and how to get people's attention as to why they should read something about hurricanes." A little later, the problem is compounded: "I'm still trying to find a transition between the opening paragraph of what I'm . . . you know . . . just trying to get the reader's attention at the moment and trying to find a transition between . . . discovery and formation."

Rob has set himself a difficult task. Rather than simply gathering facts from the source text (a predictable response to this artificial writing situation), he wants to give purpose and meaning to these bits of information. This goal leads him to ask questions of the reading: he tries to understand the connection between the two topics Alan had identified, history (how hurricanes were discovered) and definition (how they form). In an effort to explain to his readers why recent advances in hurricane tracking are important, he goes back and asks himself, *"why* do they track?" He is working hard to make sense of a poorly structured source text and a poorly defined writing task. But he is engaged and encouraged: "okay . . . we're not doing too bad . . . we're in good shape . . . I can't say we're halfway done but we're in good shape."

Listening to Rob's tape, we are engaged and encouraged as well. We are encouraged by his sensitivity to the interests and needs of his audience ("would the common average yuk reading this know what a gale-force wind would be?"), by his willingness to turn a mundane task into a worthwhile learning experience ("I just try to make it interesting for myself . . . keep my mind awake"), by his generally active and purposeful approach to this highly constrained school writing task. Rob is an active learner.

Rob's response is all the more striking when we consider the conditions under which he's writing. He and Alan are participating in a writing study that is not associated with their current writing courses and for which they will not receive a grade. Alan's mechanical response to this task is perhaps what we should expect students to do under these conditions. But unfortunately Alan's response is not unusual even in "real world" academic writing situations. Alan illustrates the passive learner stereotype that has come to represent the norm for many education critics. If we want to help students move away from this passive learner stance, we need to consider why they may adopt it in the first place.

Clearly there might be a number of reasons behind students' failure or reluctance to become actively engaged in a particular academic task or setting. If we assume the passive learner is simply unmotivated or that the task or topic or situation is not inspiring, then we will try to change these conditions. We'll work to create a more engaging writing environment, perhaps by ensuring more student-teacher or student-student interaction, by designing more purposeful writing tasks and targeting "real-world" audiences, or by helping students choose more personally important topics for inquiry.

If this passive stance is more deeply rooted, however, in basic attitudes toward learning, in a lack of self-confidence or a sense of alienation in school settings, or simply in a general lack of familiarity with academic tasks and texts—then changing the writing environment is not likely to be enough. Even in the most supportive and comfortable environments, students will not be able to adopt the active learner role if they don't know what active learners do—that is, if they haven't seen writers like Rob at work. We are continually impressed by the active, creative learning that students like Rob engage in, learning that can be observed through think-aloud protocols, through conference transcripts and process logs, and through other process tracing measures developed in recent years. We think Alan would be impressed too, and we want to give him the opportunity to observe and explore these processes himself.

Why Study Reading and Writing Processes in the Classroom?

The lessons learned through cognitive research have taken us quite far in our understanding of reading and writing processes. Examining the processes of composing has helped us recognize, for example, that students have well-developed strategies for school-sponsored writing tasks, strategies that rarely include extensive planning or revision (Emig, 1971). Research has demonstrated that when writers do attempt more difficult conceptual tasks, their control over the basic components of grammar and syntax may suffer due to limits on cognitive capacity (Flower, 1979). At the same time, their well-rehearsed writing strategies and evaluative criteria may fail them: the knowledge-telling strategies that helped students succeed at simple writing tasks do not help them cope with more complex assignments that demand knowledge transformation (Bereiter & Scardamalia, 1987). Even experienced writers sometimes frustrate their own efforts by turning helpful heuristics into counterproductive rules or requirements (Rose, 1980).

Cognitive research has helped us see the relationship between how writers think about a process and how they engage in that process, as in the striking correlation observed between writers' descriptions of the revision process (as simple editing or as "re-seeing") and the types of revisions they make (Sommers, 1980). Studies have demonstrated that writers' and readers' goals and strategies are importantly influenced by their perceptions of the rhetorical context (Flower et al., 1991; Haas & Flower, 1988). Together with other empirical approaches, cognitive research has identified a number of factors influencing the development and exercise of expertise in writing (see Hayes, 1990, for a recent review).

In short, this type of research has shown us that the way students think about writing affects the way they write and determines the ease and confidence with which they engage in reading and writing tasks. We can help students become better writers not by simply telling them what or how to write but by helping them understand how writing works. Sommers' findings on revision, for example, suggest we can help students use writing as a means for learning if we help them understand revision as "re-seeing"; to change their behavior we must broaden their perception. Rose's study of writer's block demonstrates that writers who are aware of their own strategies and are flexible in their choices are often able to circumvent writer's block by recognizing and removing self-imposed obstacles. To help "blockers" write more easily, we need to help them recognize goals or strategies that may stand in their way.

It seems self-evident that students as well as teachers and researchers should be conducting inquiry into the processes of composing. Like other researchers, students need to develop a reflective mindset that asks not what *should* writers do, but what do writers do, and what might they do? The student who asks "What should I do?" is looking to authority for answers, techniques, algorithms, but as many writing experts have observed, writing is not rule governed (cf. Young, Becker, & Pike, 1970). This important fact about writing is what makes critical awareness and reflection so essential to writers. Instead of looking to us for formulas such as the five-paragraph theme or the authoritative opening quote, we want students to observe a writer choosing an opening move and to ask why that move was chosen — what goals or circumstances led to that choice? We want them to understand that writers make choices and that these choices are motivated and constrained by a number of influences.

A writer does not choose a strategy, an example or a line of argument by formula; she chooses in response to the needs and expectations of her audience, the conventions of genre, discipline, and culture, the specific demands established by the teacher and institutional setting, and in accordance with her personal goals, needs, and history. Sensitive inquiry into the processes of composing encourages students to notice and examine these influences and gives them methods and opportunities for doing so.

This book aims to provide the groundwork for such inquiry. Our goal in this volume is to bring together the insights that cognitive process research has generated, in laboratory and classroom settings, and to describe the ways in which these findings have influenced our thinking and our teaching. Focusing on the tasks and contexts of the university, we suggest ways for students to recognize and explore the complexity of academic reading and writing. We introduce a concept of classroom research in which students become researchers: they may reflect on their writing choices in process logs, interview other students about their writing decisions, read transcripts of themselves or others thinking through a writing problem or interpreting a difficult text. In each case, they are observing what writers and readers are doing and reflecting on why. They are asking questions of the process.

The ultimate value of cognitive research lies not just in what students can discover about writing and reading through questions and reflection, but in the realization that these processes can be questioned and reflected upon, even altered. Knowledge, strategy, and critical perspective come together in the research-based classroom: in learning how others work and examining their own goals and strategies, students develop a critical perspective on learning. They learn that there are options, multiple interpretations, multiple goals — and they also discover learning strategies that can help them pursue their own goals and recognize the goals and constraints that have shaped the texts they read. The student becomes an active, critical learner, rather than a seeker/recorder of right answers. We want students to ask questions and make demands of education, not just look for answers. We want them not just to take our advice but to test it out, to see where it works and where it doesn't and what factors make the difference, to examine where it came from. As John

Dewey, Paolo Freire, Jerome Bruner, Maxine Greene, and others have persuasively argued, asking such questions is central to the process of becoming educated. The development of a critical perspective on learning is at the heart of the education process.

If, as educators, we are sincere in the claim that we want to empower students politically, socially, personally, then we must also aim to empower them cognitively. We must help them develop the powers of careful observation and critical reflection, those habits of mind that enable them to examine not only the issues and influences shaping their world but also the mechanisms through which these issues are negotiated and these influences are felt: we need to help students reflect on the essential processes of language. Before students can begin to critically examine the values and situational constraints that shape their learning and the learning of those around them, they must come to understand that values and situations do shape learning: they influence readers' interpretations, they guide writers' choices. To help students develop an understanding of the multiple constraints governing their work, we must help them understand the complex nature of writing and reading.

The goal of process research in the classroom is to help students develop the awareness they need to become active participants in their own learning. Research on learning in a variety of domains has demonstrated that this "metacognitive awareness" is a critical component of independent learning (cf. Brown, 1980; Brown, Armbruster, & Baker, 1986; Jones, Palincsar, Ogle, & Carr, 1987; Paris & Winograd, 1990). Such research suggests that students stand a better chance of becoming independent learners if they acquire knowledge of appropriate strategies and if they learn when and why to use these strategies and how to determine when they've used them effectively (Beal, 1989; Garner, 1987; Weinstein & Mayer, 1986). To become independent writers, students must be able to examine their writing goals, to recognize and invent new strategies, and to understand the conditions under which these goals and strategies may be useful. Process research activities aim to help students develop the awareness necessary for understanding and managing the special constraints of the writing and learning situations they will encounter in the future.

The classroom activities in this volume are also grounded in a second principle of learning theory, a principle familiar to teachers and well established by cognitive research in education: simply put, learning is an active, involved process (Weinstein et al., 1979; Weinstein & Mayer, 1986). Students are not passive receptors but active interpreters of knowledge (Norman, 1980). The goal of process instruction is not simply to tell students about writing and reading processes or to model processes for them, but to design activities that will let them discover processes and principles for themselves. Teachers can create environments where active learning about writing, reading, and thinking can take place. The research-based classroom provides students and teachers the opportunity to collaborate in the inquiry process.

We believe that classroom inquiry is a critical component of good teaching. In addition to the advantages it offers students, this kind of research gives us

like a science lab

important information *about* our students—the goals they set, the strategies they rely on, the contexts they perceive, the problems they run into. We need this information in order to teach well. Approaching teaching in this way puts the emphasis on the learner, on what students need to learn rather than on what teachers need to teach. We agree with other teacher-researchers that this is where the emphasis should be (cf. Graves, 1979). As educators, whether we teach writing or literature or mathematics or chemistry, we want to teach students how to learn, how to develop strategies to fit the needs of the new learning situations they will encounter, how to recognize and choose among alternatives, how to assess their own progress and recognize success—in short, how to continue their learning after they've left our classrooms.

Principles of Cognitive Process Theory

The classroom activities described in this collection develop from a central set of assumptions about the writing process and about how students learn, assumptions based on findings from recent cognitive research. The primary assumption driving this research is that writing is a goal-directed act of cognition (Flower & Hayes, 1980, 1981). That is, writing is not simply a series of actions, but a series of decisions—a thinking process. Notice that when we speak here of "writing processes," we are referring not to overt actions or stages such as outlining or editing, but to the cognitive processes of setting goals, choosing strategies that will help us work toward those goals, and applying tests to determine whether goals are met. Writers set goals according to the constraints of the writing context, and these goals direct their thinking and their decision-making as they work. In other words, writing doesn't just happen, and it's not something that happens to us (Flower & Hayes, 1980; Flower, 1981). It's something we work at and can make some decisions about.

There are three important implications of this conception of writing. First, if writing is goal directed, then the goals we set are critical, for they determine what we do when we write. A student who sets the goal to write a careful summary of a set of readings, for example, will produce a very different paper from the student who sets the goal to analyze an issue on which the authors of those readings disagree. A writer who assumes her reader knows a great deal about the topic she's writing on may set the goal to express ideas concisely so as not to waste the reader's time, whereas a writer who assumes her reader knows little will aim to explain as fully as possible, perhaps using examples, perhaps repeating an important idea in a different way. The first text will be brief; the second will be elaborated. Different writing goals lead to radically different written products.

A second implication of the cognitive process model is that much depends on the strategies writers have available to choose from in meeting their goals. In order for the above student to decide to analyze a controversial issue from her readings, she will need to know how to represent each author's view in writing and how to recognize and highlight their differences and similarities.

Without a repertoire of comparison/contrast reading and writing strategies, she will not be able to carry out this goal, and very likely will not conceive of this approach to the assignment at all. At a more practical level, compare the writer who uses the strategy of postponing editing until his text is fully shaped with the writer who routinely edits each sentence as it is produced. If both are working under timed testing conditions, the second writer's strategy may prevent him from fully developing his argument. This writer will "fail" in this writing situation, unless he has other strategies to draw on and can recognize when they are appropriate.

A third implication of the cognitive process model is that writers need ways to test whether their goals have been met. Developing writers often rely on ineffective tests. An example familiar to teachers is the "How long does this paper have to be?" test, transformed in these computer-literate days into periodic checks of word count or print preview. Beginning writers typically have few ways of evaluating the substance of their work, and often rely simply on the "sounds right" test in rereading their final drafts. In contrast, experienced writers frequently test their texts by asking others to read them. Recent writing pedagogies encourage student writers to do the same, by providing for teacher comments or peer reviews at various stages in the writing process, but writers' understanding of the purpose of such activities may vary. For example, if writers ask readers to check for spelling and grammar errors, they will receive markedly different feedback than they would if they asked for responses to the structure or coherence of the paper. Unfortunately, developing writers typically ask for the former rather than the latter type of feedback, unaware that it is possible to request, and use, more rhetorically useful responses.

Cognitive process research explores these three key components, the goals writers set in various writing situations, the strategies they use, and the tests they apply. Recent research and theory have also explored the contexts and motivations for writing decisions, as well as the consequences of these choices (cf. Applebee, 1984; Langer & Applebee, 1987; Nelson & Hayes, 1988; Sitko & Flower, in press). Process research in the classroom offers an opportunity for students to explore these processes firsthand, and to examine their contexts and consequences.

Issues for Classroom Research

As researchers, we have learned a great deal from our observations of students writing, reading, and learning. Through think-aloud protocol transcripts, we've witnessed their frustrations as they struggle for coherence in their drafts or try to figure out what a vaguely worded assignment requires of them. We've heard students stumble when reading, missing central points or controversies because they are driven by a fact-finding goal; we've seen the spark of insight when a reader stops to reflect on the purposes and motivations behind the text, when he pauses to consider the conditions under which the author wrote, the pressures she was responding to. In process logs and conference transcripts we've heard apathy and resentment in response to ill-conceived or purposeless assignments, and we've seen the enthusiasm generated by reader feedback or the prospect of presenting ideas to fellow students. We've read in students' process logs reports of failure and procrastination, but we've also witnessed the excitement of a new idea or a favorable response, the satisfaction of finally hitting on the logic of the whole.

As teachers, we've begun to turn our writing courses into research-based classrooms. As the chapters in this collection will demonstrate, many process research methodologies are easily adapted for the classroom, where students can use them to study their own and others' writing, reading, and thinking processes. Through process logs and think-aloud protocols, students are able to "listen in" on their own reading and writing processes, and to see how other writers handle similar academic tasks and choices. Transcripts of writing conferences and collaborative work sessions provide a means for examining the interactions of writers and readers. As students listen to each other's plans and reflect on each other's choices, they begin to discover basic principles for themselves—they find that changing a goal changes the product, that our comprehension of texts is shaped by our background knowledge and our purpose in reading, that different readers may interpret the same text or assignment differently. And these discoveries give rise to lively discussions of what writers and readers do and of what writing and reading can do for us.

In this volume, we've brought together the best of what we've read and tried and imagined. In each chapter, we begin by highlighting what we've discovered in our own research and from reading and discussing the work of others—at conferences and workshops, in journals, in our classrooms and hallways. Then we illustrate these findings and their implications with examples from real students, some from our writing studies, some from our classrooms. Lastly, we describe how we see these principles operating in the classroom. We talk about what we've tried and what might be tried as we work toward the goal of developing active, critical writers and readers.

In **PART I, "Interpreting Reading and Writing Tasks,"** the role of task interpretation is explored in a variety of academic tasks, from reading for comprehension to writing reports to developing arguments. The authors in this section examine student responses to these common tasks, discuss factors that may influence those interpretations, and suggest ways to help students expand their notions to include more challenging and purposeful interpretations. **Christina Haas** (Chapter 2) examines how readers' sensitivity to rhetorical context influences their reading strategies and comprehension. Recent research and theory suggest that an understanding of the rhetorical context is as critical a component in reading as it is in writing. Experienced readers frequently reflect on such factors as the writer's background and motives, the conditions under which the text was created, and the anticipated reactions of other readers (cf. Haas & Flower, 1988). Haas examines parallels between reading and writing and demonstrates ways to help students understand the rhetorical dimension of both processes.

Helping students recognize the rhetorical context of the works they read serves the dual purpose of enhancing their comprehension and of increasing their sensitivity to rhetorical constraints in their own work. In exploring the relationship between reading and authorship, **Stuart Greene** (Chapter 3) proposes a direct pedagogical link between reading and writing. He describes ways to help students engage with their reading as true authors, "mining" the texts they read for strategies that may be useful in their own writing.

Most academic tasks, from summaries to original theses, require students to draw even more directly upon the work of other writers. **Ann Penrose** (Chapter 4) examines how student writers make use of source text material in a report writing task. She demonstrates how students' interpretations of such tasks shape their reading and writing strategies and, consequently, their comprehension of the material they write about. Her chapter describes ways to help students understand that the choices they make in writing have consequences for their learning.

Lorraine Higgins (Chapter 5) further examines students' use of source texts, focusing specifically on the ways in which writers transform source materials into written arguments. Noting that most precollege writing serves a reporting or display function (Applebee, 1981; 1984), Higgins argues that students need to learn more about how writers interpret and construct arguments if they are to develop arguments of their own. She demonstrates common interpretive strategies and suggests ways to help students examine and adapt their own approaches to argument tasks.

Jennie Nelson (Chapter 6) shifts attention to an earlier stage in the writing process by examining how students locate and select sources for "research paper" projects. Whereas experienced writers have a range of purposeful strategies for finding relevant sources or supporting evidence, some novice writers report that they select source material according to its availability or the size of the books on the library shelf (Nelson & Hayes, 1988). Nelson examines contextual factors influencing students' planning and search strategies (e.g., the use of drafts or oral presentations as support activities) and discusses the effects of these factors on the goals students set. Her chapter describes ways to help students examine their own goals and their tacit assumptions about research writing.

The chapters in Part I highlight a variety of factors influencing writers' goals and strategies, including writers' sensitivity to rhetorical context, their prior experience with academic texts and tasks, the writing assignment itself, and the instruction provided in support of that assignment. Each of these influences implies a strong social dimension to writing and reading. Writers' goals and strategies are always influenced by others, sometimes indirectly as when we adhere to disciplinary conventions, assume shared values, or anticipate reader expectations, but often through more immediate or direct social interactions, with collaborators, teachers, editors, prospective readers. The social context in which writing is situated can have a powerful influence on writers' processes and products.

In **PART II, "Writing in Classroom Contexts,"** we look specifically at types of social interaction afforded in the writing classroom. Here we listen to writers in social contexts — writing collaboratively, learning to internalize their audience, using feedback from readers to revise, working one-on-one in the student-teacher conference. The authors in this section discuss features of successful (i.e., supportive) interactions and describe ways to help student writers understand and take best advantage of their immediate social context.

Collaborative writing requires writers to integrate their own representations of the task, their goals, and their strategies with those of other writers. **Rebecca Burnett** (Chapter 7) provides examples of a special kind of collaboration, coauthoring a paper. She examines several approaches to collaborative decision-making and argues that students can become more effective collaborators if they understand alternative patterns of interaction and their effects on the writing process. Her chapter suggests ways to help student coauthors explore these options.

Revision is another process strongly influenced by the social context. Given the prevalence of writing for teacher as examiner (Britton et al., 1975; Applebee, 1984), students may learn to revise for teachers without learning the kinds of strategies they will need to revise for readers unfamiliar with their topics. **Karen Schriver** (Chapter 8) shows that the ways in which students represent the task of revising influence the kinds of changes they make to their text: whole text (rhetorical, organizational) changes or local (sentence or word) changes. Schriver presents practical methods for teaching students to imagine the needs of their readers and to review their texts in accordance with those needs.

Feedback is a way of directly testing whether an intended goal has been met. As noted earlier, however, students often ask for feedback only on the correctness of their text, ignoring the potential of feedback for evaluating content and purpose (Freedman, 1987). **Barbara Sitko** (Chapter 9) presents this more powerful use of feedback in forms accessible to students. She focuses students' attention on revising after feedback as a decision-making process. Her chapter offers specific ways to help students analyze and respond to feedback from readers.

When feedback takes the form of a conference with a teacher or tutor, the social context includes the relationships of the participants, their respective representations of the task, their goals, and their differing strategies. **Betsy Bowen** (Chapter 10) discusses the difficult social balance that must be maintained in this context if teachers are to support and not usurp students' authority over their goals and texts. Her chapter suggests that conferences can be more effective if both participants understand the nature and purpose of the interaction. She describes features of successful conferences and demonstrates ways to examine patterns of interaction between students and teachers when they talk about writing one-on-one.

The various process research methodologies described in these chapters are further discussed and compared in the **Appendix** to this volume, entitled "Conducting Process Research." In that section, we describe two categories of verbal reports, retrospectives and concurrent protocols. We discuss the logistics of collecting process data and briefly overview recent uses and discussions of formal process methodologies.

The Advantage of the Research-Based Classroom

Writers vary a great deal in their understanding of reading and writing and in the amount of control they have over the many processes and interactions described above. The classroom research activities described in this volume, from process logs to conference transcripts to think-aloud protocols, are all designed to increase student awareness of their processes, to enable them to engage in reading and writing tasks more purposefully and more critically. We see classroom process research as a natural outgrowth of the now well-established multiple draft approach to writing instruction (cf. Elbow, 1973; Murray, 1979), which has long provided teachers with a means for helping students gain insights into the nature of composing. In the following process log excerpt we see a student reflecting on the generative potential of such an approach:

> Chris: The next step was going back and making all those corrections on the computer. This was kind of difficult because I had to make an entirely new introduction. From the new introduction, a whole new thought process followed, so I had to go back through what I had done in the rough draft and incorporate my new material into my old material. This might sound kind of long and tedious but I actually think it helped me clarify some of the main points in my paper. Instead of going through something only once, which is what I have typically done in previous papers, I went through it twice, so I had a chance to say things twice, only in different ways.

We believe Chris's testimony about the generative nature of writing is far more persuasive than our lectures about the writing process could ever be. Classroom research activities give students the opportunity to discover and articulate such insights for themselves and for their classmates — to recognize the problems and the potential of reading and writing. Process research in the classroom provides us, students and teachers alike, the opportunity to pause and "hear ourselves think," and in so doing, to help ourselves learn.

References

Applebee, A. N. (1981). *Writing in the secondary school* (Research Rep. No. 21). Urbana, IL: National Council of Teachers of English.

Applebee, A. N. (1984). *Contexts for learning to write: Studies of secondary school instruction.* Norwood, NJ: Ablex.

Beal, C. (1989). Children's communication skills: Implications for the development of writing strategies. In C. McCormick, G. Miller, and M. Pressley (Eds.), *Cognitive strategy research: From basic research to educational applications* (pp. 191–214). New York: Springer-Verlag.

Bereiter, C. & Scardamalia, M. (1987). *The psychology of written composition.* Hillsdale, NJ: Erlbaum.

Britton, J., Burgess, T., Martin, N., McLeod, A., & Rosen, H. (1975). *The development of writing abilities (11-18).* London: Macmillan Education.

Brown, A. L. (1980). Metacognitive development and reading. In R. J. Spiro, B. C. Bruce & W. F. Brewer (Eds.), *Theoretical issues in reading comprehension* (pp. 453–481). Hillsdale, NJ: Erlbaum.

Brown, A. L., Armbruster, B. B., & Baker, L. (1986). The role of metacognition in reading and studying. In J. Orasanu (Ed.), *Reading comprehension: From research to practice* (pp. 49–75). Hillsdale, NJ: Erlbaum.

Elbow, P. (1973). *Writing without teachers.* New York: Oxford.

Emig, J. (1971). *The composing processes of twelfth graders* (Research Report No. 13). Urbana, IL: National Council of Teachers of English.

Flower, L. (1979). Writer-based prose: A cognitive basis for problems in writing. *College English, 41,* 19–37.

Flower, L. (1988). *Problem-solving strategies for writing* (Third Edition). New York: Harcourt Brace Jovanovich.

Flower, L. & Hayes, J. R. (1980). The cognition of discovery: Defining a rhetorical problem. *College Composition and Communication, 31,* 21–32.

Flower, L. & Hayes, J. R. (1981). A cognitive process theory of writing. *College Composition and Communication, 32,* 365–387.

Flower, L., Stein, V., Ackerman, J., Kantz, M. J., McCormick, K., & Peck, W. C. (1991). *Reading-to-write: Exploring a cognitive and social process.* New York: Oxford.

Freedman, S. (1987). *Response to student writing.* Urbana, IL: National Council of Teachers of English.

Garner, R. (1987). *Metacognition and reading comprehension.* Norwood, NJ: Ablex.

Graves, D. (1979). Research doesn't have to be boring. *Language Arts, 56,* 76–80.

Haas, C. & Flower, L. (1988). Rhetorical reading strategies and the construction of meaning. *College Composition and Communication, 39*(2), 167–184.

Hayes, J. R. (1990). Individuals and environments in writing instruction. In B. F. Jones and L. Idol (Eds.), *Dimensions of thinking and cognitive instruction* (pp. 241–263). Hillsdale, NJ: Erlbaum.

Jones, B. F., Palincsar, A. S., Ogle, D. S., & Carr, E. G. (1987). *Strategic teaching and learning: Cognitive instruction in the content areas.* Alexandria, VA: Association for Supervision and Curriculum Development.

Langer, J. A. & Applebee, A. N. (1987). *How writing shapes thinking: A study of teaching and learning* (Research Report No. 22). Urbana, IL: National Council of Teachers of English.

Murray, D. (1979). The listening eye: Reflections on the writing conference. *College English, 41,* 13–18.

Nelson, J. & Hayes, J. R. (1988). *How the writing context shapes students' strategies for writing from sources* (Tech. Rep. No. 16). Berkeley, CA: The Center for the Study of Writing.

Norman, D. A. (1980). What goes on in the mind of the learner? In W. McKeachie (Ed.), *New Directions for Teaching and Learning, vol. 2: Learning, cognition, and college teaching* (pp. 37–49). San Francisco: Jossey-Bass.

Paris, S. & Winograd, P. (1990). How metacognition can promote academic learning and instruction. In B. F. Jones and L. Idol (Eds.), *Dimensions of thinking and cognitive instruction* (pp. 15–52). Hillsdale, NJ: Erlbaum.

Rose, M. (1980). Rigid rules, inflexible plans, and the stifling of language: A cognitivist analysis of writer's block. *College Composition and Communication, 31*(4), 389–401.

Sitko, B. & Flower, L. (in press). *Meta-knowledge in writing: The fruits of observation-based reflection* (Tech. Rep.). Berkeley, CA: The Center for the Study of Writing.

Sommers, N. (1980). Revision strategies of student writers and experienced adult writers. *College Composition and Communication, 31,* 378–388.

Weinstein, C. E. & Mayer, R. E. (1986). The teaching of learning strategies. In M. C. Wittrock (Ed.), *Handbook of research on teaching* (pp. 315–327). New York: Macmillan.

Weinstein, C. E., Underwood, V. L., Wicker, F. W., & Cubberly, W. E. (1979). Cognitive learning strategies: Verbal and imaginal elaboration. In H. F. O'Neil and C. D. Spielberger (Eds.), *Cognitive and affective learning strategies* (pp. 45-75). San Diego: Academic Press.

Young, R. E., Becker, A. L., & Pike, K. L. (1970). *Rhetoric: Discovery and change*. New York: Harcourt Brace.

Further Readings on Cognitive Process Theory

Flower, L. & Hayes, J. R. (1984). Images, plans and prose: The representation of meaning in writing. *Written Communication, 1*(1), 120-160.

Flower, L. (1989). Cognition, context, and theory building. *College Composition and Communication, 40*, 282-311.

Gardner, H. (1985). *The mind's new science: A history of the cognitive revolution*. New York: Basic Books.

Glover, J., Ronning, R., & Bruning, R. (1990). *Cognitive psychology for teachers*. New York: Macmillan.

I

INTERPRETING READING AND WRITING TASKS

2

Beyond "Just the Facts": Reading as Rhetorical Action

CHRISTINA HAAS

All English teachers are teachers of reading *and* of writing. Whether a teacher's scholarship, instruction, and institutional identity lie primarily within literature or within composition, the day-to-day business of English classrooms is inherently bound up in texts: student texts, teacher texts, canonical texts, marginal texts. These texts are read and reread, written and rewritten, as teaching and learning proceed. Despite this fact, a great deal of recent scholarship in English, aimed at understanding the learning that goes on in our classrooms, has focused almost exclusively on writing and writing processes. In a recent *College Composition and Communication* article, Russell Durst points out that fully 62% of the articles cited in the *Research in the Teaching of English* bibliographies since 1984 have focused on written composition (Durst, 1990). Although 9% of the articles focused on literature, Durst noted none that specifically dealt with reading or reading processes. Similar results would no doubt be found for other publications written for college teachers of English.

Yet, as teachers and as researchers, we know that reading and writing are closely tied. In a variety of literacy contexts—within and outside educational settings—much real writing arises in response to reading, and students' reading is often challenged, enriched, and evaluated by having them write. Further, the trend in language teaching today is toward placing students in rich reading and writing contexts, rather than teaching them isolated skills. In such contexts, the acts of reading and writing are dynamically woven together, as they are in the worlds of public and private discourse beyond the classroom walls.

But reading and writing are more than acts that occur together; they are acts that share an essential nature. Research from a number of disciplines has illuminated different aspects of these essential ties between the acts of reading and writing. For example, Tierney and Shanahan (1990) examine work in education that examines the relationship between reading and writing, while Brandt (1990) provides an overview of relevant work from literacy studies. Kaestle (1985) examines some reader-writer relationships from an historical perspective, and a collection edited by Bogdan and Straw (1990) connects theories from reading research with current critical theory. In a recent review article, Smagorinsky and Smith (1992) draw connections between the theoretical positions of researchers in composition and in literary understanding. Brent (1992) seeks to connect concepts of authorship from classical rhetoric with more recent studies of discourse processing. In the first section below, I sample some of this work to show how reading—like writing—is a constructive, rhetorical, choice-making activity. I then present a demonstration, useful for students as well as teachers, that illustrates the complex constructive nature of reading. This section is followed by a brief discussion of classroom activities that can enrich students' understanding and practice of reading in academic settings and beyond.

Aspects of Reading: Insights from Theory and Research

Reading is a complex discourse act. Recent research suggests that, like writing, reading is constructive and rhetorical, and that it often involves conscious decisions and choices on the part of the reader.

READING IS A CONSTRUCTIVE ACT

It is obvious, of course, that a writer constructs a text—an artifact that exists on paper or on a computer disk. This written artifact provides evidence that writing is, literally, constructive. Indeed, the written artifact makes the study of writing somewhat easier: a novelist's original manuscript and a student's successive drafts of a research paper both provide rich sources for textual analyses. The written artifact also grounds the study of writing which uses other observational or process-tracing methods. Reading, with no concrete constructed object for study, is more elusive. A student's reading of a story, or a teacher's reading of a student text, are fleeting and temporal, leaving no physical trace for study and analysis.

Despite the elusiveness of real-time reading processes, readers do construct meaning out of language. Although we may not be able to see and examine these constructed meanings, readers do indeed construct complex understandings woven out of textual cues, prior knowledge, social conventions, and cultural expectations. The most obvious illustration of the constructive nature of reading may be the reader who is also a writer, engaged in a reading-to-write task (Flower, Stein, Ackerman, Kantz, McCormick, & Peck, 1990) that requires incorporating existing texts into a new or novel contribution to an existing textual "conversation" (Kaufer & Geisler, 1989).

These reading-to-write tasks are familiar in academic settings: students respond to literary texts in English classes, synthesize disparate texts in science classes, analyze theoretical texts in history classes. Many of their exams include short answers or essay questions that draw explicitly and directly (some might say *too* explicitly and directly) from assigned readings. In such tasks students of all ages build upon, and depart from, texts they have read as they compose their own texts. In one sense, any document a writer produces can be seen as the product of innumerable historically previous texts, as writers write and readers read in an "intertextual space" (Porter, 1986) of ongoing meaning-making.

However, in a great number of reading situations—probably even the majority of reading situations—readers do not produce a written text, at least not immediately or directly. But even in those situations in which readers don't write, they are still constructing a meaning, a meaning consistent with their understanding of "cues" provided by the text, their prior experiences with similar texts, their knowledge about the world, and the social constraints and cultural expectations of that world.

Literary texts offer the most obvious example of texts that may be constructed in vastly different ways by different people—and in some sense the power of a literary work lies in its ability to be read in richly diverse ways. Indeed, reader-response theories of literary criticism have been quite powerful and influential in helping us understand how readers, in dynamic relationship both with written texts and with authors, produce meaning (Bleich, 1975; Fish, 1980; Iser, 1978; Rosenblatt, 1978). All of these reader-response theorists build upon the notion that readers are active agents of meaning-making, although they differ somewhat in how they view the relative power of the reader and of the text. An exchange between Iser and Fish in the pages of *Diacritics* in the early years of this decade provides a particularly lively example of some of these differences (Kuenzli & Iser, 1980; Fish, 1981; Iser, 1981). For most reader-response theorists, a reader is not a passive receptor or decoder of a text's meaning; rather these critics seek to correct the notion of closed, referential meanings contained within texts.

Of course, literary texts are not the only texts that require an active construction of meaning by the reader. Although the precise relationship between literary reading and other kinds of reading is not clear, expository, and particularly argumentative, texts require constructive action by the reader as well. Readers construct and revise "models" of texts as they read, models of both content information and structure (Collins, Larkin, & Brown, 1980). Meyer (1982; 1985) has examined how the organizational structures that readers build match the organizational structures suggested by the expository texts they read. Sometimes readers seem to construct inferences to make sense of seemingly disparate ideas in expository text (Bransford & Franks, 1971). They may construct content to "fill out" a given text structure or form (Spivey, 1990a; 1990b) or, conversely, they may ignore "irrelevant" ideas in a text as they strive to construct a coherent reading (Van Dijk, 1979). In a study of college-age readers, Linda Flower and I (1988) identified different reading strategies that readers used to construct a meaning for a persuasive text and found that using a range of these constructive strategies led to greater success in recognizing the kinds of claims that an author was making, whereas readers who employed fewer strategies did not recognize claims as well. Both recent theoretical work and results of research suggest that readers "build" meanings in a number of ways—in short, that reading is constructive. (See Greene, this volume, for further discussion of the constructive nature of discourse acts.)

READING IS A DECISION-MAKING ACT

Recognizing the constructive nature of reading, we turn our attention to examining *how* readers construct meaning and what part of this constructive process is open to examination and instruction. As educators, we are most interested in those literacy acts that can be taught, those literacy acts that can be brought to conscious attention, examined, and adapted to meet particular tasks and goals. In an act as cognitively complex as reading, certain aspects of the process (such as letter and word recognition in fluent readers or verbalizing by beginning readers) may not rise to conscious attention. This is in fact what makes certain readers "efficient": The process of reading may often proceed **without** conscious attention to the choices or decisions involved.

But in certain reading situations, as, for example, when incongruous or unexpected material is introduced, or new words or concepts encountered, we bring our reading processes under more conscious control, employing a repertoire of strategies to construct coherent meanings. In such situations, we may infer a relationship to explain incongruous material (Bransford, 1984), or draw upon conscious strategies to decode an unfamiliar word or examine an unfamiliar concept. In fact, part of what may distinguish "better" and "poorer" readers is the ability to bring the process of reading under conscious metacognitive control, to make it a true act of decision-making (Brown, 1982; Baker & Brown, 1984). Better readers may have more strategies upon which to draw when they are reading new, difficult, or problematic texts (Olshavsky, 1977). Similarly, readers need to devote conscious attention to the situations surrounding the texts they read and make decisions about the text based on those situations (Haas & Flower, 1988). For instance, whether an essay on gender relations was written in 1950 or in 1990 may have a profound influence on how we interpret that essay, and how we judge its author. In sum, the choices readers make—what features of texts to attend to, what knowledge and strategies to bring to bear, and how to judge the claims of an author — determine the richness and depth of their constructed meanings for texts.

READING IS A RHETORICAL ACT

The constructive process of reading is also by nature a rhetorical process. That is, the meanings that readers construct are inherently bound up in social relations between author and audience, reader and writer. Language is, after all, a social tool, used to establish, maintain, and further human relationships (Vygotsky, 1962). Written texts, like oral exchanges, arise out of rhetorical situations — the dynamic interplay of purposeful writers and readers and the worlds they share (Kinneavy, 1971; Kucer, 1985).

Adept writers, of course, adapt their texts to the needs and knowledge of the reading "audience." "Audience" is a complex and wide-reaching concept, used to refer to immediate hearers (Aristotle), to intended and actual readers of a text (Schriver, this volume), to diverse and dispersed "addressed" readers (Ede & Lunsford, 1984), to readers "implied" in the text (Iser, 1978), even to readers *constructed by* writers themselves (Ong, 1975). Readers, for their part, may also attribute identity or intention to a writer in order to understand or account for a text. This may be particularly true when encountering texts with strong claims.

Social constructionist theories of discourse tell us something about how the rhetorical exchanges between readers and writers occur. These theories posit that writers and readers work together — sharing conventions, expectations, and ways of knowing — to construct discourse (Nystrand, 1986; 1990). Dyson (1986, 1988) has examined the "text worlds" that young children construct together, alternating between roles as readers and as writers. When a student learns to write (and, presumably, learns to read) he or she learns the social conventions of communication within particular groups of people (Bizzell, 1982; Bartholomae, 1985).

While most social constructionist research has examined the way that rhetorical situations impact on writers, some scholars have looked specifically at how *readers* are influenced by social situations and relationships. Researchers interested in social cognition postulate that skill in reading and writing has an important relationship with an individual's ability to construct social situations around texts (Bonk, 1990; Kroll, 1985). Social cognition, according to Rubin and his colleagues (1984), includes attention to the values, interests, and skills of readers — and, I would add, of writers.

Related work in the sociology of science also contributes to our understanding of reading as a rhetorical act. Latour (1987) examined the kinds of rhetorical moves (a rhetorician might call them "tropes") used by authors of scientific texts. His analysis of rhetorical moves is instructive for readers as well as writers: just as the writer benefits from understanding how to employ an "argument from authority" or how to undermine and qualify another scientist's claims, so the reader of such texts is better able to interpret the argument if he or she can recognize how authors use authority-based arguments or qualification strategies. In a more empirical study, Bazerman (1985) studied several physicists as they read complex texts in their field. He found that these sophisticated readers did not read research reports straight through, looking for facts and information. Rather, their interpretation of the content of the piece was closely tied to rhetorical concerns—the authors' motivation and their previous work, the particular lab in which the authors worked, the way the findings and the conduct of the research might bear upon the readers' own research plans.

This attention to the motives and contexts of both writers and other readers I have termed *rhetorical reading*. When readers read rhetorically, they use or infer situational information—about the author, about the text's historical and cultural context, about the motives and desires of the writer—to aid in understanding the text and to judge the quality and believability of the argument put forth in it.

The Act of Meaning Construction: Three Reading Strategies

It should be clear, then, that reading is a profoundly complex discourse act, a constructive attempt at meaning-making, requiring a great deal of active choice and mental work. In one of its most sophisticated forms, the interpretation of argument, reading requires careful attention to the rhetorical aspects of discourse. However, student readers—and indeed student writers—often view texts as bodies of information or collections of facts, rather than as complex social and rhetorical acts. In a study of college readers and older, more experienced readers (Haas & Flower, 1988), we found that student readers devoted much of their reading effort to identifying this information, to determining "what the text is about." On the other hand, more experienced readers used a variety of strategies, including attention to the rhetorical situation out of which the text arose. These more experienced readers did not **ignore** information in the text so much as **interpret** it in light of its source: the situation that gave rise to it and the argument it served. So, while students may be quite adept at identifying the "facts" in a piece, they may often fail to consider more rhetorical aspects of the text—the author's identity and "agenda," the response of other readers to the argument, other texts with similar or diverse perspectives. It is these rhetorical skills, rather than a focus on content information alone, that students will need as they face complex reading tasks in college, in their disciplinary careers, and in the world of public discourse beyond the university.

The following "mystery text,"* an excerpt from a longer preface to an educational psychology textbook (Farnham-Diggory, 1972), will serve as a

---

*The "mystery text" and many of the examples that follow were originally presented in Haas & Flower, 1988.

means of identifying common reading strategies and will provide a basis for thinking about the varieties of ways that people go about constructing meaning for the texts they read. In a previous study, readers were instructed to read aloud, verbalizing their questions and comments, and to stop at specific points (indicated here with double slashes) to answer the question, "How do you interpret the text now?" For our illustrative purposes, you may want to jot down your responses to that question at the indicated points as you read.

But somehow the social muddle persists. Some wonderful children come from appalling homes, some terrible children come from splendid homes. Practice may have a limited relationship to perfection—at least it cannot substitute for talent. Women are not happy when they are required to pretend that a physical function is equivalent to a mental one. Many children teach themselves to read years before they are supposed to be "ready." // Many men would not dream of basing their self-esteem on "cave man" prowess. And despite their verbal glibness, teenagers seem to be in a worse mess than ever. //

What has gone wrong? Are the psychological principles invalid? Are they too simple for a complex world? //

Like the modern world, modern scientific psychology is extremely technical and complex. The application of any particular set of psychological principles to any particular real problem requires a double specialist: a specialist in the scientific area, and a specialist in the real area. //

Not many such double specialists exist. The relationship of a child's current behavior to his early home life, for example, is not a simple problem—Sunday supplement psychology notwithstanding. // Many variables must be understood and integrated: special ("critical") periods of brain sensitivity, nutrition, genetic factors, the development of attention and perception, language, time factors (for example, the amount of time that elapses between a baby's action and a mother's smile), and so on. Mastery of these principles is a full-time professional occupation. // The professional application of these principles—in, say a day-care center—is also a full-time occupation, and one that is foreign to many laboratory psychologists. Indeed, a laboratory psychologist may not even recognize his pet principles when they are realized in a day-care setting. //

What is needed is a coming together of real-world and laboratory specialists that will require both better communication and more complete experience. // The laboratory specialists must spend time in the real setting; the real-world specialist must spend some time in a theoretical laboratory. Each specialist needs to practice thinking like his counterpart. Each needs to practice translating theory into reality, and reality into theory. //

Here are two very different "readings," developed at this point in the mystery text by two different readers. The first reader is a college freshman; the second, a third-year PhD student in engineering.

Reader One: Well, basically, there seems to be a problem between the real-world and the laboratory, or ideal situation versus real situation, whatever way you want to put it—that seems to be about it.

Reader Two: OK, again, real world is a person familiar with the social influences on a person's personality—things they read or hear on the radio. . . . And laboratory specialist is more trained in clinical psychology. And now I think this article is trying to propose a new field of study for producing people who have a better understanding of human behavior. This person is crying out for a new type of scientist or something.

These contrasting readings of the same text differ in a number of ways: the first interpretation centers on content alone, "what the text is about." The second reader is also concerned with content, but he goes beyond the text to add details (elaborating "social influences" to include reading and listening to the radio) and to speculate on the motives of the author of the text — proposing a new field of study and "crying out" for a new kind of scientist. To understand these diverse readings of this text, we can examine the strategies that readers bring to bear upon this task, the ways that they use the text to construct meaning.

Your own reading of this passage probably illustrates a number of different reading strategies. Like most readers, you probably were confused by the text at first, but as you struggled to make sense of it, you probably brought several strategies to bear: you were concerned with *content* as you tried to interpret and analyze the "facts" presented in the text; you probably identified particular *features*, as examples or as an introduction, for instance; and you probably tried to account for the *rhetorical situation* of the text, wondering about the source of the text, the author's purpose and motivation (maybe even his or her identity), the reactions of other readers as well as your own reactions. In general, we found three broad categories of reading strategies operating when writers tried to interpret this text (Haas & Flower, 1988).

CONTENT STRATEGIES

These reading strategies focus on content, topic, and information. The reader's goal in using content strategies can range from getting "just the facts" to understanding and constructing a gist for the piece. In our study, students spoke aloud and transcripts of the reading sessions showed how these strategies were used. Notice how in each case the reader uses the word "about."

I guess this is **about** problems, social problems.

It's talking **about** children coming from different homes — good and bad children — and women.

I think it is **about** changing social conditions, like families in which both parents work.

FUNCTION OR FEATURE STRATEGIES

This strategy focuses on the conventional, generic functions or features of discourse — identifying parts of the text, or their function within it. When using this strategy, readers try to identify and name a part of the text. They also frequently tried to determine the functions of those parts: "explaining," "contrasting," "summarizing." In the following examples of function/feature strategies, the text feature or function identified by the reader is highlighted. Function/feature strategies represent a progressive enlargement of the reader's vision of the text: they build upon the content of the text and connect it (through conventional features) to other texts. Some of these conventional functions and features are highlighted in the examples.

I'm not sure of the **main point** he's making, but these **examples** of homes, and practice, and talent, and mental and physical things are part of an **introductory paragraph**.

This **list** of statements about women and mental and physical abilities, and about men and their "cave man" abilities, I presume are **examples** of how psychological principles don't hold.

RHETORICAL STRATEGIES

These strategies are "rhetorical" in the sense that, in using them, readers attend to author, purpose, context, and audience (Bitzer, 1968; Kinneavy, 1971). Rhetorical strategies go beyond, or, more accurately, "behind," the text to the author that created it, to the situation (including other texts) to which it is a response, and to other readers who may read it. Again, these rhetorical strategies build upon an interpretation of the informational content of a text or its conventional features. Following each example of rhetorical strategies below, the aspect of the rhetorical situation of the text to which the reader is attending is in parentheses.

I wonder if it [the article] is from *Ms.* (context).

The author is trying to make the argument that you need scientific specialists in psychology (author's intention).

I think this might make a day-care worker mad (audience reaction).

I wonder, though, if this is a magazine article, and I wonder if they expected it to be so confusing (context, author's intention).

Teachers of college English would probably not be surprised to find students' strategies for reading expository text to be primarily content based. In our own work, we found that experienced readers — like the engineering student above — used the full range of strategies, but that college freshmen seemed to focus primarily on content — specifically on facts and information — as they read the mystery text. Indeed, many college students are "good" readers in the sense that their automated processes of word recognition are often well developed. Such students may also be quite adept at furnishing a short gist-like summary of what a text is "about." When it comes to understanding and judging sophisticated textual arguments, however, many college students may fall short; they may have similar problems in writing such arguments. (See Higgins, this volume, for further discussion.)

Given the emphasis placed on content reading and summary writing in typical high school English curricula (Applebee, 1984), it is not surprising that many college students focus their attention on content information. The culture of schooling in this country has often encouraged an attention to "just the facts" as students are taught to locate, identify, and remember factual information. "Doing school" often means locating, memorizing, and reproducing isolated bits of information—important dates in history classes, Latin names for familiar plants and animals in biology classes, characters' names and plot chronologies in English classes. This is not to suggest, of course, that high school teachers are misguided pedagogically or remiss in their duties as educators. Rather, the current educational and political environment may encourage if not mandate a focus on facts and information, easy to quantify and easy to test.

When students arrive at college, however, and particularly as they move into the study of particular disciplines and out of college into the worlds of public discourse and debate, attention to facts and information alone may not be sufficient. Reading, in college and beyond, requires students to analyze, synthesize, and criticize the texts they read. While college students may not arrive in our classrooms completely prepared to interpret arguments, to read rhetorically, there are aspects of the constructive, rhetorical process of reading that we can bring to students' attention: we can lead them to see what kinds of reading strategies they use, the value of those strategies in various reading situations, and ways to increase the "repertoire" of reading strategies at their disposal (McCormick, 1990).

Expanding Students' Views of Reading

As we have seen, recent theory and research have greatly expanded our own views of reading, as we have come to see reading as a rich constructive and rhetorical act. Our students' views of reading, however, may be quite different. A critical first step in helping our students move beyond the exclusive use of information-based strategies in their reading is to help them see that reading may be a more complicated act than they had thought. After elementary school, most students don't receive explicit instruction in reading. Although they may have had several years of literature courses before college, they probably have not learned about reading in their history or biology or psychology courses, in high school or in college, despite the fact that these courses tend to require a great deal of reading.

A useful first step is to help students learn about their own conceptions of reading. We—and they—often find that these conceptions are somewhat limited, not reflecting what constructive theories tell us about reading. Students can interview one another, or write about themselves, asking and answering questions like, "What kind of reading do you do in college?" "What is your reason for reading these texts?" "What are you expected to do with the information or knowledge you gain through reading?" "How would you define a **good reader**?" Students' purposes for reading (especially at the freshman and sophomore level) may include "passing tests," "remembering information," even "doing what the teacher assigned." And their definitions of good reading may be quite content based: "good readers remember information," "good readers understand all the terms used in a text," "good readers get the ideas from a text quickly."

After a discussion of these interviews (or written responses), students might work together to define two or three characteristics of a **good reader**. These characteristics can provide interesting material for discussion after students have read a particularly difficult text, such as the "mystery text" above. Reading this difficult text requires more than content-reading: students may "know all the words" and "remember the main idea" but meeting these requirements may not satisfy their desire to truly "understand" the text. Class discussion might focus on how and why the characteristics of **good readers** identified earlier didn't seem to students to be sufficient to understand this text. This kind of activity provides a useful starting point; follow-up activities might focus particularly on the constructive, decision-making, and rhetorical nature of reading.

HELPING STUDENTS SEE HOW READING IS CONSTRUCTIVE

Students can read the same essay (or parts of an essay), but with different information about the author or the text or the time period in which it was written. For example, I give students excerpts from King's "Letter from Birmingham Jail," but do not tell them that it was written by King. Rather, I put a different author's name on different copies of the letter, so that some students read the excerpt thinking it was written by King, while others receive information that the same excerpt was written by Charles Manson, or John Kennedy, or Malcolm X. As students discuss their differing interpretations of the text, they are at first astonished with the interpretations of other students. As it is gradually revealed that they have conflicting information about the text's author, they see how expectations about authors and situations profoundly influence what the text "means" for them.

Teachers can also have students conduct "field research," interviewing other readers reading the "Letter" (or other texts). Students might provide readers with different author or situation information to elicit different kinds of readings. This activity can then provide the basis of class discussion. Students are able to share with their classmates some specific examples of how readers use information about discourse situations to construct meaning for a text.

HELPING STUDENTS UNDERSTAND THAT READING
IS A SERIES OF CHOICES

Students can keep logs of the problems they encounter as they read texts for their courses and how they choose to go about solving those problems. Students will recognize, for example, that they have particular strategies for dealing with a failure to understand a particular passage: they may decide to reread it, they may decide to keep reading to see if later text makes the troublesome passage clearer, they may go to outside sources to clarify what they don't understand.

Students might also work together to research the background of a text they have read and "reconstruct" the kinds of decisions that went into writing the text. What kinds of decisions—from global text strategies to local word choice—did the author make? Why has he or she made these decisions? What can we learn about his or her situation, background, and purposes that may have led to these decisions? How was he or she influenced by prevailing social trends or cultural beliefs? Who was the author's intended audience? How is it different from the actual audience? What kind of reaction was the author hoping for from the intended audience? Is the reaction of the actual audience different? Class discussion can then focus on how information about an author helps readers decide how to react to, interpret, and act upon a text.

HELPING STUDENTS RECOGNIZE THE SOCIAL AND RHETORICAL NATURE OF READING

Students can observe oral discourse situations—friendly conversations, flirting, friendly (or not so friendly) disagreements—and note the cues they use to determine the speakers' and listeners' motives and intentions. Class discussion can focus on comparing what students find about verbal situations to reading/writing situations: What are the similarities and differences? What happens when we don't take into account the listener or other speakers in a verbal situation? What happens if you ignore them in reading and writing? Students are certainly savvy interpreters of this kind of verbal, real-world discourse; teachers can help them see how these interpretive strategies can be applied to academic texts and situations as well.

Students may also find it easier to recognize reading as rhetorical in "everyday" situations: they may read cereal labels rhetorically, recognizing that nutritional claims on the front of the box were probably written by the cereal manufacturer and may not be entirely consistent with the nutritional tables on the back of the box. Students certainly think about the authors of class syllabi and assignments and are usually quite good at assessing those authors' (their teachers') motivations and desires. They recognize the situations surrounding other "everyday" texts, from love letters to car ads, where they use information about the author and situation to help them interpret, evaluate, and use these everyday texts.

Students can also conduct field research in their own areas of study, interviewing readers and writers of specific discourse communities. Based loosely on Bazerman's 1985 research on physicists, such interviews might focus on how and why members of a discipline choose the texts they read; the actual processes they go through in reading (or skimming or skipping) current publications; how they "use" (or ignore) such texts in their own writing. Students will probably find that readers within their fields of study have a great deal of information about the authors of publications, that they use this information to attribute motives and to judge the quality and applicability of the argument.

The classroom activities briefly outlined here rest on both a theory of discourse, outlined in the early section of this chapter, and an assumption that students' understandings and use of written texts, particularly in an educational setting, can be enlarged and enriched. Students need not be passive "receptors" of factual information; as teachers of reading and writing we can encourage them to be active, rhetorical agents — building a construction of textual meaning that includes not only content information, but an understanding of motivated arguments and of the human situations behind those arguments.

References

Applebee, A. (1984). *Contexts for learning to write*. Norwood, NJ: Ablex Publishing.

Aristotle. (1959). *Art of Rhetoric*. Cambridge, MA: Harvard University Press.

Baker, L. & Brown, A. (1984). Metacognitive skills and reading. In P. D. Pearson, M. Kamil, R. Barr, & P. Mosenthal (Eds.), *Handbook of Reading Research*. New York: Longman.

Bartholomae, D. (1985). Inventing the university. In M. Rose (Ed.), *When a Writer Can't Write: Studies in Writer's Block and Other Composing Process Problems*. New York: Guilford.

Bazerman, C. (1985). Physicists reading physics: Schema-laden purposes and purpose-laden schema. *Written Communication, 2*, 3–23.

Bitzer, L. (1968). The rhetorical situation. *Philosophy and Rhetoric, 1* (1), 1–14.

Bizzell, P. (1982). Cognition, convention, and certainty: What we need to know about writing. *Pre/Text, 3* (3), 213–242.

Bleich, D. (1975). *Readings and feelings: An introduction to subjective criticism*. Urbana, IL: National Council of Teachers of English.

Bogdan, D. & Straw, S. B. (1990). *Beyond communication: Reading comprehension and criticism*. Portsmouth, NH: Boynton/Cook.

Bonk, C. J. (1990). A synthesis of social-cognition and writing research. *Written Communication, 7* (1), 136–163.

Brandt, D. (1990). *Literacy as involvement*. Carbondale: Southern Illinois University Press.

Bransford, J. (1984). *Cognition: Learning, understanding, and remembering*. Belmont, CA: Wadsworth Publishing.

Bransford, J. & Franks, J. J. (1971). The abstraction of linguistic ideas. *Cognitive Psychology, 2*, 193–209.

Brent, D. (1992). *Reading as rhetorical invention: Knowledge, persuasion, and the teaching of research-based writing*. Urbana, IL: National Council of Teachers of English.

Brown, A. L. (1982). Learning how to learn from reading. In J. Langer & T. Smith-Burke (Eds.), *Reader meets author: Bridging the gap*. Newark, DE: International Reading Association.

Collins, A., Larkin, K., & Brown, J. S. (1980). Inference in text understanding. In R. J. Spiro, B. C. Bruce, & W. Brewer (Eds.), *Theoretical Issues in Reading Comprehension* (pp. 385–410). Hillsdale, NJ: Erlbaum.

Durst, R. K. (1990). The mongoose and the rat in composition research: Insights from the *RTE* Annotated Bibliography. *College Composition and Communication, 41* (4), 393–408.

Dyson, A. H. (1986). Transition and tensions: Interrelationships between the drawing, talking, and writing of young children. *Research in the Teaching of English, 20*, 379–409.

Dyson, A. H. (1988). Negotiating among multiple worlds: The space/time dimension of young children's composing. *Research in the Teaching of English, 22*, 355–390.

Ede, L. & Lunsford, A. (1984). Audience addressed/audience invoked: The role of audience in composition theory and pedagogy. *College Composition and Communication, 35* (2), 155–171.

Farnham-Diggory, S. (1972). *Cognitive processes in education: A psychological preparation for teaching and curriculum development*. New York: Harper & Row.

Fish, S. (1980). *Is there a text in this class? The authority of interpretive communities*. Cambridge: Harvard University Press.

Fish, S. (1981). Why no one's afraid of Wolfgang Iser. *Diacritics, 11* (March), 2–13.

Flower, L., Stein, V., Ackerman, J., Kantz, M., McCormick, K., & Peck, W. (1990). *Reading-to-write: Exploring a cognitive and social process*. New York: Oxford University Press.

Haas, C. & Flower, L. (1988). Rhetorical reading strategies and the construction of meaning. *College Composition and Communication, 39* (2), 167–184.

Iser, W. (1978). *The act of reading: A theory of aesthetic response*. Baltimore: Johns Hopkins University Press.

Iser, W. (1981). Talk like whales: A reply to Stanley Fish. *Diacritics, 11* (September), 81–87.

Kaestle, C. (1985). The history of literacy and the history of readers. *Review of Research in Education, 12* (1), 11–53.

Kaufer, D. S. & Geisler, C. (1989). Novelty in academic writing. *Written Communication, 6*, 286–311.

Kinneavy, J. L. (1971). *A theory of discourse*. New York: W. W. Norton.

Kroll, B. M. (1985). Social-cognitive ability and writing performance: How are they related? *Written Communication, 2* (3), 293–305.

Kucer, S. B. (1985). The making of meaning: Reading and writing as parallel processes. *Written Communication, 2*, 317–336.

Kuenzli, R. E. & Iser, W. (1980). Interview: Wolfgang Iser. *Diacritics, 10* (June), 57–74.

Latour, B. (1987). *Science in Action*. Cambridge: Harvard University Press.

McCormick, K. (1990). The cultural imperative underlying cognitive acts. In Flower, L., Stein, V., Ackerman, J., Kantz, M., McCormick, K., & Peck, W. (Eds.), *Reading to Write: Exploring a cognitive and social process* (pp. 194–218). New York: Oxford University Press.

Meyer, B. J. F. (1982). Reading research and the composition teacher: The importance of plans. *College Composition and Communication, 33*, 37–49.

Meyer, B. J. F. (1985). Prose analysis: Purposes, procedures, and problems. In B. K. Britton & J. Black (Eds.), *Understanding expository text* (pp. 11–64). Hillsdale, NJ: Lawrence Erlbaum.

Nystrand, M. (1986). *The structure of written communication: Studies in reciprocity between writers and readers*. Orlando: Academic Press.

Nystrand, M. (1990). Sharing words: The effects of readers on developing writers. *Written Communication, 7*, 3–24.

Olshavsky, J. (1977). Reading as problem-solving: An investigation of strategies. *Reading Research Quarterly, 12*, 654–671.

Ong, W. J. (1975). The writer's audience is always a fiction. *PMLA, 90*, 9–21.

Porter, J. E. (1986). Intertextuality and the discourse community. *Rhetoric Review, 5*, 34–47.

Rosenblatt, L. M. (1978). *The reader, the text, the poem: The transactional theory of the literary work*. Carbondale: Southern Illinois University Press.

Rubin, D. L., Picher, G., Michlin, M. L., & Johnson, F. L. (1984). Social cognitive ability as a predictor of the quality of fourth-graders' written narratives. In R. Beach & L. S. Bridwell (Eds.), *New Directions in Composition Research*. New York: Guilford.

Smagorinsky, P. & Smith, M. W. (1992). The nature of knowledge in composition and literary understanding: The question of specificity. *Review of Educational Research, 62* (3), 279–305.

Spivey, N. N. (1990a). *The shaping of meaning: Composing and comparing* (Technical Report). Berkeley: Center for the Study of Writing at Berkeley and at Carnegie Mellon.

Spivey, N. N. (1990b). Transforming texts: Constructive processes in reading and writing. *Written Communication, 7*, 256–287.

Tierney, R. J. & Shanahan, T. (1990). Research on the reading-writing relationship. In R. Barr, M. L. Kamil, P. Mosenthal, & P. D. Pearson (Eds.), *Handbook of reading research, volume II* (pp. 246–280). New York: Longman.

van Dijk, T. A. (1979). Relevance assignment in discourse comprehension. *Discourse Processes, 2*, 113–126.

Vygotsky, L. S. (1962). *Thought and Language*. Cambridge: MIT Press.

3

Exploring the Relationship Between Authorship and Reading

STUART GREENE

Attempts to integrate reading and writing in literature or composition courses have brought into focus the extent to which comprehending, like composing, is a constructive, rhetorical act. In turn, we have begun to consider some of the ways we can enhance students' understanding of what they read, making them aware that reading is a strategic process that entails reconstructing some of the choices and decisions writers make in a given situation. This renewed interest in how readers construct meaning is important in thinking about how to foster the development of critical literacy; but I want to go a step further by thinking about students as authors who have opportunities to contribute knowledge to a community of readers.

Constructivist theories of reading, which call attention to comprehension as an active process of composing meaning, can provide a useful framework for understanding how a sense of authorship can motivate and influence reading, that is, how people read in order to further their own rhetorical intentions as writers and define a position from which they might speak (cf. Bartholomae, 1985). As Spivey (1990) has observed, readers use what they know together with textual cues to organize meaning in a text, select information based on some relevance principle, and make connective inferences between the information they select in reading and the content they generate from prior knowledge. Writers can embellish what they read with examples and counter-examples (Stein, 1990), thinking critically about what they read in light of their goals as writers. Thus a constructivist framework can help us understand

the ways in which writers think their way through rhetorical problems, negotiate their own goals in a given social situation, and structure information in
order to develop intellectual projects of their own (Flower & Higgins, 1991).
This kind of negotiation is illustrated in Bazerman's (1985) research in the
sociology of science where he points to the constructive nature of reading and
writing—a process shaped by an individual's schema or personal map of the
field. This map consists of consensual knowledge about the field, its methods
and current practices, the problems on which the field is working, and the
ways problems are worked out. Meaning, he suggests, seems to come from
being able to integrate new information into what one already knows. Readers
selectively evaluate and connect information from texts in order to enter a
scholarly conversation.

It follows, at least pedagogically, that we can help students to think critically
about what they read and to establish an intellectual project of their own. In
this chapter, I explore some of the ways teachers have tried to foster students'
sense of authorship and then propose a set of strategies that underscore the
relationship between reading and writing that constructivist theories help us
to understand. Of particular interest are two questions: How do writers make
use of what they read in furthering their goals as authors? And, what do
writers attend to in reading their own texts?

How Reading Can Inform Writing

IMITATION AND IMMERSION: SOME PEDAGOGICAL
AND THEORETICAL ASSUMPTIONS

Reading has played an important role in the writing classroom because we
believe that students can learn about writing through imitating models of well
wrought prose. The expectation is that students will internalize the style, grace,
and correctness that make these works exemplary. Though such an approach
has been criticized in composition, imitation has a venerable tradition in classical rhetoric (Corbett, 1971). And, as Bazerman (1980) points out, "teachers of
other academic disciplines still find the model attractive, because writing in
the content disciplines requires mastery of disciplinary literature" (p. 657).
Teachers have faith that when students write about disciplinary subjects, using
a field's preferred genres and styles, they will absorb knowledge about discourse features and the acceptable "commonplaces" (Bartholomae, 1985) in
that field. Others conclude that reading can inform writing through more
direct instruction that consists of analyzing stylistic features of written products, an approach that implicitly assumes that writers can infer process from a
written text and that form can precede content (Church & Bereiter, 1984; cf.
Bereiter & Scardamalia, 1984). Yet one might wonder if students can articulate
or apply the discourse knowledge they tacitly learn through imitation to their
writing in different situations and across a number of varying tasks. Will imitation serve our students when they must transform their knowledge in order to contribute something new to an ongoing conversation in a given field?

At a more basic level, in imitating models, what would we expect students to attend to as they read in light of their purposes as writers?

Perhaps a more productive line of research has begun to examine the ways in which a knowledge of content *and* strategies contributes to the construction of meaning in reading and writing. Smagorinsky (in press) has suggested that reading can inform writing when "writers . . . understand the relationship between form and content." Thus a "model seems to be most beneficial when learners have appropriate content knowledge and learn how to transform it; the model can illustrate how to relate the bits of knowledge in a coherent structure" (cf. Hillocks, 1986). From this perspective, models may be useful, but the issue is when to introduce models to students in an instructional sequence and how we might use these models to describe for students the ways in which reading can inform writing.

As an alternative to imitation, some teachers foster the development of writing ability by immersing students in what Atwell (1985, 1987) calls a "literate environment." Here writers share their writing and evolving interpretations of literary works, meet with one another in groups, and develop portfolios of their writing over time. The assumption is that by immersing students in a social process they can learn certain features of discourse and adapt their writing to the needs of an audience in a literate environment. In short, they can begin to see the social purposes of writing: contributing to the growth and development of a community. This assumption is based, in part, on Vygotsky's (1962) theoretical framework for learning, one that underscores the social origins of individual activity and appears to imply that writers will internalize knowledge about texts through social interaction (Bruffee, 1984; cf. Wertsch & Stone, 1985). Seen in this way, collaboration provides a kind of instructional scaffolding (Vygotsky, 1978; see also Burnett, this volume) that supports students in their attempts to balance their purposes as writers with their perceptions of a reader's background knowledge and goals for reading (Nystrand, 1986). Thus social context enables students to see that texts are made, evolving through conscious choices and decisions. Still, though interaction between readers and writers may heighten writers' awareness of their choices, research on collaboration suggests that "awareness itself may not insure that students will reflect critically on those choices" (Higgins, Flower, & Petraglia, 1992).

MINING TEXTS: A CONSTRUCTIVIST APPROACH TO READING AND WRITING

An emphasis on the mindful study of texts, either through imitation or immersion, is of value, but these approaches have tended to neglect the active role readers play in constructing meaning in both comprehending and composing. Moreover, studies of instruction have not accounted for the ways in which individual learners use what they know in reading to further their own goals as writers. This knowledge remains tacit. If we want to help students understand the decisions and processes that a sense of authorship requires, then we need to build upon and go further than traditional approaches. We can teach students to mine texts, helping them to engage in critical, conscious reflection as they read in their role as writers.[1]

Mining suggests a strategic process that consists of mapping out the territory by examining the situation or *context*. It also entails imposing some sort of *structure* based on informed guesses about where the object or objects of inquiry might lie, as well as exploring possible options and choices by representing one's plan in different ways in *language*. Language can provide a lens through which we can understand something in a particular way. And subtle changes in language alter the ways we locate meaning. Such a process requires one to plan, selectively evaluating and organizing information in order to get a sense of the topography, and to reflect upon one's choices and decisions about how to use accumulated knowledge to best effect. For this excavation, the miner uses certain "tools" appropriate to the situation to help uncover what is most desired. For the reader who is also a writer, this means using strategies to reconstruct context, infer or impose structure, and see choices in language. In these ways, a reader can begin to make informed guesses about how to use the ideas or discourse features of a given text in light of his or her goals as a writer. Such an "excavation" can be a selfish endeavor for it serves the individual in his or her search for "nuggets" of information. But in excavating knowledge an author uses the object of inquiry to make a contribution to the community that shapes and constrains what is said and how it is communicated.

Whereas teachers often encourage a critical reading of individual texts as an end in itself, mining is part of an ongoing effort to learn specific rhetorical and linguistic conventions. The strategies students observe in reading can become part of their own repertoire for writing on different occasions. Perhaps the best way to illustrate the contrast between mining texts and a more traditional critical reading of a text is through two examples. In providing these two examples — really just thumb-nail sketches — I wish to demonstrate two different approaches to reading a text, not to suggest that one kind of reading is better than another. The key point is that each type of reading reflects a different sense of purpose. In the first, a student thinks aloud, revealing some of her thoughts as she reads a passage from John McPhee's (1969) book *The Pine Barrens.*

> All throughout the essay McPhee makes a point of showing how this area, the Pine Barrens, are incongruous with the rest of the country. Along with having unpolluted water, he makes a point of saying how the Pine Barrens occur in the middle of New Jersey, which a lot of people think is very industrial, very busy and there's lots of transportation and a lot of activity. . . . He directly contrasts the Pine Barrens with the rest of New Jersey. . . . And he kind of marvels at how the Pine Barrens are still undamaged.

Here the reader takes on what Britton (1982) has called the role of a "spectator," observing with some deference the way McPhee uses a point of contrast to urge the reader into agreeing that the Pine Barrens should be saved from development. The primary goal is to understand how McPhee orchestrates his argument, a goal the reader achieves by staying close to the text, not by consulting her own experiences, nor by reflecting on her own goals as a writer. In the second example, a different reader engages the text in a more active way, taking on a "participant's" role—she mines the text:

> If he presented his argument more up front he would have captured the reader's interest faster. The whole idea of it in telling a story, giving the argument and then telling more of the story does get the point across, if you're interested in the Pine Barrens. . . . In my own paper I would definitely use support, like he [McPhee] does—Joseph Wharton, the underground water, and how it can be used in the future. But I would expand on that more than he did.

Most telling in this example is that in taking an authorial stance the writer challenges the approach that McPhee has taken in developing his argument, motivated by her own goals as a writer. She writes the text that has yet to be written, using her experience as a writer to select what is most relevant or important, balancing a text-based strategy with a purpose-driven strategy. More specifically, she focuses on McPhee's attempts to support his argument in the text; but she also imagines the use of support in a much different context—her own writing shaped by a given set of goals—though this context remains undefined here.

Though mining a text emphasizes students' use of strategies to acquire knowledge about discourse, such a process does not ignore the importance of comprehending the content or substantive issues in reading. As other researchers in this volume affirm (e.g., Haas, Higgins, Nelson), students' readings of texts are often motivated by a search for content, informed by a legacy of schooling that values recitation of given information (Applebee, 1984; Barnes, 1976), rather than the sort of *writerly* reading that mining promotes. My concern as a teacher and researcher is to give students the means to make informed choices about how to adapt others' rhetorical strategies to further their own intentions as authors within a given community.

Examining How a Sense of Authorship Can Inform Reading

One way to understand how a sense of authorship can inform reading as students selectively evaluate texts and adapt others' rhetorical strategies is to look closely at what writers do as they mine a text. In early observations of students, I saw them mining texts in the three distinctive ways described in the previous section: reconstructing context, inferring or imposing structure, and seeing choices in language. Examples from the think-aloud protocols that I collected from six students illustrate how they used two of these strategies in reading John McPhee's "The Woods from Hog Wallow," the first chapter of his book *The Pine Barrens*.[2] As part of a class assignment, students were given the essay and told that they would be asked to write an argumentative essay on any issue they were interested in, one that mattered to them. In addition, they were told that their paper did not need to focus on the issue that McPhee wrote about, nor should they see his text as an exemplar that they could or should imitate. "The Woods from Hog Wallow" was simply an example of how one might write an argumentative essay. Further, they were reminded of the range of journal articles and essays they had read during the semester. They could draw upon their reading of other works in producing their own texts. After they read McPhee's essay and felt they understood the substance (i.e., the content) of his argument, they were asked to consider the issue he had written about and the techniques he used to further his purpose and goals, mining the text for whatever they might use in writing their essays.

Transcripts of think-aloud protocols revealed that students attended to both context and structure when they attempted to understand McPhee's rhetorical plan. In a sense, they "mapped out the territory" by selectively evaluating information in the text or from prior experiences of how discourse works, organizing textual meaning in order to get a sense of the "topography," and reflecting upon different options as they composed a reading in their role as authors. These students also focused on context and structure as they looked ahead to writing their own texts. This marked an important shift in students' attention from their initial understanding of McPhee's rhetorical plan to developing their own plans for writing.

MAPPING OUT THE TERRITORY IN READING TO WRITE

When students like Janet (see below) mapped out or represented the writer's rhetorical plan in thinking aloud as they read, they made inferences about context, speculating about why a writer chose the subject he did and how he might have gone about collecting information. The emphasis here is less on the actual text and more on the rhetorical situation and method of inquiry. Students like Andy (see below) focused primarily on the text in representing McPhee's rhetorical plan. They searched for explicit references that showed McPhee's attempts to set up a context for discussing a given issue: presenting background information or providing a rationale for writing.

> Janet: . . . he's going in, I think, he got this idea from some outside source and he was interested in the water supply in this area or interested in possibly just the area itself. So he went in, he had this urge or desire as a writer to go in and find out more about it and write about it. So he goes into this area, he does some studies on the area. He meets these people he's going to spend time with.

> Andy: It's very structured because he starts out in the beginning and he's setting it up. . . . He's describing what the place [the Pine Barrens] is like. Logically, now he's going to defend all this beauty that he's describing here. It sets up the context, a reason for arguing.

One could argue that Janet has lost sight of the text in her concern for where the writer got his idea for writing and the methods he used to initiate the process of inquiry. In contrast, Andy appears to be a "good" reader who has also mined the text, imposing a structure that helps him organize his ideas about what the writer tries to accomplish at the outset of his text. Yet one could argue that both Janet and Andy use strategies that teach us about how to read in the role of writers. Neither approach to reading is better than the other. Indeed, students use cues from a text in order to build a coherent representation of meaning. They also make inferences, considering the importance of situation and method in setting out to construct their own texts. Individual differences in mining texts suggest that there are options that students can weigh. A text-based strategy, like Andy's, can be quite powerful, reinforcing comprehension, and can complement the kind of theorizing that someone like Janet engages in as she reconstructs the process that shaped McPhee's final text.

Part of mapping out the territory also included students' attempts to infer or impose some kind of structure or pattern on the source text. Such a move suggests the fluid nature of structure. Structure may be perceived as a kind of textual space (Nystrand, 1986) created by both readers and writers. At times, students considered the writer's goals in using a particular rhetorical device, a given organizational pattern, or mode of argument. For instance, both Janet and Brian engage in a kind of critical reading, focusing on a specific feature of a text—structure. Yet, in representing purpose, Brian illustrates an important characteristic of mining. His selective attention is focused on what McPhee tried to accomplish in his writing, not solely on what McPhee said or how McPhee structured his ideas.

> Janet: Going through this essay seems to have three major parts. The first part would be setting up, giving background information as to what the Pine Barrens are. The second part would be showing what life in the Pine Barrens is through Bill and Fred's eyes. And then the other part is showing the modernization, the potential that the Pine Barrens have. In addition to showing the water supply that it can supply, points are also brought out about how industry could locate around there, how an air force base could be located near the top of the woods—a jetport. So the essay seems to focus on background, past, present and future.

> Brian: He goes from a comparison of how beautiful it all is to how already it's gotten smaller. I got the idea that he was trying to make it seem like a beautiful esthetically pleasing place so that the reader would tend to go on his side . . . it makes you kind of think that it's beautiful and you can't ruin it . . . he adds the people to the essay to make you get a more personal feeling of what's going on and that's why he puts the characters in . . . you get a stronger feeling of how someone can get attached to a place.

In this instance, Janet imposed a structure on the source text, using a text-based strategy, while Brian emphasized McPhee's use of a rhetorical technique as a means for achieving his purpose in writing. Moreover, I would stress that the strategies Brian and Janet use complement one another. To learn about writing through reading, students should attend to how a writer structures his ideas and the relationship between certain ordering principles and rhetorical purpose.

MAKING A WRITING PLAN

Finally, comments referring to a student's writing plan reflect a shift in attention from McPhee's rhetorical plan in the source text to developing their own arguments; that is, students read with their own rhetorical concerns in mind. The following examples also suggest the extent to which a writing plan affects what students selectively evaluate as they read and decide whether or not to adapt another's strategy in writing their own texts.

> Lauren: In the beginning of the essay he starts out with a scenario. I think that would be good if I gave a scenario about someone having to deal with writer's block. Then people can get a better idea of what direction I'm going to take . . . I could start out with a scenario. Then I could make my argument saying that the five cognitive dimensions do cause anxiety, giving examples like McPhee does.

> Colleen: In my own paper, I definitely would use support, like he [McPhee] does. But I would expand on that more than he did. I would also state a thesis telling people that "This is the problem." I would bring out the importance of it [the water in the Pine Barrens] not being polluted, that it is fresh water, and that you can drink it right out of the pump . . . I'd bring that out and show the importance of not having it polluted . . . I'd expand on that and get away from the story.

Perhaps the critical difference between how Lauren and Colleen evaluated what they read depended on their own plan for writing. Lauren read the source text knowing that she would be writing an essay on writer's block, so that she mined the text for what she could use in fulfilling her own goals as a writer. McPhee's use of a scenario inspired her to employ the same strategy to help "make her argument." She imitated McPhee and did so purposefully, aware that this rhetorical technique could help her achieve her goals as a writer. Colleen, however, did not read the source text with a writing plan of her own. Thus she did not mine the text for what she could use, but imposed her own criteria for writing an argument, assuming authority over what she read as a writer. In the end, both Lauren and Colleen demonstrate purposeful, though different, goal-directed strategies. These strategies reflected an important meta-awareness about writing and what could be achieved through reading and writing.

MINING ONE'S OWN TEXT AS A READER AND WRITER

As students read McPhee's essay, their comments reflected the extent to which they were beginning to look ahead to writing their own essays. After writing an argumentative essay as part of a class assignment, students provided retrospective accounts that detail some of the choices and decisions they made in writing their own texts. These accounts demonstrate that practice in mining seems to have made some of them more sensitive to their own rhetorical choices and the potential effects that their decisions might have on a reader.[3]

In the example that follows, Lauren implicitly reconstructs the context of her paper, providing a rationale for the argument she tried to advance. Here she considers both the content she included and why she made the choices she did in writing an introduction to her paper on writer's block.

> Lauren: What I tried to prove was that there are five cognitive dimensions that lead to writer's block. And they lead to writer's block because they first lead to

anxiety. And anxiety leads to writer's block. And in the beginning of my paper what I did was I just introduced what I was going to talk about . . . I didn't explain them, I just listed what they were. I just wanted to introduce what I wanted to do. Then went on in my paper and I was still introducing certain other things like that. I used the writing model developed by Flower and Hayes and I did this just so the reader would have an idea of what I was talking about. So I didn't really start my argument on the first page. I just spoke about what I was going to be arguing about.

When students attended to structure, they often described the organizational pattern of the essay; at times, students considered the rhetorical structure, certain kinds of evidence, or specific images. Students began with a text-based strategy that focused their attention on what they said, but moved away from the text, demonstrating an awareness of why they approached the issues in the ways that they did:

Brian: My essay's not structured to where I develop different points or to where I have to be very persuasive . . . I don't think you'll find anybody who's a drinking and driving advocate . . . It's more along the lines of a narrative, a story about what happens to a group of people.

Lauren: I mentioned that studies were done to prove that apprehension leads to writer's block . . . I did that so the audience can see. The reader can say that my argument was based on fact and not just on my beliefs and ideas . . . I was saying that this was proved in an experiment. I'm not just throwing all of this information together. So my argument would be more solid.

Some students also focused on choices about language, why certain words or phrases might be appropriate or not; interestingly, students referred to language only in reading their own work, not McPhee's chapter.

Brian: He's just sitting there. He's frozen completely but his mind is going and he's thinking about this thing. And I have him say, "He thought surprisingly clearly to himself." "Surprisingly clearly," describing his thought because I wanted to make it very clear that what Brad was thinking is basically what I think.

Andy: I don't want to narrow this down to one particular situation. I sort of want to allow everyone to compare themselves to this. So you know I don't want to nail down one time and one place. But it's helpful to give little images here and there. That's basically what I'm trying to do with phrases like "nervously fingers the bridge of his glasses" and "smiles blindly with dry lips into the glare of the stage lights" . . . while it's not really specific it does begin to give you a picture of what's going on, what he's feeling.

Finally, I noted episodes in these retrospective accounts when students reconstructed the choices and decisions they made about content — what to include or not to include in the essay in light of their goals. These comments reflected an important meta-awareness about writing, suggesting a sense of control on the part of the writer who knew both what he or she wanted to say and why certain details and ideas may or may not have been appropriate.

Brian: I didn't go into detail about the car that was wrapped around a tree. I didn't go into things like that or the shock of the drivers or anything like that. I just went into, I said, you know, this is what happens and two people were killed and that's it. That's all I need to say and the rest can be left up to your imagination and because things like that aren't pleasant to imagine. They shouldn't be for the essay. I think I can spare people the gore, I can make my point completely without it . . .

Taken as a whole, the examples of students mining texts in reading to write support some earlier speculations about the conditions under which students will and will not read like writers. The think-aloud protocols and retrospective accounts suggest that when students read with a sense of authorship, knowing that they will be expected to produce texts of their own, they use the source text as a heuristic for structuring and developing their own ideas. This was evident when Lauren observed that McPhee uses a scenario at the outset of his essay and believes that using such a technique would be effective in her own work. Similarly, Colleen used McPhee's approach to writing an argument as a point of departure for writing her own essay, making choices about how she would develop an effective argument that would sustain a reader's interest. Of course, the extent to which students read in the role of writers depends on their having an occasion to write, having a fairly well-developed plan for writing when they read a source text, and having strategies for making use of what they read in composing. Interestingly, Colleen, troubled by the way McPhee structured his essay, approached reading as a means for solving a problem. In turn, she "rewrote" the text, applying her own criteria of how to structure an argument. Yet when students have difficulty grasping the meaning of a text, as was the case when Janet first started reading McPhee's chapter, they will attend to content, not how they can adapt what other writers are doing in writing their own texts. At the same time, source content can help create a writer's goals. Goals may emerge, change, or be discovered while reading.

Teaching Students to Mine Texts

The goals of teaching students to mine texts are, first, to encourage students to develop a sense of the options they have as writers and, second, to enable them to articulate their reasons for making the choices they do in different situations. To help students achieve these goals, we can teach strategies directly by *modeling* the process of analyzing discourse features, giving students opportunities to *practice* individually or in groups, and then gradually *fading*, so that students are actively engaged in their own learning (cf. Collins, Brown, & Newman, 1989).

Within such a sequence, we can help students locate issues, determine the forms and conventions of a discipline, and establish ways to enter a conversation. In doing so, we can model for students a rhetorical reading (Haas & Flower, 1988) of a text. This can entail showing them how writers in a discipline invoke context by establishing the importance of an issue, use citations to demonstrate their knowledge of the field, and create a research or problem space that provides an opportunity for contributing to a scholarly conversation (cf. Swales, 1984). An analysis of structure can also underscore the contextual nature of writing, since structure can be linked to the ways of knowing in a given discipline. The report form in the sciences is a case in point, reflecting the kind of work that scientists carry out: establishing the importance of a certain area of study, defining a problem, situating their work in a network of prior research, determining the methods of conducting a study, analyzing data, and so on. The form embodies the scientific method and principles of knowing that characterize the way scientists see the world (cf. Bazerman, 1985; Myers, 1990). Moreover, we can show students how writers like E. B. White, Joan Didion, or Tracy Kidder achieve more personal goals in writing, at the same time pursuing issues about impending nuclear war in the late 1950s, the political climate in El Salvador, or the role of advanced technology in contemporary American society.

In turn, students can practice using strategies for mining texts in small groups, each taking on the "role" of a given strategy in order to make this kind of thinking visible (cf. Brown & Palinscar, 1989). For example, one group could compose a reading by mapping out the situation, showing how a given writer established the context, and suggesting some of the social and historical forces that shaped a writer's choices and decisions in writing. What are the writer's purposes? What issues concern the readers of this text? Another group could discuss text structure—how a writer moves from one idea to another and how that writer sets up significant points. This group might also consider whether there could be other, more effective ways to structure the text. What are some alternative ways to move from one idea to another? A third group would talk about language. What kinds of language does the writer prefer? Common words? Jargon? Slang? What is the level of speech? Streetwise? Educated? What options does a writer have in deciding how to frame his or her ideas in language?

Discussions like these could occur in writing workshops in which students share their own work with one another. "What if?" could become a familiar refrain as students read with a sense of authorship. Once students become more comfortable with the strategies associated with mining a text, instructional support can fade, so that students can begin to take control over their own learning.

To learn more about how a sense of authorship can inform reading, students can also keep logs and develop handbooks in which they discuss relationships between discourse strategies and the purposes these strategies serve in furthering a writer's rhetorical intentions. Students in this study kept logs that consisted of descriptions of how writers from different fields establish context, structure their reports and journal articles, and use the language of a given disciplinary community. (See Appendix I for the assignment students received.) One student noted that to establish the context for his own writing he could use background knowledge, particularly when he believed his "audience ha[d] limited knowledge of the subject. . . . [This] works well when describing 'technical subjects.'" From his reading, he learned that another strategy for establishing context entailed giving a brief overview of "what has been said on your topic until now." Further, he wrote in his log that this strategy was "especially useful in describing the reasons for the evolution of your field" and for revealing the "motivation behind your [own] study." It is important to see that this student forges links between the knowledge he acquires about discourse and the meta-awareness he develops about when the use of a given strategy might be appropriate. (This student's log appears in Appendix II.)

From their research, students developed their own repertoire of strategies and shared their handbooks with one another in order to explain how writers across the curriculum construct texts. In addition, students began mining texts in an ongoing process of reading, analyzing, and authoring that recognizes the social nature of discourse. Each piece of writing that a student reads or writes is a contribution to an ongoing written conversation. To reconstruct the context of a text requires an understanding of how an author frames a response appropriate to a given situation and an author's own purpose. Mining also fosters the kind of comparative analysis that can enable students to see, as Bazerman (1980) has observed, how "previous comments provide subjects at issue, factual content, ideas to work with, and models of discourse appropriate to the subject" (658). In reading in the role of writers, students make judgments about the most appropriate way to make their own contribution in writing.

If our goals as teachers consist of enabling students to take control over their own learning, then it makes sense to help them to develop a knowledge of what mining texts means, when to employ these strategies, and how to manage these strategies in order to direct their own reading-writing process. At the same time, I would offer one caveat: teaching students to mine texts — to attend to certain text features in reading and writing — should be part of an ongoing process of reading situations and of representing the demands of a given context for writing. In these ways, mining texts emerges as a means of weighing options and choices in light of what is required in a given situation. As one student reflected:

> The usefulness of [mining a text] depends on your own purpose for reading. If you're reading in order to gain ideas for our own writing then reading like a writer is useful. Otherwise, it is more of a burden. For example, if you were reading a physics textbook in order to learn how to do your physics homework assignment, then reading like a writer . . . would just get in the way. If you were planning on writing your own textbook, then perhaps you would want to read other texts like a writer in order to get a feel for what your task will entail and to get an idea of how you will write your book. Examining the choices the authors of other books made could, indeed, strengthen your own text.

Two points are worth emphasizing in this student's observation. First, he calls attention to the important relationship between purpose and strategy. It is one thing to develop a repertoire of strategies; it is quite another to understand the circumstances under which one might use these strategies to best effect. Second, he makes an implicit distinction between recitation and contribution. If students are to read in the role of writers, we need to give them opportunities to write — to enter conversations.

Finally, we can share with students transcripts of think-aloud protocols and retrospective accounts such as those discussed in the previous section. By reading transcripts, students can see how others translate a set of strategies flexibly into actions they can take in reading to write. In this way, students are encouraged to reflect upon their own decision-making process as readers and writers relative to how others make decisions, set goals, and choose certain paths. Perhaps most important, students can help us generate new knowledge about how a sense of authorship can inform reading.

Conclusion

In learning to mine texts, students recognize that the choices and decisions they make as writers vary according to the social context in which they write. This is an important distinguishing feature between the notion of mining texts and other pedagogical approaches that treat writing as invariable across different social situations. Moreover, the notion of mining texts embodies a valued process that can enable students to fulfill the cycle of literacy. Such a cycle enables them to be more than "deferentially literate" (Newkirk, 1982), that is, politely observing what other authors have accomplished in their writing. Instead, students are given the promise of contributing as authors.

Notes

1. Portions of this chapter are included in Greene (1992) and appear with permission. This earlier piece includes a more complete analysis of the theoretical issues raised here.

2. For a discussion of the validity of think-aloud protocols, please see the Appendix at the end of this volume.

3. See Greene & Higgins (in press) and the Appendix for a discussion of the reliability of retrospective accounts.

References

Applebee, A. (1984). *Contexts for learning to write*. Norwood, NJ: Ablex.

Atwell, N. (1985). Writing and reading from the inside out. In J. Hansen, T. Newkirk, & D. Graves (Eds.), *Breaking ground: Teachers relate reading and writing in the elementary school* (pp. 147–165). Exeter, NH: Heinemann Educational Books.

Atwell, N. (1987). *In the middle: Writing, reading, and learning with adolescents*. Portsmouth, NH: Heinemann.

Barnes, D. (1976). *From communication to curriculum*. Hammondsworth, UK: Penguin.

Bartholomae, D. (1985). Inventing the university. In M. Rose (Ed.), *When a writer can't write* (pp. 134–165). New York: Guilford.

Bazerman, C. (1980). A relationship between reading and writing: The conversational model. *College English, 41*, 656–661.

Bazerman, C. (1985). Physicists reading physics: Schema-laden purposes and purpose-laden schema. *Written Communication, 2,* 3–23.

Bereiter, C. & Scardamalia, M. (1984). Learning about writing through reading. *Written Communication, 1,* 163–188.

Britton, J. (1982). Spectator role and the beginnings of writing. In G. Pradl (Ed.), *Prospect and retrospect: Selected essays of J. Britton* (pp. 46–67). Upper Montclair, NJ: Boynton/Cook.

Brown, A. L. & Palinscar, A. S. (1989). Guided, cooperative learning, and individual knowledge acquisition. In L. B. Resnick (Ed.), *Knowing, learning, and instruction: Essays in honor of Robert Glaser* (pp. 393–451). Hillsdale, NJ: Erlbaum.

Bruffee, K. A. (1984). Collaborative learning and "The conversation of mankind." *College English, 46,* 635–652.

Church, E. & Bereiter, C. (1984). Reading for style. In J. Jensen (Ed.), *Composing and comprehending* (pp. 85–91). Urbana, IL: ERIC Clearinghouse on Reading and Communication Skills.

Collins, A., Brown, J. S., & Newman, S. E. (1989). Cognitive apprenticeship: Teaching the crafts of reading, writing, and mathematics. In L. B. Resnick (Ed.), *Knowing, learning, and instruction: Essays in honor of Robert Glaser* (pp. 453–494). Hillsdale, NJ: Erlbaum.

Corbett, E. P. J. (1971). The theory and practice of imitation in classical rhetoric. *College Composition and Communication, 22,* 245–250.

Flower, L. & Higgins, L. (1991). Collaboration and the construction of meaning. (Tech. Rpt. #56). Center for the Study of Writing at Carnegie Mellon and University of California, Berkeley.

Greene, S. & Higgins, L. (in press). Once upon a time: The role of retrospective accounts in building theory. In P. Smagorinsky (Ed.), *Verbal reports in the study of writing.* Newbury Park, CA: Sage Press.

Greene, S. (1992). Mining texts in reading to write. *Journal of Advanced Composition, 12.1,* 151–170.

Haas, C. & Flower, L. (1988). Rhetorical reading strategies and the construction of meaning. *College Composition and Communication, 39,* 167–183.

Higgins, L., Flower, L., & Petraglia, J. (1992). Planning text together: The role of critical reflection in student collaboration. *Written Communication, 9,* 48–84.

Hillocks, G. (1986). The writer's knowledge: Theory, research, and the implications for practice. In A. Petrosky & D. Bartholomae (Eds.), *The teaching of writing* (pp. 71–94). Chicago: The University of Chicago Press.

McPhee, J. (1969). *The Pine Barrens.* New York: Farrar, Straus & Giroux.

Myers, G. (1990). *Writing biology: Texts in the social construction of knowledge.* Madison: University of Wisconsin Press.

Newkirk, T. (1982). Young writers as critical readers. In T. Newkirk & N. Atwell (Eds.), *Understanding writing: Ways of observing, learning, and teaching* (pp. 106–113). Chelmsford, MA: Northeast Regional Exchange.

Nystrand, M. (1986). *The structure of written communication.* Orlando, FL: Academic Press.

Smagorinsky, P. (in press). How reading model essays affects writers. In J. Irwin & M. Doyle (Eds.), *Research in making reading-writing connections.* Newark, DE: IRA.

Spivey, N. N. (1990). Transforming texts: Constructive processes in reading and writing. *Written Communication, 7,* 256–287.

Stein, V. (1990). Elaboration: Using what you know. In L. Flower, et al., *Reading-to-write: Exploring a cognitive and social process* (pp. 144–155). New York: Oxford University Press.

Swales, J. (1984). Research into the structure of introductions to journal articles and its application to the teaching of academic writing. In J. Swales & J. Kirkman (Eds.), *Common ground: Interests in ESP and communication studies* (pp. 77–86). New York: Pergamon Press.

Vygotsky, L. (1962). *Thought and language.* Trans. E. Hanfmann & G. Vakar. Cambridge, MA: MIT Press.

Vygotsky, L. (1978). *Mind in society*. Trans. M. Cole & S. Scribner. Cambridge, MA: Harvard University Press.
Wertsch, J. & Stone, C. A. (1985). The concept of internalization. In J. Wertsch (Ed.), *Culture communication and cognition* (pp. 162-179). New York: Cambridge University Press.

Appendix I: Handbook Assignment

One goal of the course consists of learning to read like writers, to mine texts in light of your own goals as writers. As you know by now, this type of reading encourages you to attend to important features of the texts you read, so that you can develop a well-defined set of strategies that you can use as writers. Mining texts also means looking at what is not written, reconstructing the choices a writer might have considered in producing a text in a given rhetorical situation. Importantly, we have begun to see that reading like a writer is an action, a series of steps that you can take in writing texts of your own.

The literary journalists help us to see that an impetus for writing — curiosity, interest, the need to solve a problem or to make people aware of something they need to know about — leads to a series of actions. They engage in informal talk and conduct interviews, search the stacks in libraries, observe people and events, and take field notes. Yet what happens when writers begin to write? What choices must they make? How do they make their decisions? When do writers make these choices and decisions? For now, I would simply wager the guess that there are certain choice points in the process of writing that force writers to consider their options — the information they have, the context they want to establish, the most effective organizational pattern for conveying issues and ideas, and the language that is appropriate for a given audience (e.g., disciplinary community). I have suggested that at various choice points writers make decisions like users on a computer select options from a pop-up menu on a screen and then sort through the different options available to them, though this decision-making process may not be altogether conscious:

Context	**Structure**	**Language**
Historical	Narrative	Discipline-
Political	Scientific	Specific
Social	Report	Academic

During the remainder of the term, I would like you to help me understand the ways we can translate the notion of mining texts into a set of things we can do when we read and write. More precisely, as you read and write in this course and others, I would like you to build your own *private* set of strategies. By the end of the term, you should have developed a handbook that can serve as a guide, suggesting when mining texts might be most useful and what sorts of options might be most helpful in writing different kinds of papers in different situations. This project will culminate in your final paper, an analysis of your own reading and writing process. Perhaps more important, the analysis and handbook are part of a collaborative effort to make sense of what it means to mine texts.

Appendix II: Brian's Handbook

CONTEXT

Genetics of Psychopathology – **David Rosenthal**

The book establishes context in the first 3 chapters. Chapter 1 gives a brief history of how man has tried to explain psychopathic disorders. It talks about Greek "logical" explanations, "discoveries" from medieval times to the nineteenth century, etc. Chapter 2 ties psychopathology into the field of evolution. It describes how the fact that we reproduce sexually helps our species grow and adapt, but it also gives rise to "mutations" in our genes. Chapter 3 is a general background on genetics. Miosis, mitosis, mutation, and DNA are topics covered.

"Travels in Georgia" – John McPhee

- Never clearly establishes context, basically starts right in with his story and lets you get the idea
- Tells what Carol and Sam stand for in the encounter with Chip Crusey
- In this same section McPhee talks about why this creek is being disturbed. Fills us in about the Soil Conservation Service and about making a "water resource channel improvement." This gives us some background, and some idea of what Carol and Jim do.

Philosophy of Natural Science – **Carl Hempel**

Sets up the book in Chapter 1 entitled "Scope and Aim of this Book." In this chapter he describes what the natural sciences are, and what the book will deal with. Mostly in the last paragraph of the chapter he tells in detail what he is going to write about.

STRATEGIES FOR ESTABLISHING CONTEXT

1. Background information – good for situations where your audience has limited knowledge of your subject. Ideally, you should supply enough background information so that your audience has a solid knowledge of the field you're discussing and/or a general idea of what motivates your characters. Works well when describing "technical" subjects (i.e., "Flying Upside Down").
2. Jumping in – basically not establishing context. Useful when dealing with subject matter that is somewhat bizarre or out of the ordinary. Helps ease people into what is potentially a "shocking" subject or idea. Works especially well in narrative because it creates a sort of curiosity (i.e., "Travels in Georgia" and "Invasive Procedures").

3. History—establishing context by giving a brief overview of "what has been on your topic until now." Especially useful in describing the reasons for the evolution of your field. For example, (in psychology) introspectionism didn't cut it, so the Behaviorist view emerged. This movement helped, but it didn't explain internal thought processes. Thus, cognitive psychology was born . . . (then go on about cognitive psychology). Also useful because in giving a brief history often the motivation behind your study is revealed or at least more readily understood.

4. Establish importance—establishing context by telling why what you have to say is important. Helpful when the value of your information is not completely obvious (i.e., why study auctions? . . . then deal with why, in fact, anybody would want to study auctions).

5. "Shocker"—closely related to jumping in except the easing in part is intentionally skipped in order to shock the reader. Useful when the author's tone is one of disapproval and he wants this tone to be instilled in the reader (i.e., *Brave New World*).

FORM

Genetics of Psychopathology

After the 3-chapter introduction the book's following chapters all take a similar form. First they give a general background of the disorder to be discussed. Then they talk about how widely the disorder is "distributed" among the population. Finally, they describe studies that reflect a genetic influence on the disorder.

Brave New World — Aldous Huxley

Divided into 3 basic parts:

- Episode where the students are touring the "Central Cordon Hatchery and Conditioning Center." This gives background information as to what the world is like.
- The main plot about the savage and his condition, he does not fit in BNW or on the reservation. In addition, this deals with other characters' interaction with the savage and his effect on them.
- The savage's talk with Mustupha Mond ("a world controller")

These parts are divided into chapters. In Chapter 3 Huxley describes 3 different occurrences (Mond's lecture, Lenina and Fanny's conversation, and Bernard's thoughts) all at once. Each event is divided into parts and interrupted by the other events in between parts. This shows the contrasts between the ideas and the seclusion of Bernard.

Philosophy of Natural Science

Each chapter is broken into sections that deal with separate but related topics. Generally with each section he describes a certain theory of conviction, and he elaborates on this with the use of examples of actual scientific laws or hypotheses.

STRATEGIES WITH FORM

1. Outline — useful for information or educational materials (textbooks), when the data lends itself to hierarchical structure.
2. Dialogue/Description — good in narratives. Basically switching back and forth from description of area, characters, etc. to actual dialogue (found in almost all the literary journalists' stuff).
3. Flashback — breaking off in the middle of something and describing events that happened earlier. Useful as a sort of colorful way of describing characters. Also, at times it is a necessity in dramatic writing. Sometimes you need to describe earlier events but don't want to give a "history" of everything that has gone on in the character's past.
4. Sections — much like outlining except that the information does not fit into a hierarchy. Also widely used in textbooks. Good for situations where the information is related but not ranked by importance.
5. Definition, Argument, Example — done throughout philosophy. The definition part clarifies exactly what the author is talking about (so there can be no debate about the actual subject). The argument section expresses the author's views on his topic. The examples help show the practicality or usefulness of the ideas the author has introduced. This form is good for persuasive papers.

LANGUAGE

"Flying Upside Down" — Mark Kramer

- Points out the unique uses of common words or expressions within the group of engineers such as "no muss, no fuss," "quick and dirty," "wars," "shootouts," "hired guns," "the win," etc.

"Growth and Slowdown in Advanced Capitalist Economies" — Angus Maddison

- Very technical — uses the language of the field. Words and acronyms appear that you are assumed to have knowledge: GDP, OECD, Growth accountancy, incremental output, ratio, etc.

On Liberty — John Stuart Mill

- Sentences are long-winded, lots of commas, complex thoughts
- Words of philosophy: truism, individuality, judgment, approbation, infallibility, etc.

Philosophy of Natural Science — Carl Hempel

His sections are interwoven with technical terms from different scientific laws and hypotheses. He talks as if you should know what he is referring to. It seems as if he thinks he is writing to a fairly knowledgeable audience.

STRATEGIES FOR LANGUAGE

1. Giving examples—sometimes the language of the characters in the story is just slightly different from our own everyday speech. In this case, it's OK just to give examples of this unique language to give people a taste of the difference between "how we think" and "how they think."
2. Using "their" language—good for when you are trying to create a different setting. You just start in with the characters using their own language. This helps create a "separate" atmosphere and lets people know that these characters are "different" than they are.
3. Audience question—whenever you write something that is supposed to inform someone else about a subject, you must always take into account your audience's knowledge of your topic. This knowledge will determine how much of the "language of the field" you use in your paper.

4

Writing and Learning: Exploring the Consequences of Task Interpretation

ANN M. PENROSE

Teachers across disciplines and grade levels have discovered that writing can serve many purposes in the classroom. Writing-across-the-curriculum theorists suggest a variety of write-to-learn activities, from free writing in journals to summarizing class lectures to working with papers through multiple drafts. In the composition literature, support for these activities has come largely from intuitive arguments about the value of writing as a way to learn. Emig, for example, in her seminal essay "Writing as a Mode of Learning" (1977), argued that one way writing helps us learn is by forcing us to engage actively with our material. Shaughnessy (1977) suggested that this activity embeds the material more "deeply" in memory. Others have described writing as a "connective" activity, arguing that the process of writing forces us to discover and articulate relationships between what might otherwise be discrete bits of knowledge (e.g., Murray, 1980; Britton, 1981) and encourages us to go beyond the text, to engage in imaginative and speculative thinking (cf. Fulwiler, 1982). From our own experiences as writers, and from observing our students' ideas develop as they write, we have come to believe that writing encourages us to be precise, to make connections, to speculate, to examine our subject from multiple perspectives. We have only recently begun to accumulate research evidence that can help us verify or refine these intuitions.

What We Know About Writing as a Way to Learn

We know writing can enhance student learning in important and exciting ways, but we also know that the value of writing as a means for learning varies from one writing task to another, from one classroom to another, and from one student to the next. Research to date suggests four key variables in the relationship between writing and learning: the type of learning desired, the nature of the material to be learned, the nature of the writing task, and characteristics of writers themselves.

The Value of Writing as a Means for Learning Varies According to the Type of Learning Desired

Studies of writing-to-learn have defined "learning" in a number of ways. The easiest type of learning to test, of course, is simple comprehension, particularly factual recall, and most experimental studies have included measures of this sort. Results on this type of learning have been mixed. When compared with nonwriting activities such as answering multiple-choice questions, writing does appear to help students remember and use facts from their reading (Copeland, 1985, working with sixth graders). However, research has demonstrated no clear advantage for extended or essay writing over shorter, more text-based writing activities when it comes to factual recall or application measures. In one of the first studies of this type, Newell (1984) compared learning gains across three writing activities: note taking, answering study questions, and essay writing. He found no effect of task on eleventh graders' ability to recall simple facts and relationships or to answer application questions; none of the three activities consistently resulted in higher scores on these measures. In my own research with college freshmen (Penrose, 1989), essay writing actually led to lower factual recall and application scores when compared with a direct studying task in which students chose their own study and note-taking strategies.

These few studies suggest that the benefits of writing as an aid to basic comprehension may disappear as students mature, perhaps indicating that younger students benefit from the extra concentration and time-on-task that writing activities require. As students become more familiar with academic studying, however, they develop efficient study strategies of their own. Requiring advanced learners to use essay writing instead of their normal study strategies may then interfere with, rather than enhance, their learning of basic facts and concepts.

Beyond the level of factual recall, extended writing shows much more promise as a means for learning. Newell (1984), in the study mentioned above, and Langer (1986), in a similar study, found that essay writing significantly influenced the organization of students' concept knowledge when compared with note taking and answering study questions. Further analyses of Newell's data (Newell & Winograd, 1989) revealed that the essay task led to more coherent recall of the "gist" of the original passage, prompting Newell and Winograd to hypothesize that because essay writing involves global planning it requires more extensive manipulation of the source material, leading to "an enduring mental representation of passage gist" (p. 211). In my study as well, the essays students wrote revealed higher levels of learning that were not captured by the low-level comprehension measures I employed. Examples from that study, included later in this chapter, will illustrate the reflective and analytic thinking that essay writing enabled students to engage in. Higher order thinking is clearly more difficult to measure than simple comprehension, but research thus far suggests that writing holds far greater potential as an opportunity for higher level learning than as an aid to factual recall. Taken together, these findings suggest further that the value of writing as a means for learning will depend on the type of material we ask students to write about.

The Relationship Between Writing and Learning Varies with the Nature of the Material to Be Learned

In keeping with the above trends, research has demonstrated that essay writing is more helpful when students are working with abstract material than with factual material (Penrose, 1992), and when they're working with difficult rather than "easy" texts (Langer & Applebee, 1987). In the latter study, Langer and Applebee found that the effectiveness of particular essay writing tasks depended in part on the type of material in the source passage: writing activities were more effective than simply rereading and studying when students were working with difficult text material, but studying was equally as effective as writing when the source text was easier to understand.

Marshall (1987) found essay writing tasks particularly useful in helping students understand literary texts. Also working with eleventh graders, Marshall designed two essay writing tasks that students completed after reading a short piece of fiction: a Personal Writing task in which students were to explain and elaborate upon their responses to the story, and a Formal Writing task, in which they gave an extended interpretation of the story, drawing inferences from the text. These tasks were compared with short answer questions and with a no-writing condition. When students were later tested for their understanding of the story, those who had completed short-answer questions scored similarly to those who had done no writing at all and both groups scored significantly lower than the two essay writing groups. Marshall concluded that the short-answer task may actually have interfered with students' "developing impression of the stories' plots, characters and central meanings" (p. 57) because it encouraged them to shift focus from one isolated aspect of the text to another. The extended writing tasks presumably encouraged students to connect and integrate their observations, enabling them to focus on larger issues and on the relationships between parts of the text, rather than on the parts alone.

Such analyses offer strong support for the assumption that writing offers opportunities to connect and integrate. In generalizing from these findings, however, it's important to note that different essay writing tasks encourage different amounts and types of integration.

The Interaction of Writing and Learning Will Vary According to the Nature of the Writing Task Itself

If we want to fully understand the relationship between writing and learning, we need to look closely at the learning that takes place as writers write different kinds of texts. Researchers have begun to examine both the products and the processes of different writing tasks in an effort to describe the types of thinking that various tasks encourage.

For example, in comparing summary writing with analytic writing, Langer and Applebee (1987) found that summary writing led to rather generalized effects on learning but involved only superficial manipulation of the material. That is, students learned much of the information in the passage they read, but they learned it at a relatively superficial level. In analytic writing tasks, on the other hand, students focused on a smaller body of information but learned it more thoroughly. Langer and Applebee point out that the effects of analytic writing are limited and therefore potentially limiting: the process of writing an essay does not necessarily encourage a more careful review of all the material at hand, as we often assume (p. 130).

In order to learn more about the specific learning benefits of particular writing tasks, other studies have examined writers' texts and think-aloud protocol comments in an effort to describe the cognitive operations that different tasks encourage. Durst (1987), for example, found analytic writing to encourage more questioning, more high-level planning, and more construction of new meaning than summary writing; Applebee, Durst, and Newell (1984) observed different patterns of logical operations in the two tasks (e.g., time sequence was more common in summary writing; classification and contrast in analytic writing). Newell and Winograd (1989) used the Applebee, Durst, and Newell system to examine logical patterns in the study cited above, and Marshall (1987) also included some analysis of reasoning operations in his study of personal and formal essay writing.

This line of research is helping us identify both the potential and the limitations of particular writing activities. These analyses of the types of reasoning encouraged by different tasks point to specific benefits rather than generalized effects of writing (Newell & Winograd, 1989, p. 211; Schumacher & Nash, 1991), underscoring the critical role of the writing assignment itself. The assignment we develop is a critical variable in the write-to-learn process, and it is the only variable the teacher can directly control. These early findings suggest that the type of writing assignment we choose to give our students will — to some extent — determine the type of learning they engage in.

But we know from experience that different students will handle our assignments in different ways. Definitive comparisons of writing tasks are difficult to achieve due to the wide range of variation among writers.

The Value of Writing as a Means for Learning
Is Also a Function of Individual Writers'
Goals, Skills, and Assumptions

There is, of course, plenty of research evidence to support the assumption of individual differences among writers — not just between novices and experts, but within these groups as well. Research has demonstrated differences in planning strategies (Flower & Hayes, 1981), in organizing (Bereiter & Scardamalia, 1986), in revising (Sommers, 1980; Faigley & Witte, 1981; Flower, Hayes et al., 1986), and in many other aspects of the composing process, any of which can be expected to influence how a writer interprets a particular task and what he or she ultimately writes. Other studies have examined the role of task interpretation more directly (Langer, 1984; Flower, Stein et al., 1990; Nelson & Hayes, 1988; Nelson, 1990), in each case discovering a wide range of interpretations of the particular task under study.

This understanding of learner characteristics suggests that students given the same assignment will, in effect, do different tasks — because they differ in reading and writing ability, in prior knowledge of the topic, in how they interpret the assignment, and in many other ways. Sometimes these differences are inconsequential; at other times they are large and important. Studies of the composing process have shown that such differences affect the quality of students' written work, and it seems reasonable to expect the quality of their learning to be affected as well. Differences in knowledge, skill, and experience may enable students to reap different benefits from particular writing tasks, as the examples in the next section of this chapter will illustrate.

The research reviewed here suggests that writing will be most beneficial as a means for learning when the following conditions hold:

- *The writing task matches the learning goal.* In designing writing-to-learn assignments, we need first to determine the types of learning we'd like students to engage in. Only then can we decide whether writing will be the most effective means for helping students achieve those learning goals, and only then will we be able to design writing tasks to meet the goals we've identified.
- *Students understand both the learning and the writing goals.* Once we've articulated our learning goals for ourselves, it seems sensible to let students in on that information. As the first chapter in this volume has argued, we stand a better chance of helping students take control of their learning if we help them develop a range of strategies and a sense of when and how to choose among them. They cannot make sensible choices if they do not know the goals we want them to accomplish. We need to tell them not just what kind of paper to write but why we've chosen this particular task and how it will move them toward the larger goals of the

course. Students will be less likely to "misinterpret" our tasks if we share our own interpretations with them.

- *Teachers provide support throughout the writing process.* Teacher support is of course vital in any writing situation and is emphasized in each of the chapters in this volume, but this crucial factor becomes even more important as students encounter writing assignments across the disciplines. Not only must students learn the forms and conventions of writing in each of the disciplines they encounter, they must also recognize the types of learning that are expected in each (cf. Herrington, 1985; Faigley & Hansen, 1985; McCarthy, 1987; Walvoord & McCarthy, 1990). It is important for teachers as well as students to realize that writing and learning goals may vary across the disciplines; students will need special support in interpreting and carrying out assignments in these varied territories. (In this volume, Nelson illustrates the influence of process supports such as drafts and oral presentations on students' work on a research paper in psychology; Higgins describes ways in which students were encouraged to adopt argumentation rather than recitation strategies in response to an American history assignment.)

Examining the Consequences of Task Interpretation

We can learn more about the relationship between writing and learning by examining real students' interactions with real writing tasks. Consider the following drafts written by college freshmen, each working with the same source text. The source is a 1200-word passage on the concept of paternalism; it provides an extended definition of the concept and a discussion of cultural systems that operate on this principle. The beginning of the text appears below, followed by portions of three student drafts. The complete texts are included in the appendix to this chapter.

As will become evident, the students used the source material in quite different ways. In each case, speculate about what type of writing assignment the student had been given.

Source Text
Paternalism, according to Webster's Seventh Collegiate Dictionary, is "a system under which an authority treats those under its control in a fatherly way, especially in regulating their conduct and supplying their needs." In the United States, there are some economic relationships that can be aptly described as paternalistic. For example, affluent families hire domestic servants who sometimes come to be regarded and treated as family members. But such relationships do not describe the mainstream of the American economy. For the most part, workers in America are protected by union contracts and legal rights. They do not routinely look upon their employer as a fatherly or parental figure who will attend to their general welfare and happiness in return for the services they render.

In cultures where there is no strong, centralized government to define and protect the rights of common individuals, however, "parental concern" is often a vital bond holding together the culture's major social and economic relationships. Instead of looking to the government for rights, protection, and support, individuals in these cultures routinely turn to the wealthy, powerful, and privileged. Historians and sociologists have described such relationships as "paternalistic." Studies of paternalism have explored European feudalism, landlord/tenant relations in India, manager/worker relations in the Japanese factory, plantation master/slave relations in Brazil, and corporate paternalism in early capitalist America when industry had to attract workers away from the comfort and security of the family farm. . . .

Jack's Draft
Paternalism is "a system under which an authority treats those under its control in a fatherly way, especially in regulating their conduct and supplying their needs." In the U.S., some economic relationships can be described as paternalistic. For example, domestic servants of affluent families sometimes regarded and treated as family members. Such relationships not common in American economy. Workers in America are protected by union contracts & legal rights. They do not routinely look upon their employers as a fatherly or paternal figure.

   In cultures where there is no strong, centralized government, "parental concern" is often a vital bond. Individuals look to the wealthy, powerful & privileged instead of the government for rights, protection & support. Such relationships are described as "paternalistic." Some examples include European feudalism, landlord/tenant relations in India, manager/worker relations in the Japanese factory, plantation master/slave relations in Brazil, and corporate paternalism in early America. . . .

Ned's Draft
Paternalism is a word that most people are familiar with, however, they are really only familiar with one definition. They would describe paternalism as the relationship between a father and child. They would go on to give an example, probably from their household or somebody they know household, where the father is the highest figure and has the last say in any situation. Though this is a very general term it does complete the task of defining the word.

   With this definition in mind, I would like to give the other important definition that many of us don't even know. Imagine a company, such as Alcoa or Ford, where there are many people working for the company. We will be very specific and only describe those people that have low-level jobs, such as the factory workers. These people, many who have probably worked for the company for a while, have a dependence upon that company. They work for the company, recieve their paychecks weekly, and with this money, they are able to feed their family, pay the bills and hopefully have a little extra to spend on leisure or save. This worker is in a very similar position to that of a child in the above genetic paternalism relationship. He has a very large dependence upon a fatherly figure, which in this case is the owner or board of trustees of the company. He depends on these people to keep his welfare alive. Thus one can see that there is a so called paternalistic relationship in the economic world. . . .

Ruth's Draft (in its entirety)
Paternalism is very beneficial to some countries and economics systems. But there some flaw in the paternalistic systems. Japan is one country that has benefitted from the paternalistic system, yet in America the idea of paternalism would cause dissention between the government and the people.

As in the relationship of a father and child, the father is looking in child's best interests. He wants his child to broaden their horizons and reach their goals on the ladder of success. In the economic paternalism, the employer or one in control, is only looking out for his best interests. He will do anything to keep his "good, little" worker from straying too far. He will treat the worker in a fatherly way and also carry that father-figure too far by controlling the worker as if he were the employers child. You see how economic paternalism can take the features of a father/child relationship.

The only advantage I can see for having a economic paternalistic system in a country is the country will be unified. This unification is great for the government, but how does it affect the workers? These workers may not have the same opportunity to asceed to their goals due to ignorance or the always present put down from the employer/government, so they are stuck in this type of relationship.

The paternalistic system may be good for countries like Japan, but I'm glad this type of system is not in the U.S. It is wrong for a person to keep another person 'a child' in the sense of word. An employer can show the same type of affection or caring a parent shows for their child, but they can also let that child reach for their goals.

Most readers conclude from these drafts that Jack was asked to write a close paraphrase of the source text, that Ned was told to summarize and explain the main ideas of the passage, and that Ruth was asked to write an evaluative response to the content of the passage. In fact however, the three students were responding to the same assignment. Jack, Ned, and Ruth were among forty students participating in a writing study (Penrose, 1989; 1992). The students were given one hour to read the passage on paternalism and "write a paper" on that topic. They were told the paper should be "an informative essay, focused around the key issues or concepts that you think someone should know from the reading."

The drafts themselves demonstrate that this generic writing task was interpreted by students in a variety of ways, but more direct evidence of interpretation can be found in the students' descriptions of their writing goals. After they had completed their drafts, students wrote answers to the following questions: "What kind of paper did you write? What kind of paper did the assignment call for?" Jack responded, as his essay suggests, that he was to "Try to paraphrase article. To inform reader about article's topic." Ned, parroting the task directions, stated that he wrote an "informative essay giving the main points from the reading," and noted that the instructions "really didn't say" what kind of paper he was to write. Lastly, Ruth explained, "I wrote a more personal essay. I put a lot of my beliefs of the subject matter, but I also used the facts from the paper. I think the paper assignment called for a more informative paper. It was to summarize the paper's content!"

What is striking about these comments is how closely they match the goals that readers typically infer from students' written products. The comments reveal the intentions behind these products. Jack didn't just happen to write a close paraphrase in response to this assignment: he set out to paraphrase. Jack's comments convey a clear sense of purpose; Ned's indicate frustration at not being able to ascertain the "real" purpose of the task. Ned recognized that the task directions were vague and tried his best to make sense of the few clues he was given — that the essay should be "informative" and should include the "key issues or concepts" from the reading. Both writers' comments indicate an awareness of their interpretation of the task.

Ruth's comments go a step further, revealing an awareness of alternative interpretations. Ruth's comments are perhaps the most telling, for they suggest not only that Ruth knew she was writing a personal response, but also that she knew such a response was inappropriate. She felt the assignment called for an objective summary rather than the more evaluative piece she wrote. What is interesting here is not that Ruth knowingly "misinterpreted" the assignment, but that she was able to envision more than one response to this particular assignment and that she made a choice from among these alternatives.

Ruth's active interpretation of the task directions can be seen even more clearly in the comments she made during the writing task itself. Students in this study gave think-aloud protocols as they worked; that is, they spoke aloud into a tape recorder as they read the source text, took notes, composed sentences, daydreamed, and so on. Thus we have a running record of what they were thinking about as they worked.* The transcripts of these tapes, along with the written material students produced, enable us to develop a profile of each student's writing and reading processes. Ruth's transcript, for example, shows she is an active and astute reader. Of the three students described here, Ruth seemed to have the easiest time understanding the paternalism passage. She read quickly, jotting key phrases and sub-topics in her notes, and pausing often to reflect on the content of the passage. The following excerpt from her think-aloud transcript shows Ruth thinking about what kind of essay she will write. She has just finished a first pass through the source text, reading and making notes.

> okay . . . so . . . I'm worried about . . . okay when . . . let's see . . . all right . . . hmm . . . what is this? . . . can't write about this . . . it's so repetitious . . . all right . . . ah . . . let's see . . . paternalism is a nice way of stabbing workers in the back . . . all right . . . ah . . . okay . . . how are we going to start this . . . "a system of which an authority treats" . . . well I can write about how I feel about this . . . I think I will . . .

In this brief excerpt, Ruth complains about the boring source text, considers starting her own essay in a similar boring way (the quoted segment is based on the source text), and decides instead to write about how she feels. Like the retrospective comments mentioned earlier, Ruth's transcript shows us what her written text could not — that she recognized alternatives and chose among them.

Ned's transcript also reveals more than his final product. Most readers see Ned's essay as the most thorough and elaborated of the three; a comparison

---

*For further discussion of the think-aloud protocol technique and the instructions these students received, see the Appendix, "Conducting Process Research," at the end of this volume.

of his full draft with the source text will reveal that he carefully follows the structure of the original passage but often adds examples and explanations for the reader. His paper is seen as informative and non-evaluative, clearly taking the objective stance that he (and Ruth) felt the assignment called for. What his essay doesn't reveal, however, is that Ned developed strong opinions on the topic of paternalism, as the following transcript excerpt demonstrates.

> okay ah . . . it's true what he's saying in the last paragraph but I disagree with it totally . . . I mean because we have this big thing . . . big thing with ah . . . how everybody should have their own rights . . . and I mean . . . with this paternalistic connection . . . I don't think you're doing anything with human rights . . . just actually . . . certain people need a figure . . . and ah . . . you know maybe some people will always need that figure . . . not that it's bad or good . . . but it's just going to help them keep on track and feed their family whatever . . . so now I read through . . . okay . . . I'm going to make an outline . . .

Unlike Ruth, Ned did not include his opinions in his "informative" paper, presumably considering such personal response inappropriate for this assignment. Because the transcript contains no explicit discussion of this alternative, we have no way of knowing whether Ned made a conscious decision not to include his own views or whether this was simply a default assumption about academic writing, perhaps exacerbated by the experimental context. We know only that Ned has insights that would have enabled him to write a very different essay on the topic of paternalism, had he chosen to do so.

In contrast to Ned and Ruth, Jack's transcript reveals virtually no reflection on the task at all, or on the topic of paternalism, though he spent more time on this task than either of the other two writers. Jack took a methodical, indeed mechanical, approach to this assignment, proceeding essentially sentence by sentence through the source text, paraphrasing or copying each segment first into his notes (omitting connectives and modifiers) and then from his notes into his draft (often reinserting connectives omitted earlier).

Jack's painstaking approach contrasts sharply with Ruth's holistic and subjective response to the topic, and to Ned's careful analysis and elaborations. Again, we have no way of knowing what other options Jack had available to him, if any — perhaps Jack doesn't know that it's okay to add to source material, as in Ned's elaborations or Ruth's statements of opinion; perhaps he doesn't feel comfortable doing so; perhaps he doesn't know how. In this study, students were screened for prior knowledge about paternalism, so we can assume that none of these students had extensive knowledge of the topic, but we must also assume that the students differed from each other in many ways — perhaps in reading ability, in writing skill, in experience with academic tasks. In addition, and perhaps as a consequence, these students differed in their interpretation of this reading/writing task. Certainly Jack, Ned, and Ruth set different goals for this assignment and wrote quite different essays as a result.

But we're interested here in what these students *learned* about the concept of paternalism. It seems reasonable to expect these varied approaches to the writing task to facilitate varied types of learning as well. We might predict, for example, that Ruth developed a more complex understanding of paternalism than Jack, since she had reflected on the material and its implications while Jack simply transferred information from the source text to his own. Indeed, this hypothesis is supported by results of comprehension tests that students took after they had written. Of the three students, Jack scored the highest on simple recall items, questions that called for individual facts from the source text (Jack answered 57% of these questions correctly, Ruth 43%, Ned 29%); but his score was the lowest on complex recall questions, which required students to recall and relate information from different parts of the passage (Ruth 78% correct, Ned 44%, Jack 33%). Conversely, Jack (73%) and Ned (64%) were much better able to answer questions about the structure of the original passage than Ruth (27%), who, unlike the other two writers, had paid little attention to that structure in writing her own text.

Jack's close paraphrase strategy apparently helped him learn isolated facts from the source passage but did not encourage him to see connections among those facts. Ned, too, had difficulty making connections within the text, though his essay suggests he made many connections to outside knowledge and experience. On the other hand, Ruth's evaluative approach seems to have enabled her to "see the big picture," though it may have distracted her from attending to the specifics of the passage or its structure. She may have difficulty reconstructing this particular author's argument, but she understands the concept of paternalism and its applications quite well.

Other factors undoubtedly contributed to these comprehension differences, for, as noted above, these students differed in many ways. But the fact remains that Jack, Ned, and Ruth interpreted this particular writing task in quite different ways; they therefore wrote different kinds of papers, which focused their attention on different parts and levels of the source text material; and they learned different things through this writing experience. The choices they made in writing had consequences for their learning.

Helping Students Understand the Concept and Consequences of Task Interpretation

We need to talk with students about the decisions they make as writers and about the consequences of those decisions. As we've seen, the decision to closely reproduce a source text may help us learn the facts of the passage but prevent us from considering larger issues; the goal to write an evaluative response may distract us from attending to the logic and structure of the passage. Which of these is the "right" response, of course, depends on the instructor's goals for the assignment. Instructors in all disciplines who assign writing need to take seriously the obligation to define their goals and to let students know what these goals are. Students can choose among the various strategies at their disposal only if they fully understand what the activity is intended to accomplish.

In the writing classroom, we can prepare students to face these interpretive decisions by helping them understand the relationship between writing goals and learning consequences. One way to demonstrate the role of task interpretation is to have students examine their own interpretations and compare them with others. Students can do informal think-aloud protocols during the planning stage of a class assignment, using tape recorders while working at home (see Flower, Stein et al., 1990, for a description of large-scale classroom use of this technique). After transcribing or listening to the tapes of their planning, they can write about the goals they set, the type of essay they thought the assignment called for, the approach they planned to take in completing the assignment. Discussing their findings with others (and analyzing others' transcripts if time permits) can be an eye-opening experience for students as they discover the wide range of responses that a seemingly straightforward assignment elicited.

Once students understand that assignments, like other texts, are interpreted, other classroom research activities can help demonstrate the consequences of varying interpretations. An easy way to demonstrate the relationship between writing goals and learning outcomes is to have students analyze a range of responses to the same task, as in the previous section. I have used the sample essays in this chapter in discussing the role of task interpretation with freshman composition students. Students easily identify the distinctive features of the essays written by Jack, Ned, and Ruth, and are able to speculate about each writer's goals much as we have above. What is most important in such a discussion is that the samples are presented not as good or bad models, but as papers that meet different goals. A discussion of which is the "right" response to the assignment can make the point that different situations call for different interpretations. We can discuss with students the various types of understanding that each of these writing activities fosters and the situations in which each type may be appropriate. If an instructor wants students to learn a set of facts, for example, then the paraphrase may be adequate, but if the goal is to see whether students understand an author's argument well enough to recognize its central premises and underlying assumptions, then the paraphrase is the "wrong" response for that situation; an analysis would be better.

In addition to the essays in this chapter, sample student texts can easily be culled from existing sets of papers or from assignments early in the semester. In fact, creating sample sets of papers is a useful class activity as well, for it enables students to see firsthand the consequences of their writing decisions. We can give the class a generic writing task such as "Write a report on X," talk in class about the various ways the task could be interpreted, and then assign different groups in the class to act on each of these alternative interpretations: one group may be assigned to write a close paraphrase, another group to summarize, and another to analyze the strengths and weaknesses of the author's argument. After comparing features of the written products generated by these groups (e.g., focus of essay, level and amount of detail included, amount of outside information added), students can make predictions about the "learning consequences" of the various approaches. Or, effects on learning can be informally tested: with comprehension questions (prepared by instructor or students), in interviews between groups, by comparing written recalls of the source text. Students who simply paraphrased may be able to answer factual questions correctly but be unable to recall the author's main idea or purpose and will probably not have noticed problems or inconsistencies in the author's argument. Students who wrote analyses should be better able to answer questions about the author's point of view or the type of evidence used in the argument. It is important to point out, of course, that these essentially quantitative measures of learning are limited. Class discussion can encourage students to think about what other kinds of learning are demonstrated in essays such as Ned's or Ruth's.

Activities such as these, which enable students to examine the complex interaction of writing and learning firsthand, help them to discover that writers make choices and that these choices have consequences — not just for the quality of their writing but for the quality of their learning as well. If we can help students develop this awareness and learn to choose among alternatives, we will have helped them develop strategies for learning beyond our writing classrooms.

References

Applebee, A. N., Durst, R. K., & Newell, G. E. (1984). The demands of school writing. In A. N. Applebee, *Contexts for learning to write: Studies of secondary school instruction* (pp. 55–77). Norwood, NJ: Ablex.

Bereiter, C. & Scardamalia, M. (1986). Cognitive coping strategies and the problem of "inert knowledge." In J. W. Segal, et al. (Eds.), *Thinking and learning skills: Current research and open questions.* Vol. 2. Hillsdale, NJ: Erlbaum.

Britton, J. (1981). Language and learning across the curriculum. *Fforum, 2,* 55–56, 93–94.

Copeland, K. A. (1985). The effect of writing upon good and poor writers' learning from prose. Paper presented at the annual meeting of the National Council of Teachers of English, Philadelphia.

Durst, R. K. (1987). Cognitive and linguistic demands of analytic writing. *Research in the Teaching of English, 21*(4), 347–376.

Emig, J. (1977). Writing as a mode of learning. *College Composition and Communication, 28,* 122–128.

Faigley, L. & Hansen, K. (1985). Learning to write in the social sciences. *College Composition and Communication, 36*(2), 140–149.

Faigley, L. & Witte, S. (1981). Analyzing revision. *College Composition and Communication, 32*(4), 400–414.

Flower, L. & Hayes, J. R. (1981). Plans that guide the composing process. In C. H. Frederiksen and J. F. Dominic (Eds.), *Writing: The nature, development and teaching of written communication,* Vol. 2 (pp. 39–58). Hillsdale, NJ: Erlbaum.

Flower, L., Hayes, J. R., Carey, L., Schriver, K., & Stratman, J. (1986). Detection, diagnosis, and the strategies of revision. *College Composition and Communication, 37*(1), 16–55.

Flower, L., Stein, V., Ackerman, J., Kantz, M. J., McCormick, K., & Peck, W. C. (1990). *Reading-to-write: Exploring a cognitive and social process.* New York: Oxford University Press.

Fulwiler, T. (1982). The personal connection: Journal writing across the curriculum. In T. Fulwiler & A. Young (Eds.), *Language connections: Writing and reading across the curriculum.* Urbana, IL: National Council of Teachers of English.

Herrington, A. (1985). Writing in academic settings: A study of the contexts for writing in two college engineering courses. *Research in the Teaching of English, 19*(4), 331–359.

Langer, J. A. (1984). The effects of available information on responses to school writing tasks. *Research in the Teaching of English, 18*(1), 27–44.

Langer, J. A. (1986). Learning through writing: Study skills in the content areas. *Journal of Reading, 29*(5), 400–506.

Langer, J. A. & Applebee, A. N. (1987). *How writing shapes thinking: A study of teaching and learning* (Research Report No. 22). Urbana, IL: National Council of Teachers of English.

Marshall, J. D. (1987). The effects of writing on students' understanding of literary texts. *Research in the Teaching of English, 21*(1), 30–63.

McCarthy, L. P. (1987). A stranger in strange lands: A college student writing across the curriculum. *Research in the Teaching of English, 21*(3), 233–265.

Murray, D. (1980). Writing as process: How writing finds its own meaning. In T. R. Donovan & B. W. McClelland (Eds.), *Eight approaches to teaching composition* (pp. 3–20). Urbana, IL: National Council of Teachers of English.

Nelson, J. (1990). This was an easy assignment: Examining how students interpret academic writing tasks. *Research in the Teaching of English, 24*(4), 362–396.

Nelson, J. & Hayes, J. R. (1988). How the writing context shapes college students' strategies for writing from sources (Tech. Rpt. No. 16). Berkeley, CA: Center for the Study of Writing.

Newell, G. E. (1984). Learning from writing in two content areas: A case study/protocol analysis. *Research in the Teaching of English, 18*(3), 265–287.

Newell, G. E. & Winograd, P. (1989). The effects of writing on learning from expository text. *Written Communication, 6*(2), 196–217.

Penrose, A. M. (1989). Strategic differences in composing: Consequences for learning through writing (Tech. Rpt. No. 31). Berkeley, CA: Center for the Study of Writing.

Penrose, A. M. (1992). To write or not to write: Effects of task and task interpretation on learning through writing. *Written Communication, 9*(4), 465–500.

Schumacher, G. M. & Nash, J. G. (1991). Conceptualizing and measuring knowledge change due to writing. *Research in the Teaching of English, 25*, 67–96.

Shaughnessy, M. P. (1977). *Errors and expectations.* New York: Oxford University Press.

Sommers, N. (1980). Revision strategies of student writers and experienced adult writers. *College Composition and Communication, 31*(4), 378–388.

Walvoord, B. E. & McCarthy, L. P. (1990). *Thinking and writing in college: A naturalistic study of students in four disciplines.* Urbana, IL: National Council of Teachers of English.

Appendix: Texts

Paternalism Source Text*

Paternalism, according to Webster's Seventh Collegiate Dictionary, is "a system under which an authority treats those under its control in a fatherly way, especially in regulating their conduct and supplying their needs." In the United States, there are some economic relationships that can be aptly described as paternalistic. For example, affluent families hire domestic servants who sometimes come to be regarded and treated as family members. But such relationships do not describe the mainstream of the American economy. For the most part, workers in America are protected by union contracts and legal rights. They do not routinely look upon their employer as a fatherly or parental figure who will attend to their general welfare and happiness in return for the services they render.

In cultures where there is no strong, centralized government to define and protect

---

*Adapted from "Introduction to Paternalism," D. S. Kaufer, class handout, Carnegie Mellon University, 1985.

the rights of common individuals, however, "parental concern" is often a vital bond holding together the culture's major social and economic relationships. Instead of looking to the government for rights, protection, and support, individuals in these cultures routinely turn to the wealthy, powerful, and privileged. Historians and sociologists have described such relationships as "paternalistic." Studies of paternalism have explored European feudalism, landlord/tenant relations in India, manager/worker relations in the Japanese factory, plantation master/slave relations in Brazil, and corporate paternalism in early capitalist America when industry had to attract workers away from the comfort and security of the family farm.

Too often, however, the term misleads. Describing such systems as paternalistic causes us to overlook important characteristics of these relationships. Though these cultural systems have much in common with the genetic parent-child relationship from which the word *paternalism* derives, they differ from genetic paternalism in significant ways. Unless these differences are acknowledged, theorists who use the term in describing social or economic systems run the risk of seriously misrepresenting the true nature of these relationships.

Broadly understood, paternalism is a metaphor for the father/child or parent/child relationship as it manifests itself across a culture at large. For every metaphor, however, there are features that transfer and features that do not. When we say that Ajax was a lion in battle, for example, we wish to transfer certain features from the source domain, lions, to Ajax. We wish to say, perhaps, that Ajax was strong, ferocious and brave. But we do not wish to say that Ajax walked on four legs, lived in the African bush, or lusted after female lions. Analogously, when we speak of a cultural act, practice or attitude as paternalistic we wish to transfer certain features of the father/child relationship to that act, practice, or attitude — and not transfer others. But which features do we wish to transfer and which not?

According to traditional stereotype, parents' behavior toward their children is, on the one hand, wise, altruistic, benevolent, and protective. On the other hand, it is autocratic and not to be questioned. Parents are caring protectors, providers and guides, but they are also stern shepherds who tolerate little opposition as they raise their flock. They have only their children's best interests at heart, but they alone are usually left to decide what those best interests are. A parent is a charismatic authority and model to whom respect is often freely given. Yet parents are also in a position to command respect and obedience should they not be forthcoming. "Father knows best."

The parents' power over their children diminishes as the child develops and gains independence. As children advance in years, they become better decision-makers. Their cognitive and self-regulatory powers increase. They acquire a longer and more focused attention span; they can plan ahead and set long-term goals. They come increasingly to reject behaviors that give immediate pleasure but threaten long-term goods. They acquire a stronger, more coherent, sense of self, and they gradually come to understand the authority of their parents.

We now need to ask what features of the original parent/child relationship transfer to the notion of social or economic paternalism. First, there is the notion of a power hierarchy existing between two social actors or classes of actors. In the genetic domain, the parent exerts power over the child. In the domain of these cross-cultural studies, there is a paternalist who exerts social or economic power over less powerful targets. Second, there is the notion of the more powerful actor taking an interest or concern in the general welfare of the target. In the genetic domain, this notion is obvious. But it is also apparent in the domains of these cross-cultural studies where the paternalistic master, boss, or lord claims an interest in the general well-being of the slave, employee, or peasant in at least partial exchange for the latters' services. Third, there is the notion that the less powerful targets require care and protection because of deficiencies that limit their decision-making. In the genetic domain, these deficiencies are associated with the child's immaturity and lack of experience. In the social or economic domain, they are associated with the worker's ignorance, poverty, isolation, lesser age or status, or general vulnerability.

Despite these similarities between the parent/child relation and cultural paternalism however, there are also important dissimilarities, features that do not comfortably transfer or whose transfer is a matter of controversy. In the genetic relation, the parent has intimate contact and, at least in the early years, altruistic motives toward the child. The parent gives the child love and protection in exchange for no immediate goods and services. And parents work hard to make their children independent.

On the other hand, economic and social paternalists do not—and cannot possibly—share the same degree of intimate contact and plan the same evolving relation toward their workers as parents plan toward their children. Paternalistic systems are usually thought to benefit the paternalist more than the worker. Though such systems can evolve to give greater freedom to the worker, they usually do so against the wishes of the paternalist. These systems have associated with them the notion that the paternalistic dependencies are built-in and permanent. Economic paternalists in most cultures work hard to preserve dependencies. They are often guilty, moreover, of lame reasons for maintaining the dependencies. American slavery was often justified on the grounds that blacks had permanent "child-like" mentalities and were uneducable. Such arguments were used to keep blacks from receiving the education that could have made them a greater threat to the plantation owner.

It should not be inferred from this that cross-cultural studies of paternalism uniformly condemn or find little value in paternalistic systems. Many American economists credit the greater paternalism in Japanese industry with the ability of that country to overtake America in manufacturing markets world-wide. Paternalism can encourage employees to work for longer hours with less pay and still with higher efficiency and morale than American workers. Employees work harder, presumably, because they trust that whatever profits the company will eventually profit them. Employment security in the Japanese firm is typically high, as employers try to protect employees from fluctuations in their economic fortunes and often provide non-wage benefits such as housing, schooling, and medical care; in return, management benefits from a far lower rate of employee turnover.

Despite these attractions, paternalistic systems frequently arouse much suspicion and repugnance in contemporary America. There is a strong tradition in our culture to protect the freedom of individuals against interferences from others. The idea that an individual should look upon an employer (or any outsider) as a trusting father figure who knows what's best strikes many Americans as absurd, not to mention undemocratic, socialistic, and even totalitarian.

Jack's Draft

Paternalism is "a system under which an authority treats those under its control in a fatherly way, especially in regulating their conduct and supplying their needs." In the U.S., some economic relationships can be described as paternalistic. For example, domestic servants of affluent families sometimes regarded and treated as family members. Such relationships not common in American economy. Workers in America are protected by union contracts & legal rights. They do not routinely look upon their employers as a fatherly or paternal figure.

In cultures where there is no strong, centralized government, "parental concern" is often a vital bond. Individuals look to the wealthy, powerful & privileged instead of the government for rights, protection & support. Such relationships are described as "paternalistic." Some examples include European feudalism, landlord/tenant relations in India, manager/worker relations in the Japanese factory, plantation master/slave relations in Brazil, and corporate paternalism in early America.

The term "paternalism" misleads. It causes us to overlook important characteristics. Cultural systems differ from genetic paternalism. Paternalism is a metaphor for father/child or parent/child relationships. Some features we want to transfer and some we do not. But how do we decide which ones?

A traditional stereotype is that parent's behavior toward their children is, on one hand, wise, altruistic, benevolent, & protective; on the other hand, autocratic, and not to be questioned.

The parent's power diminishes as the children grow up & become better decision-makers.

What features of the original parent/child relationship transfer to social or economic paternalism? First, the notion of power hierarchy. In the genetic domain, the parent exerts power over the child. In cross-cultural, there is a paternalist who exerts social or economic power. Second, the notion of the more powerful actor taking interest or concern in general welfare of target. This is apparent in both. Third, the notion that the less powerful require care & protection.

Despite these similarities, there are also dissimilarities. The parent has intimate contact, altruistic motives, and gives love & protection. The parents work hard to make children independent. Economic and social paternalists do none of the above.

It should not be inferred that cross-cultural condemns paternalistic system.

Despite attractions, paternalistic systems arouse suspicion & repugnance in contemporary America.

Ned's Draft

Paternalism is a word that most people are familiar with, however, they are really only familiar with one definition. They would describe paternalism as the relationship between a father and child. They would go on to give an example, probably from their household or somebody they know household, where the father is the highest figure and has the last say in any situation. Though this is a very general term it does complete the task of defining the word.

With this definition in mind, I would like to give the other important definition that many of us don't even know. Imagine a company, such as Alcoa or Ford, where there are many people working for the company. We will be very specific and only describe those people that have low-level jobs, such as the factory workers. These people, many who have probably worked for the company for a while, have a dependence upon that company. They work for the company, recieve their paychecks weekly, and with this money, they are able to feed their family, pay the bills and hopefully have a little extra to spend on leisure or save. This worker is in a very similar position to that of a child in the above genetic paternalism relationship. He has a very large dependence upon a fatherly figure, which in this case is the owner or board of trustees of the company. He depends on these people to keep his welfare alive. Thus one can see that there is a so called paternalistic relationship in the economic world.

Though there are two definitions for the same word, they do have different meanings in a sense. Many of the ideas in the first definition transfer to the second definition, however, there are those which don't transfer.

One can see that in both of the definitions there is one figure which seems to have the power and respect over the other figure. In the genetic definition there is the child-father relationship, with the father having the respect from the son. In the economic definition, there is the worker having the respect for the owners or supervisors. Another idea that transfers is that as the lower figure grows and gains knowledge, the need for the powerful figure grows less. This can undoubtedly be seen in the genetic sense by just looking at yourself. As you grew from a child to a young adult and then onto an adult your need for your parents became less and less. You learned to make decisions for yourself and live on your own. This concept can be seen in the economic sense in that a worker climbs the "business" ladder as he progresses. Whe he first started he had a lot of respect for the power figure. However, as he climbed he learned alot about the company and soon enough didn't need the power figure all that much.

Just as some of the ideas transfer, there are some which don't. Take for instance the idea of why the power figure has concern for the lower figure. In the genetic sense, the father figure cares for his child, feeds and clothes the child and helps to develop the child with no notion that he will get something back. However in the economic sense the power figure takes care of his employees because he expects them to produce the goods they are suppose to produce. If they don't he will probably dispose of them. I can just not see this happening between a father and son.

Since I think most of us can see what is good and bad about the genetic relationship, I will show the pros and cons about the economic relationship.

In the economic relationship, a worker is paid for his duties and with this he is able to keep his welfare alive. In return for his duties, the power figure also takes care of him, by fixing any machines or other objects that the worker needs. The power figure also will usually supply a comfortable environment and atmosphere.

There are some aspects which can be considered bad. The power figure, many people will say, is using the worker only to help him achieve his goals and when the power figure doesn't need the worker he will dispose of him. Also, mainly in the United States where peoples rights are held high, many people will say that this economic relationship can be compared with that of slavery before the Civil War.

Thus, though you may have been aware of one definition of the word "paternalism" the economic definition may now be added to your knowledge. I have shown what transfers between the two definitions, and have as well, presented the pros and cons of the economic definition.

Note: Ruth's full draft is included earlier in the text.

5

Reading to Argue: Helping Students Transform Source Texts

LORRAINE HIGGINS

College students are often asked to develop arguments that address the questions and problems raised in their courses. In assessing student papers, however, instructors often remark that students seem to be indiscriminately reporting on or responding to source texts rather than using them to argue a position. This chapter explores some of the difficulties students face as they attempt to transform source texts into written arguments, and it demonstrates how instructors can model and support the interpretive strategies that underlie written argument.

What We Know About Students' Experience with Written Argument

Process tracing studies of college writers and studies of high school writing can give us some insight into the writing strategies and experiences that students bring to college assignments. This research suggests that when students enter college, they may have little, if any, experience with formal written argument; moreover, while valuable for some purposes, the general writing preparation many students have had may not be relevant for the purpose of organizing sources around an argument, one of the most highly rated college writing skills identified by university faculty (Bridgeman & Carlson, 1984).

STUDENTS MAY LACK EXPERIENCE
WITH FORMAL ARGUMENT

Although writing from sources is common in high school and in college courses, many high school graduates have not had a great deal of experience writing arguments based on sources. In a study of 11- to 18-year-old writers, Britton, Burgess, Martin, McLeod, and Rosen (1975) argued that the bulk of precollege writing assignments are reports, low-level analyses, and classification essays. Arthur Applebee's more recent research (1981, 1984) on writing in American high schools has shown that the main purpose of writing across all content areas in high school is not to argue from or to apply assigned reading but to recite or display source ideas in reports, narrative summaries, and short-answer essay exams. Unlike college students, high school students are not frequently asked to adapt their reading and writing to a wide range of purposes (Curtin, 1988). In high school, writing is frequently used to test knowledge of course content.

Younger writers may lack experience with argument in non-school contexts as well, and while older students may have some experience, it may not be relevant to the type of argument tasks they face in college. Unlike older adults, the typical 18-year-old student has had little opportunity to use writing to argue for change in the workplace or to build consensus in social or community groups. Older college students may have a great deal of experience with written argument outside of the classroom, but, even so, the type of arguments these adults write in their personal lives may differ from the formal arguments assigned in school. In a series of interviews with returning, female students (Higgins, 1992), I found that these women had used written argument to prepare themselves for court hearings and to dispute unfair bills. However, these arguments typically took the form of persuasive letters or personal notes in which the writers offered a brief claim and attached proof, in the form of testimony, receipts, or a dated list of facts and events. These situations did not require them to develop extensive reasoning from texts, and the proof they offered was often self-evident, requiring little elaboration or restructuring.

PREVIOUS WRITING INSTRUCTION MAY NOT PREPARE
STUDENTS TO ARGUE FROM SOURCES

Argument assignments in college typically require the student to transform source ideas into a series of well-reasoned claims; however, the writing assignments students encounter in high school often do not require high-level restructuring and transformation of source ideas. In Applebee's study (1984), he observed that "The task for the students was one of repeating information that had already been organized by the teacher or textbook, rather than of extending and integrating new learning for themselves" (p. 3). In writing research papers, for example, students often find the content for their essays directly in the texts they read, borrow the organizational frameworks from those texts to use in their own papers, or rely on simple text structures such as the familiar five-paragraph theme.

Students use text structures as outlines or templates that they can efficiently "fill in" with course content. These familiar text structures or schemata can streamline the writing process and help students select organizing ideas quickly (Hillocks, 1986). The five-paragraph theme is a structure that allows students to complete a research essay in five easy pieces: introduce the topic (e.g., "There are many viewpoints on paternalism . . ."); plug source ideas into three body paragraphs (e.g., "First, Plato's view is . . . . A second perspective is that of J. S. Mill. . . . And finally, a third philosopher argues . . ."); and sum up with a conclusion (e.g., "As you can see, philosophers have yet to resolve the issue of paternalism . . .").

The problem is that report writing and the type of text structures that guide it don't encourage students to adapt and organize source information for more complex purposes such as argument or analysis. Argument and analysis tasks make it difficult for students to slot information into neat and predictable structures, because students themselves must construct the interpretive framework in which they will present the information. In an analysis of high school students' texts, Applebee, Durst, and Newell (1984) found that, as students moved into more analytical writing, they had difficulty adapting source information around a synthesizing concept; these students tended to multiply detail in their texts (to list bits of information taken from their reading) and to minimize superordinate structure (they failed to create their own organizational frameworks). Students experience a similar difficulty in writing arguments. Students' persuasive essays often consist of "a list of baldly stated, unelaborated reasons" (Crowhurst, 1991, p. 315). For weaker writers, this failure to elaborate on evidence is apparent even at the college level (Cooper, Cherry, Coley, Fleischer, Polard, & Sartisky, 1984). Instead of organizing source evidence around a claim, some students simply list or display these ideas; they insert quotes, facts, or data from the sources without elaborating this evidence or offering warrants that link the source ideas they cite to the claims they have made (Higgins, 1992).

Along with depending on familiar text structures, students also enter college controlling a number of well-practiced reading strategies that help them summarize and respond to source information. Flower (1990) has documented a number of these in a large-scale protocol study of college freshmen who wrote from source texts. Many of these freshmen used a "gist and list" strategy as they read, first compiling a list of paraphrased notes or gists alongside the readings and then stringing these gists into a paper (p. 44). Flower also observed what she called the "skim and respond" strategy, which allowed students to identify points that were most interesting to them, using the text as a springboard for their own ideas (p. 45). These strategies can help students select and delete ideas for their papers.

Although these selection strategies and text structures may serve students well in high school, such strategies may not take them far enough in their college writing assignments. When students are asked to argue from sources, they need to do more than invoke a familiar text structure or fill in information that is already "known" to them or can be directly transcribed from their reading. In fact, students are often asked to address open questions and problems for which the answers are assumed unknowable, but arguable (Higgins, Mathison, & Flower, in prep.). Students need to build a case, to structure source ideas around a set of top-level claims. Consider, for example, these assignments from courses in two Pittsburgh area colleges:

Reading-to-Argue Tasks
American History: How and why did the status of Northern, middle-class women change during 1776–1876? Please draw on the assigned documents to support your claims. (Source texts: assigned historical documents and course materials).

Philosophy: Write a paper that addresses the following question: Does the U.S. government have the right to ban the use of marijuana; that is, should marijuana be legalized? Please draw on course readings to develop your argument. (Source texts: J. S. Mill's *On Liberty*, Plato's *Republic*, and a documentary on drug abuse in the United States).

Sociology: Write a paper that addresses the following question: Which theory or theories (Allport, Loewenberg, Boggs) best accounts for racism as portrayed in Terkel's interview with C. P. Ellis? (Source texts: Terkel interview with former Klansman, three different theoretical articles on the causes of prejudice and racism).

These reading-to-argue assignments invite students to become active users of knowledge, to transform source texts into well-reasoned claims that address a specific issue. But how do writers respond to invitations like these? Over the past several years, I have had the opportunity to observe and work with students in history and in writing courses both at Carnegie Mellon and at an inner-city campus of a Pittsburgh Community College. As a researcher and guest lecturer, I was invited into these classrooms to interview students about their argument assignments and to explore some methods for more direct instruction in this area. Consider how two students I spoke with interpreted the history assignment described above. Their history instructor had given them a packet of historical documents including graphs of occupational statistics over a period of years, excerpts from women's magazines of the period, personal letters from prominent female figures, and legal documents and commentaries on women's rights. After receiving these materials and the writing assignment, Jeff, a freshman, explained his writing plans to me in a brief interview. Faced with this array of information and his history text, Jeff admitted that he had difficulty knowing just what his professor expected. He explained that he didn't have any "definite steps" for this kind of paper. In the last assignment, he had relied on a trial and error approach. "I knew the first draft wasn't counted, so I put down some ideas to figure out what they wanted." Jeff depended on feedback from the teaching assistant who reviewed his draft and offered suggestions. "Mostly," he claimed, "I listen for important points from Professor _____'s lectures, and I look for them in the books." When asked how he put those ideas together in his papers, Jeff explained that he typically started with the "most obvious ideas" and then looked for support. If he found some support, he looked for more. Jeff predicted that this history assignment might be difficult because "the paper's major points are not obvious. He [his professor] wants us to base it on these documents, and I haven't found anything definite in these documents. Nothing jumped right out at me." Scott, Jeffrey's classmate, claimed to have no plans for the paper except to "read them [the documents] and do what I did with the other one—take notes on the side, anything that catches my eye and sounds like it will go well."

These interview excerpts capture a typical response to reading-to-argue tasks. Many students seem to approach these tasks as if the sources, lectures, or books themselves contain the answers or can provide self-evident proof that they can insert directly into their texts. Reading becomes a task of looking for the most "obvious ideas," the "important points." Students are frustrated to find that the answers aren't readily available for transportation into their own texts; they don't "jump out" at them. In reality, the "answer" to this assignment is a claim that students must construct themselves out of the data and that they must support with reasons they themselves develop. Students like Jeff and Scott simply may not know that college writing tasks can require more than gisting and listing the main ideas. Faced with uncertainty about what these tasks require, they rely on the recitation and response strategies learned in high school, a logical approach, given their experiences with school writing.

Flower and her colleagues (1990) observed this response in their study of freshmen writers. Their students seemed to rely on summary and response routines they had learned in high school, even though they were asked specifically to adapt and apply information for a purpose. In this study, over half of the students who wrote from sources engaged in what Flower calls "knowledge-driven planning." That is, their reading provided them with content knowledge on the topic which they then organized around a familiar text schema. These students saw writing as a process of communicating the ideas they had read, rather than adapting ideas to the larger rhetorical goals of the assignment. Working with the same set of students, John Ackerman (1990) noted that ambiguity and contradiction in the source texts had frustrated the students, because these contradictions made it difficult for them to do a neat synthesis or report. Over half relied on the familiar I agree/I disagree framework as a way to bury the conflict in their own texts. Ackerman cites this response as a symptom of the culture of recitation in our schools, where the emphasis is on the accuracy of reporting rather than on resolving conflicts with new perspectives or original arguments.

This research illustrates some key differences between the writing students do in high school and the kind of writing they will face in many college courses. College students are expected not to transmit previously known ideas but to transform ideas for a variety of purposes. They are asked to use multiple and sometimes conflicting source texts that are relevant to the assigned problem but do not provide ready-made answers. This means that students may not be able to rely solely on familiar frameworks (e.g., the 5-paragraph schema) or familiar summary strategies (e.g., abstracting gists) learned in high school. They may have to construct a new framework or set of goals in response to the rhetorical demands of the assignment.

When writers approach reading-to-argue tasks, they must do a great deal of inventional work before they ever set pen to page. They must interpret and restructure source ideas so that they can produce relevant claims, and they must construct a series of reasons and warrants that link source data to those claims. Although active reading, planning, and note taking play a crucial role in helping writers construct arguments, college writing instruction does not emphasize this stage of invention, but instead focuses on the written product, the formal parts and layout of a written argument, rather than the interpretive process one uses to create the written text.

Some instructors rely on traditional argument pedagogy, teaching students to identify the various *parts* of an argument such as data, warrants, claims, and qualifiers (see Toulmin, Rieke, & Janik, 1979). They also help students identify different argument techniques such as the use of examples, and they warn students to avoid the logical fallacies. These methods can help students understand what their own arguments should look like, and they may help students evaluate others' arguments. This product-based instruction does not, however, reveal to students the interpretive work they must do in order to begin writing. Being able to recognize the parts of a well-formed argument does not ensure that all students will know how to synthesize one from scratch. The goal of traditional, product-based instruction is often to help the student arrange ideas she is already assumed to have. But one of the most critical aspects of persuasive writing is generating content — deciding what can and must be said in the first place. If college students can no longer recite another author's ideas from a text, how do they deal with this inventional problem? Clearly they need reading and note-taking strategies that will support this knowledge transforming task and that will carry them beyond the gisting and paraphrasing strategies they have learned so well.

Transforming Sources into Arguments: Observing Writers' Reading and Note-Taking Strategies

How do writers develop source ideas into arguments? Are there some general reading and note-taking strategies that can support this interpretive process? In this section, I demonstrate how one group of experienced writers used reading and note-taking strategies to develop arguments about the efficacy of tobacco ads. A philosophy instructor ("Jonathan"), an educational researcher ("Carey"), a literary critic ("Peter"), and a graduate student in English ("Patrice") participated in this exploratory task.

These writers were provided with a set of fictional data — "facts" about the release of health-related information on smoking, and survey results and statistics about smokers and tobacco ads over a period of years. In creating these "facts," I included information that could be perceived as relevant but which was not directly related to the assigned question. I also embedded some questionable and contradictory information into the data, because I was interested in how the writers would select, connect, and transform this information for their arguments. These source data appear in Appendix A.

The writers were asked to use the source information to address this question: *Is the tobacco industry attuned to the needs, desires, and lifestyles of the public who buys its products?* The writers were asked to think aloud into a tape recorder as they read through the material, took notes, and planned a rough draft. I examined their tapes, notes, and drafts, to describe the kinds of strategies they had used to construct their arguments. All four writers engaged in a common set of interpretive strategies, which are illustrated here.

WRITERS DIVIDED THE ASSIGNED ISSUE INTO MANAGEABLE THEMES

These writers carefully attended to the issue set by their assignment. They did so by reviewing the assigned question and breaking it down into key topics or relevant themes such as "lifestyle of smokers in 1960," "typical smokers today," "health information," and "ads" to name a few. We see this strategy at work in the following protocol excerpts:

Strategy One: Breaking the Issue into Themes
Carey: (Rereads assignment question)   So now I've been through this set of unconnected facts, so, and I better start to do some organizing. So I'm gonna write down "profile of a smoker" . . .

Patrice: So we have a category of the "health hazards." Now we're gonna make a category of "who was smoking when" . . .

This strategy not only helps writers stay on their topic, but when used early in their planning, it also gives them a way to conceptualize and frame the sources. These themes give writers goals for their reading – to select and adapt sources *relevant* to the issue. The themes can later become useful labels or conceptual structures that can help writers reorganize source materials in their notes (this becomes evident in strategy two). Without such a strategy, a writer may be in danger of choosing source information indiscriminately, simply reporting on information that "catches [his] eye" (as Scott, the freshman writer, put it) rather than relating it to the assigned question.

WRITERS SELECTED AND ORGANIZED SOURCES AROUND RELEVANT THEMES

These writers used their themes as headings for their reading notes. They selectively reread sources, identifying relevant information and recording it under the appropriate headings. This strategy helped the writers restructure and transform their data around the new framework of themes they had developed. For example, Peter sifted through some facts on cigarette smoking, found a statistic that showed him that more smokers have desk jobs today, then found another that showed an increase in female smokers. He recorded these facts together under his "Lifestyle of smoker – today" theme, which allowed him to see these isolated facts together, in a new way, and to characterize the needs, desires, and lifestyles of some contemporary smokers –

women with office jobs. Patrice used this strategy to group facts about the
development of cigarette ads during the past few decades:

Strategy Two: Selecting and Organizing Source Information Around Themes
Peter:　Okay, that sort of wraps up who our smokers are. More women smokers
than men. We have teenage smokers, but we don't know if that's up or down. We
have more indoor workers than outdoor workers, so that can correlate with the
women. Fewer ivy league smokers — and that's mostly men . . .

Patrice:　The ads went from stressing name brand and quality to the celebrities to
talk against it [smoking]. We have fewer words in the ads, fewer words now, and we
footnote the hazards . . .

Figures 5.1 and 5.2 provide excerpts from two writers' notes, showing how
they categorized source ideas under the themes they had created — "profile of
a smoker" and "ads."

This strategy also makes reading a more manageable process. Rather than
tackling a mass of source material all at once, a writer can use the themes to
break her reading into sub-tasks, for instance, find information relevant to
the first theme, then the second, then reconsider what's left, how it might be
made to fit. (See Nelson, this volume, for a discussion of issue-driven strategies in research writing tasks.) In sum, these first two strategies help writers to

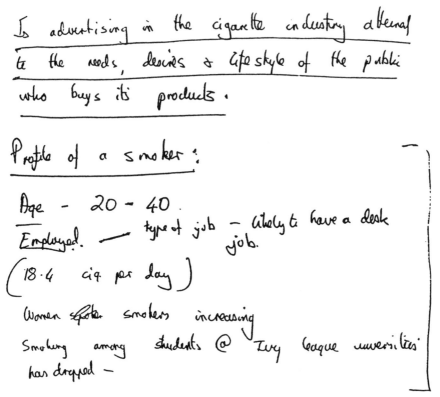

Figure 5.1. Excerpts from Carey's Notes

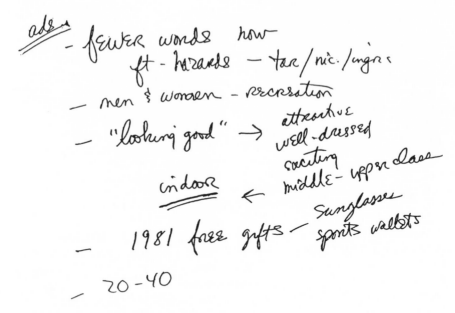

Figure 5.2. Excerpts from Patrice's Notes

create issue-relevant categories, to organize their reading and note taking, and to restructure relevant sources around their purpose.

It is interesting to note that part of this source selection and reorganization strategy was also driven by these writers' personal evaluation of the "facts" they read. Even though some of these facts might have fit logically under their themes, they were omitted when writers questioned their validity. Carey, the educational researcher, wanted far more information on the sampling methods used to collect some of these data and was quite frustrated that she would have to arrive at a general claim based only on this "bitty data," as she put it. Peter, the literary critic, was skeptical about the political and economic motivations behind the data, questioning who had conducted these surveys and for what purposes. (The writers were not told that these were fictional data.) His attention to the rhetorical context is typical of experienced readers (see Haas, this volume). Although he stayed on task, organizing the data around the assigned question as he read and took notes, Peter insisted that his real impulse was to write a scathing critique of statistical data of this sort.

WRITERS MADE INFERENCES THAT
CONNECTED SOURCE IDEAS AND LED TO CLAIMS

Once these writers' sources were laid out in a clear fashion, it became easier for them to see relationships not previously evident. In this third strategy, the writers linked concepts in their notes and used their inferences to establish claims related to the assignment. The following protocol excerpts demonstrate this powerful reasoning strategy in action. Underlined portions emphasize inferences and logical connections the writers made.

Strategy Three: Creating Inferences and Claims From Notes

Patrice: Forty-nine percent of brands offer light blends. That's another action of smoking obviously directed — brands obviously directed — at the concern about health. And final fact, that average smoker today falls into the 20–40 age bracket, employed and smokes 18.4 cigarettes per day (rereads notes). Um, in fact, this fact might be correlated with the light blend that cigarette companies are offering because people who smoke roughly a pack a day might perceive themselves as smoking a fair amount and hence be, uh . . . concerned about cancer.

Jonathan: So what's going to indicate that, um, the cigarette industry is attuned to the needs, desires, and lifestyles. Um, the depictions of men and women together smoking and recreational activities. Obviously this indicates a concern for health and the desire to view cigarettes as social activities, so we'll suggest that has something to do with it.

As the underlined portions of these examples indicate, restructuring the source data into facts about smokers, health risks, and changing advertising techniques helped these writers infer *causal* relationships. In this particular assignment, writers used logical connectors such as "because," "since," and "correlated with" as they reasoned through the data, because the assignment had asked them to evaluate whether the industry had responded to the changing market. This reasoning eventually led the writers to claims. After Jonathan engaged in the reasoning above, for example, he remarked "Yes, it appears that to some degree, the tobacco industry is aware of the consumers' needs and desires."

This third strategy reveals the constructive nature of reading and how it informs claims later made in text. Collins et al. (1980) point to the important role inference plays as readers construct hypotheses about the meaning of texts they read. This third strategy seems to be the mechanism for creating hypotheses or claims from source materials. Moreover, it lays a groundwork of reasoning that writers can offer to readers as they defend and elaborate their claims in writing.

WRITERS REVIEWED CLAIMS AND
CREATED A QUALIFIED THESIS STATEMENT

Once these writers had restructured and linked the sources, they used their claims to develop a thesis statement or synthesizing claim that appeared in their texts. This link between reading and writing becomes very apparent when we compare an excerpt from Jonathan's protocol (a remark he made when summing up his reading notes) and the text he eventually produced:

Strategy Four: Summing Up Claims With a Qualified Thesis

Jonathan's Protocol: So if we compare our smoker's profile with the typical cigarette ad, we can see that, in general, the industry is attuned to the lifestyle of the smoking public, or at least what the smoking public would like its lifestyle to be . . .

Thesis statement from Jonathan's draft:

For some time, the industry has demonstrated a consciousness of the needs, desires, and lifestyles of the public that buys its products.

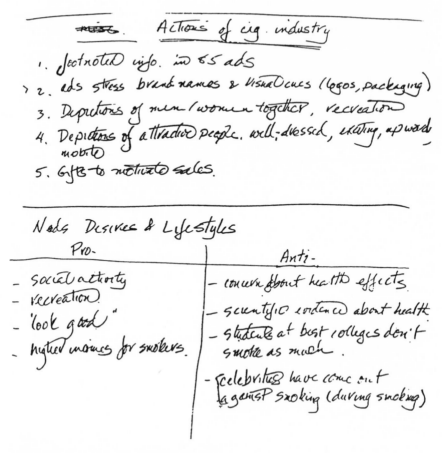

Figure 5.3. Excerpts from Jonathan's Notes

After developing inferences and tentative conclusions, a writer is better able to make a more precise thesis statement, one he can support in text by returning to his notes. Figure 5.3 provides excerpts from Jonathan's notes.

The following excerpt from Jonathan's draft reflects the influence of those notes in its structure and content:

> For some time, the cigarette industry has demonstrated a consciousness of the needs, desires, and lifestyles of the public that buys its products. Twenty years ago, ads for cigarettes stressed name and package identification to promote a consciousness of the product and to reinforce the consumer's identification with the particular brand that he/she consumed. This was just a standard advertising method, but clearly indicated the company's desire to make their product an important part of an individual's lifestyle.
>
> Over the last twenty years, the cigarette market has changed substantially (though concerns of today's consumers do overlap with those of consumers in the past). One of the most significant changes is the public's concern about the health effects of cigarette smoking. In 1964, the surgeon general determined that smoking is linked to cancer and heart disease; and the worry about the adverse effects of smoking has

steadily increased. The tobacco industry has responded to this concern by displaying legally required information about brand ingredients in mere footnotes. (In previous years this information was foregrounded in ads.) Furthermore, [despite] worries about health effects, cigarette ads now display smokers engaged in healthy open air activities. Finally, tobacco manufacturers have produced light blends of original brands. . . .

WRITERS READ AND WROTE RECURSIVELY, RETHINKING THEIR INTERPRETATIONS AND CLAIMS

These writers did not always proceed in a linear fashion from reading to note taking to text. For example, when Patrice encountered difficulty generating the next idea in text, she paused and returned to her notes and reread them. She then added boxes and arrows to these notes, linking the ideas she was trying to express (see Figure 5.4). Writers often reread sources and modify their notes as they move into text. This strategy allows a writer to continue the process of interpretation throughout writing.

Strategy Five: Rethinking Interpretations and Claims

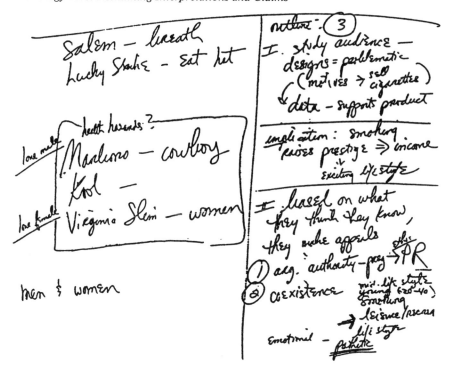

Figure 5.4. Patrice's Revised Notes

Being able to observe and describe these general, interpretive moves that underlie written argument is important, for it gives teachers a way to demonstrate the very active role that writers play as they think through a set of source ideas and transform them into claims. George Hillocks (1986) has demonstrated that direct strategy instruction has advantages over more traditional methods of teaching writing, such as providing students with examples of good texts or providing them with exercises in grammar or style. Harris (1983) has argued that strategies are best taught when instructors model expert processes directly. In teaching students to argue from sources, we can show them brief snapshots of writers' thinking—the protocol excerpts, sample notes, and arguments that other writers have produced. This type of modeling can achieve several purposes. First, it can change students' image of argument tasks by offering them interpretive strategies they might not have considered using themselves. Second, students can modify these strategies for their own purposes. And finally, as students discuss and attempt these strategies in class, teachers can gain some insight into their performance. In what follows, I will describe how teachers can help students adapt these strategies to their own ends.

Helping Students Transform Sources: Examining and Adapting the Reading and Note-Taking Strategies

When I teach as a guest lecturer in other courses, or when I teach argument in my own composition classes, I model the reading and note-taking strategies in one class period, using the tobacco ad assignment. I preview the assignment and distribute handouts of the facts on smoking and excerpts from the writers' notes and drafts. I then describe each strategy and play examples from the writers' tapes. As each strategy is modeled, students create "strategy cards," index cards on which they name the strategy, write down an example, and define it, creating a prompt they can later refer to when they work on their own argument assignments at home. Scardamalia & Bereiter (1987) developed the idea of strategy cards as a means of procedural facilitation. The cards not only serve as a support system when students tackle assignments in the privacy of their own rooms, but they also allow students ownership of the strategies in that they can define and modify them to suit their own needs. I have students share their strategy cards in class and prompt them to think about how they might be used in the arguments they will write. This approach models a strategy, coaches students as they attempt to use it, then allows students to assume responsibility for the strategies themselves. As Collins et al. (1986) have explained, this type of instructional scaffolding "externalizes processes that are usually carried out internally" (ibid, p. 3).

After the initial modeling session, I provide a practice class in which students take turns "role-playing" each strategy on another sample thesis question and a small set of source materials that are shown on an overhead or chalkboard.* Students who role play the first strategy are responsible for creating

---

*Instructors can assemble a brief list of "facts" on an issue (such as the tobacco ad data) or can piece together reading excerpts, tables, and other data related to the issue in question.

themes or categories; those who role play the second strategy are responsible for recategorizing the data in a set of notes they create on the blackboard, and so forth. This role-playing can offer students further practice with interpretation and note taking without the extra effort of producing a paper. And, as Palincsar and Brown (1984; 1985) have noted, role-playing also decomposes a task in that students share the responsibility of executing the strategies and can learn from each other in the process.

After creating their own strategy cards in class, students use the cards at home as they read, take notes, and plan for an upcoming argument assignment. I asked Jeff and Scott, the two students who discussed the American History assignment with me, to think aloud into a tape recorder as they used their strategy cards at home and to share their tapes and notes with me. The assignment they worked on required them to draw from a number of source documents that their instructor had taken from the 1981 Advanced Placement Exam in History (see Appendix B). Jeff decided to create three notecards from the modeling session. His first notecard seemed to correspond to the first strategy, Breaking the Issue into Themes (see Figure 5.5). On his strategy card, Jeff referred to the themes as "categories" and prompted himself with this reminder: "Question is broken into parts and each part becomes a category that the data is fitted under."

The following excerpt from Jeff's protocol illustrates how he used this strategy to identify several relevant themes from the assigned question, including time periods (women's lives "before" and "after" 1800) as well as status-related themes such as marital and legal status, role, and occupation.

> Okay. Back to the question, to help get categories, which would be using, using the first strategy, breaking the question into categories. Okay, question: How and why did the status of northern, middle-class women change? Uhh, suggestions for the way to proceed are first think carefully about the phrase lives and status of northern, middle-class women. Means, okay, relevant categories here would be status of, status of women. Uh, this lives can be broken down into before and after any changes. Wait'll later to do that. Let's see, status. I guess we can call that marriage, status under marriage. Uh, status is mainly legal, so we'll leave status in women's categories. Uhm, also we'll go with role as part of their lives, huuuh, role of women and we'll say occupation.

Name: BREAKING THE QUESTION INTO CATEGORIES
Description, notes:
    QUESTION IS BROKEN INTO PARTS AND EACH
    PART BECOMES A CATEGORY THAT DATA IS
    THEN FITTED UNDER. A METHOD OF SORTING
    DATA INTO NEEDED SECTIONS RELATED TO THE
    QUESTION.

Figure 5.5. Jeff's First Strategy Card

Name: DECIDE RELEVANCE TO CATEGORIES.
Description, notes:

    SEE IF DATA FITS UNDER CATEGORIES.

(IF NECESSARY, USE KNOWLEDGE OF YOUR OWN)

    (ALSO, ADD CATEGORIES RELATED TO QUESTION IF

    NEEDED)

Name: DECIDE WHAT INFO IS BELIEVABLE
Description, notes:

    1. USE OWN KNOWLEDGE TO DECIDE VALIDITY

    2. USE REPITITION OF DATA TO DECIDE   "

    3. USE SOME DATA TO DECIDE BELIEVABILITY OF
OTHER DATA. EX, MIDDLE CLASS, INDOOR WORKERS ((CORRELATION))

Figure 5.6. Jeff's Second Strategy Card

Jeff's interpretation and use of these categories became apparent as he
attempted to use his second strategy card. This card corresponded to strategy
two, Selecting and Organizing Source Information Around Themes. Jeff had
broken this card into two parts (see Figure 5.6). On one side of the card, he
had written "Decide What Info Is Believable," and on the other side he wrote
"Decide Relevance to Categories."

As Jeff began to reread the sources, he explained that he was "deciding
what information is believable as well as deciding the relevance to the categories, both parts of the second, second strategy." On his card, Jeff had given
himself several pointers for assessing source credibility — using his own knowledge, noting repetition of facts across the data, and seeing correlations (mutual support) between facts. In his reading, Jeff raised the issue of validity
twice. After reading Document K, he commented, "children here the main
responsibility. So that makes that definite." He had already read about the
obligations of motherhood in Document I, so this second reference made it
"definite." At another point, Jeff claimed that Document A was "believable"
but he didn't say why. In his text and in his reading comments, Jeff never
challenged or disagreed with any of the documents outright (as the experienced
writers did). Although this absence of criticism might suggest that Jeff simply
accepted the data at face value, his use of this strategy card told another
story. Jeff's two-part strategy card suggested that he did see credibility as an
important factor in selecting source information; however, his understanding
of credibility, at least for this assignment, seemed to center on ways to affirm

or choose the most believable facts rather than ways to discredit or question those facts. It may be that students do not question source data unless they encounter several pieces of conflicting data, unless they suspect the instructor would question the data, or unless they have a great deal of knowledge about the topic or the methods on which the source data were based. In this assignment, Jeff had no reason to question or discredit the sources his instructor had provided. In the context of other assignments, however, it might be interesting to model these critical moves, to provide students like Jeff with some contradictory and questionable data, and to see how they might expand or modify this strategy to assess credibility. One benefit of modeling and observing students' responses to these strategies is that it can give us some insight into students' interpretations of issues such as validity.

On the other side of his strategy card, Jeff had written "Decide relevance to categories." In defining this move, Jeff included a number of pointers—"See if data fits under categories" and "If necessary, use knowledge of your own" as well as "Add categories related to question if needed." Jeff used this strategy as he reread the marginal gists he had already created beside each document in his first pass through the materials. In this second pass, he organized these gists on a separate page of notes, using three category headings at the top of the page. Jeff reread every piece of information, fitting each gist under his categories.

Some of the data were apparently relevant to his categories. For example, after reviewing Document A, which began "By marriage the husband and wife are one person in law . . ." Jeff wrote "no legal existence" under his status category. After examining a table of women's and men's occupations (Document G), he concluded, "So the women are basically teachers. That would be occupation." He then wrote "teachers" under his occupation heading. But sometimes Jeff took his own advice, using his own knowledge to make the data fit. For example, when he first examined an illustration from Godey's Lady's Book (Document J), he commented, "I don't know what that has to do with anything." This illustration depicts two well-adorned women with their daughters sitting formally in a parlor. But as Jeff used his second strategy card, he made the inference necessary to *make* the document relevant. He looked at the illustration and said "Maybe one of the ideals of femininity is women looking nice. Role of women—looking nice." Document H, which explains the transition from the age of the homespun to the industrial revolution, also had no obvious relevance to Jeff's categories, but, after thinking it through, he was able to fit the information under social role:

Jeff: Clothes no longer made at home or made in the home. That brought change to home life, changes social matters to home life. So, it's the role of women—change from making clothes to, uhh, being motherly.

Jeff was no longer searching in vain for the main points. He was systematically using his categories to assess the relevance of the data and to organize it around issues central to the assigned question. But part of Jeff's success was due, in part, to the categories he created and his very faithful use of them in note taking. When Jeff used the categories to screen each document, it prompted him to explain the relevance of his sources, even when the relevance of them was not apparent or didn't "jump out at him," as he might say. This move to make the sources relevant was a powerful sign that Jeff was transforming the sources around the assigned question.

These transformations are apparent in Jeff's notes (see Figure 5.7), which contrast sharply with the notes that Scott took (see Figure 5.8). Unlike Jeff, Scott did not use his themes to organize the sources. He initially mentioned the need to look at time periods, economics, and legal issues, but when taking notes, he arranged the data only according to time periods, ignoring the other categories he had mentioned. Jeff's categories allowed him to harness the data and use it to inform his argument; but Scott only paraphrased the data, arranging it in chronological order. In doing so, Scott simply dismissed those

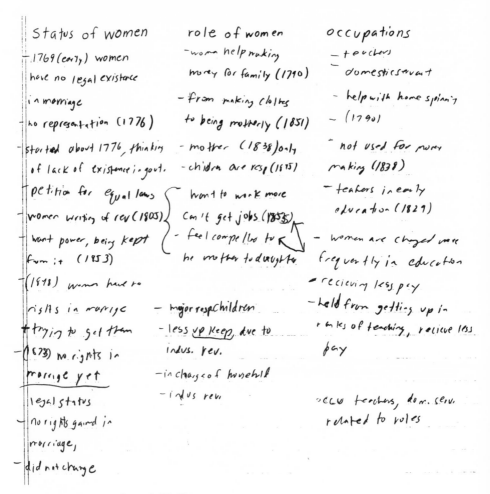

Figure 5.7. Excerpts from Jeff's Notes

documents that didn't appear, on the surface, to be important. Note that he didn't bother to record information from several documents (e.g., H, O, L, M, N), even though these documents had the potential to inform an argument about change in women's legal status and economic conditions.

Jeff's written reminder to "Change categories if necessary" suggested that he recognized the recursive nature of fitting the data to the assigned question. Jeff had initially inferred several meanings of the phrase "lives and status" that were reflected in his categories—role, occupation, lives before and after change, and legal and marital status. However, he seemed to realize that these were tentative categories that might need to be redefined or expanded once he looked more closely at the data. And indeed, after discovering that a woman's rights were often linked to her marital status, Jeff eventually collapsed marital status and legal status under the same status category, which is evident in his notes.

The variety of ways in which students have adapted this second strategy suggests that note taking itself is a rich site for further instruction and intervention. Although Jeff seemed to use his themes to take notes, for example, he might have developed a more efficient note structure. Jeff had initially planned to include "before and after" categories to note changes in earlier versus later time periods, but the note-taking format he developed (three columns) didn't lend itself to "before and after" categories. Dates were simply sprinkled throughout the columns. Several months later, when I used these history data to teach the strategies to students in another history course, they discovered that a table or matrix might work even better than Scott's chronological list or Jeff's columns. As they practiced with the data in class, these students collaboratively created a matrix-type note structure on the blackboard (see Figure 5.9).

Across the top of the board, they wrote headings responding to themes they had created from the first strategy. On the side of the matrix, students wrote in time periods—"lives before 1800" and "lives after 1800." They then selected and reorganized the documents, filling in the matrix. This allowed them to better see how certain aspects of women's status had changed over time, while others had not. In using their matrix to interpret the data, they also observed that gains or losses in certain types of status—such as jobs—were closely related to other aspects of status such as home life.

When writers attempt to assess and restructure information around relevant issues, they might do well to experiment with different kinds of note structures, depending on the logical relationships they are seeking in the sources (e.g., whether they are tracking change over time, whether they are looking for similarities between events, causal relationships, etc.). An important part of argument instruction may be getting students to consider alternative note structures as they interpret different kinds of data and address different kinds of questions.

Jeff combined the third and fourth strategies (Creating Inferences and Claims and Summing Up Claims with a Qualified Thesis) in his third strategy

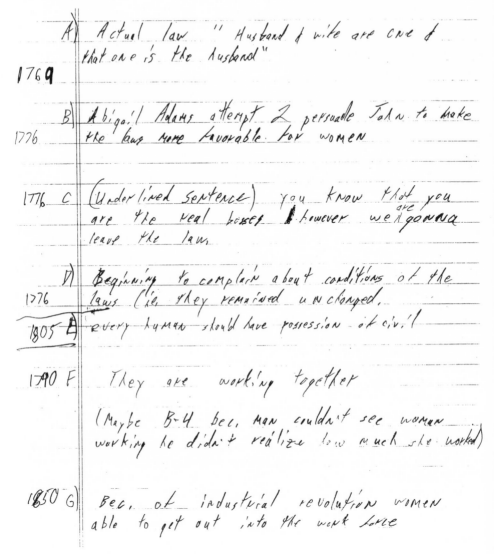

Figure 5.8. Excerpts from Scott's Notes

card, which read "Find Correlations Between Categories" (see Figure 5.10). Jeff's card reminded him to relate facts in different categories to his thesis and to explain these connections as he presented his thesis.

Jeff's use of the second strategy card had already helped him identify relationships and conflicts in the data. Using this third strategy card, he began to articulate and explain some of these relationships. For example, Jeff initially categorized Document F, a picture of women spinning, under role of women: "Women helping make money—that'll be a role." But later he put this document under occupation: "I guess, uh, that help with home spinning would

1651 H)

1838 I) wife has more move to do with the education
of the child then the father

1845 K) Against women's Movement

1829 L)

1953 M)
1860 N)

1855 P Only profession open was that of teacher.

1859 Q she can't actively partake in the Womans
Movement because she is a mother 1st

1873 R This is a law still

1848 O)

Figure 5.8. (Continued)

also be occupational." He explained this double categorization by noting the close relationship between these categories of role and occupation. He noted that women may compete for "the less important occupations, ones related to their role — teachers, domestic servants. That's because it's related to role." Jeff also noted a contradiction under his role of women category. Lucy Stone, in Document O, says she "can only be a mother" and yet, his prior note under that category (from Document P) states that women such as Lucy Stone desired a role change — to become workers and to fight for their rights. Jeff

	attitudes	jobs	home life	legal rights
lives before 1800				
lives after 1800				

Figure 5.9. An Alternative Note Structure

noted that "These are both related so I'll put them in brackets." One can see the brackets and arrows in his notes, which are later translated into a statement of causality in his draft. Jeff explained that part of the reason why women couldn't get jobs is because they felt compelled to be a mother, and this prevented them from staying with their occupations.

Jeff also used this strategy card to develop claims. He quickly read through his notes under status of women and made the claim, "So no rights gained in marriage." He was aware that he needed to create some additional support at this point: "And the reason it hasn't changed would be, uh, lets see, uh. . ." He then shifted to the other categories to see if he could come up with some explanations. In the flurry of reasoning that appears in the protocol excerpt below, Jeff began to connect women's marital rights with their socially acceptable roles and their limited occupational opportunities.

> The job of being a teacher is more like working with kids anyway—not making that much money doing it. They are just teaching children like theirs, like their role is, uh. They never really get high up in the ranks of teaching, if always with younger kids. I assume because they seem to change the number of different teachers—much more for females than males—and receiving less pay, and therefore that assumption seems correct that they are not staying on the job very long. Which could be tied to feeling compelled to be a mother, uhhm, feel compelled to be motherly tied to the fact that they can't get jobs. So the reasons they can't get jobs is because, uh, cuz

Name : FIND CORRELATIONS BETWEEN CATEGORIES (A)
Description, notes :
        USE KNOWLEDGE YOU HAVE TO RELATE FACTS IN
DIFFERENT CATEGORIES TO THE THESIS. THE CORRELATION
BETWEEN CATEGORIES WILL NEED EXPLAINED WITH
YOUR OWN CONNECTIONS. DIRECTLY RELATED TO
THESIS,

Figure 5.10. Jeff's Third Strategy Card

<u>their main responsibility is to be mother.</u> Once they become mother they quit their job so they're not going to get a job that requires continual work. Maybe. Haa. . .

Jeff finally tied these inferences together, claiming that a woman's role was not just related to her occupation and legal status, but that socially accepted roles were responsible for a lack of change in all of these areas:

<u>So women are not gaining rights because their main role would be to raise children.</u> <u>So the changes in their roles, uh, [does] not justify change in their [legal] status</u> because the role basically changes from helping the man run the household to <u>run[ning] the household on their own.</u> Uh, which is basically now raising children. And the reason the husband left the home to go out working would be because of the industrial revolution. So the men were doing the industrial revolution jobs and women were doing things such as being teachers and domestic servants.

Because Jeff had tracked changes in occupations and roles as well as legal rights, he was able to come up with a qualified thesis, arguing that, in some respects, women's status had changed, while in other respects it had not. Jeff's qualified claim turned up in the introduction of his draft:

The lives and status of Northern middle class women changed during the nineteenth century. Noticeable changes occurred in women's roles and their attitudes toward legal status and occupation. Married women began to feel oppression from their husbands under the legal bind of marriage. Also women felt as if their occupational choices were limited. By the end of this period, women did not make all the advances which they hoped for.

Jeff argued that women's legal status remained largely unchanged, because their social role did not necessitate legal change or call previous laws into question. We can see the origins of this argument in watching Jeff use his third strategy card:

Women were being hired to jobs to which they were, uh, set up to do. And, uhhh, I don't know, let's see. So the women's status did not change legally, but their role changed as they were <u>becoming more responsible for their household duties and that</u> <u>was due to the industrial revolution. That did not justify changes in their [legal]</u> <u>status, so they weren't really given a change in their status.</u>

This reasoning informs the last paragraph of Jeff's text. There, he explains not only the changes women experienced, but he offers his conclusions of why this is so:

In the early stages of the period from 1776 to 1876, the role of the women began to change. At the same time, there was also a change in the woman's attitude toward her education, job opportunities, and rights. These changes were mainly brought about by the industrial revolution. This new attitude was counteracted by her need to be a mother and rear her children. Many of the women's attitudes were changed upon the entry of her child into the world. The resulting conflict limited the opportunities presented to women. Since men believed that it was a women's job to care for children and there was little evidence to show that her job should be otherwise, the men of the time did not feel a need to grant women as many opportunities as the women wanted. As a result, the legal status of women, especially in marriage, did not change during the nineteenth century.

Prior to this training, Jeff had relied on his teachers to show him the ideas he should use in his papers. He also looked for important ideas in the sources themselves. But in this assignment, the important points were not obvious, as Jeff pointed out. As Jeff experimented with these strategies, though, he began to take ownership over the process of interpretation, using the strategies to transform the documents into claims about change in legal status, social role, and occupation. Being able to manage and organize this diverse source information allowed Jeff to take interpretation one step further, to concentrate his efforts on finding connections and developing reasons and claims. In the end, Jeff did not stumble upon the important points he initially set out to find in the data; he developed those points himself.

Conclusions

Students' initiation into argument tasks may be difficult, especially if they expect to rely on the reading, note-taking, and writing strategies that worked so well for them in the past. Although these recitation and response strategies are quite useful, they alone cannot help students transform source texts into claims. In this chapter, I have suggested that teachers might better support this constructive process by helping students recognize and try out some optional strategies for reading, note taking, and planning their arguments.

My purpose here has not been to prove the effectiveness of modeling as compared to other ways of teaching argument. Although the students I have worked with have generally found this type of modeling useful (especially at the note-taking phase), certainly other instructional methods (e.g., Toulmin's data-warrant-claim model) might be better for teaching other aspects of the task (e.g., identifying weak or unelaborated claims in your draft). And of course, as in any method, some students are able to take more from the modeling sessions than others. However, I do want to argue that this combination of observing, modeling, and adapting strategies can enlarge the possibility of reflection and learning in our classrooms. As teachers and students observe and experiment with the interpretive strategies that underlie argument, they become aware of alternative approaches and can pinpoint those particular strategies that may be most difficult for them. Scott, for example, had trouble turning his themes into a usable note-taking strategy, and both Jeff and Scott might have benefited from some exposure to other types of note structures such as the matrix. This combination of observation, modeling, and adapting strategies allows teachers to gain access to and intervene in the reading and note-taking strategies that often remain hidden when students do this interpretive work in the privacy of their own rooms.

When students don't perform well on the tasks we assign, we are often too quick to generalize that they are somehow incapable of meeting these challenges. In some cases, we even lower our expectations. However, when we bring research into the classroom and watch students respond, we often gain a sense of the strategic knowledge students already possess. Jeff, a B student at a very competitive university, was a capable writer to begin with, a student who had fared well in high school. But up until this history course, Jeff had never been asked to write an argument from sources of this nature. So what did modeling do for Jeff? In a post-task interview, Jeff himself said it best: "It (the strategies) set me in the right direction I needed to be going. I knew these strategies but I didn't know to use them." Indeed, Jeff had the ability to see connections in the data, draw inferences, and construct a set of relevant claims. At some level, he and most other students "know" these strategies. What they may not know, however, is when to use them or how they might take shape in the context of reading and planning an argument paper. Jeff and students like him may just need a procedural map and a set of prompts to help them do what they are already quite capable of doing.

References

Ackerman, J. (1990). Translating context into action. In L. Flower, V. Stein, J. Ackerman, M. Kantz, K. McCormick, & W. Peck, *Reading-to-write: Exploring a cognitive and social process* (pp. 173-193). New York: Oxford University Press.

Applebee, A. (1981). *Writing in the secondary school*. (Research Monograph No. 21). Urbana, IL: National Council of Teachers of English.

Applebee, A. (1984). *Contexts for learning to write*. Norwood, NJ: Ablex.

Applebee, A., Durst, R., & Newell, G. (1984). The demands of school writing. In A. Applebee (Ed.), *Contexts for learning to write*. Norwood, NJ: Ablex.

Britton, J., Burgess, T., Martin, N., McLeod, A., & Rosen, H. (1975). *The development of writing abilities*. London: Macmillan.

Bridgeman, B. & Carlson, S. (1984). Survey of academic writing tasks. *Written Communication, 1*, 247-280.

Collins, A., Brown, J., & Larkin, K. (1980). Inference in text understanding. In R. Spiro, B. Bruce, & W. Brewer (Eds.), *Theoretical issues in reading comprehension*. Hillsdale, NJ: Erlbaum.

Collins, A., Brown, J. S., & Newman, S. (1989). Cognitive apprenticeship: Teaching the craft of reading, writing and mathematics. In L. Resnick (Ed.), *Knowing, learning, and instruction: Essays in honor of Robert Glaser* (pp. 453-494). Hillsdale, NJ: Erlbaum.

Cooper, C., Cherry, R., Coley, B., Fleischer, S., Pollard, R., & Sartisky, M. (1984). Studying the writing abilities of a university freshman class: Strategies from a case study. In R. Beach & L. Bridwell (Eds.), *New directions in composition research* (pp. 19-52). New York: Guilford.

Crowhurst, M. (1991). Interrelationships between reading and writing persuasive discourse. *Research in the Teaching of English, 25*, 314-338.

Curtin, E. (1988). *The research paper in high school writing programs: Examining connections between goals of instruction and requirements of college writing*. Unpublished doctoral dissertation, Carnegie Mellon University, Pittsburgh.

Flower, L. (1989). *Negotiating academic discourse*. (Technical Report. No. 29). Berkeley, CA: Center for the Study of Writing, University of California at Berkeley and Carnegie Mellon University.

Flower, L., Stein, V., Ackerman, J., Kantz, M., McCormick, K., & Peck, W. (1990). *Reading-to-write: Exploring a cognitive and social process*. New York: Oxford University Press.

Harris, M. (1983). Modeling: a process method of teaching. *College English 45*, pp. 74-78.

Higgins, L. (1992). *Argument as construction: A framework and method*. Unpublished doctoral dissertation. Carnegie Mellon University. Pittsburgh, PA.

Higgins, L., Mathison, M., & Flower, L. (In prep). The rival hypothesis stance (Tech. Report). Pittsburgh, PA: Center for the Study of Literacy in Science.

Hillocks, G. (1986). *Research on written composition*. Urbana: National Conference on Research in English.

Kaufer, D. & Geisler, C. (1989). Novelty in academic writing. *Written Communication, 8*, 3 (286-311).

Kaufer, D., Geisler, C., & Newirth, C. (1989). *Arguing from sources: Exploring issues through reading and writing*. San Diego: Harcourt Brace Jovanovich.

Norman, D. A. (1980). What goes on in the mind of the learner. *New Directions for Teaching and Learning, 2,: Learning, cognition, and college teaching* 37-49.

Palincsar, A. & Brown, A. (1984). Reciprocal teaching of comprehension-fostering and comprehension monitoring activities. *Cognition and Instruction, 1* (2), 117-175.

Palincsar, A. & Brown, A. (1985). Reciprocal teaching: Activities to promote "reading with your mind." In T. Harris and E. Cooper (Eds.), *Reading, thinking and concept development*. New York: The College Board.

Scardamalia, M., Bereiter, C., & Steinbach, R. (1984). Teachability of reflective processes in written composition. *Cognitive Science, 8*, 173-190.

Scardamalia, M. & Bereiter, C. (1987). Knowledge telling and knowledge transforming in written composition. In S. Rosenberg (Ed.), *Advances in applied linguistics*. New York: Cambridge University Press.

Spivey, N. (1987). Construing constructivism: Reading research in the United States. *Poetics, 16*, 169-192.

Toulmin, S., Rieke, R., & Janik, A. (1979). *An introduction to reasoning*. New York: Macmillan.

Voss, J., Greene, T., Post, T., & Penner, B. (1983). Problem solving skills in the social sciences. In G. Bower (Ed.), *The psychology of learning and motivation: Advances in research and theory* (Vol. 17). New York: Academic Press.

Appendix A: Source Materials—Cigarette Ads

1. A survey of popular magazines including *Time, People, Newsweek* and *Life* revealed that cigarette ads in those magazines during 1973 were 19.7 words longer than the 1985 ads. The earlier ads foregrounded information on brand ingredient and percentage of tar and nicotine. This information was footnoted in the 1985 ads.

2. One study conducted by the American Heart Association showed that from 1966 to 1970, cigarette ads on television stressed name brand and quality. On the average, brand names were repeated 7.3 times per commercial and brand packaging or logos were shown during 78% of commercial time.

3. The Department of Health claims that there are fewer smokers now than there were in 1970, but more women are smoking now than were in 1970.

4. In 1964 the Surgeon General determined that smoking is hazardous to good health and may be linked to heart disease and cancer.

5. 75% of today's cigarette ads in the magazines previously mentioned show men and women smokers together, usually engaging in some type of recreational activity.

6. Over 60% of teenage smokers interviewed in a 1984 study reported that "looking good" was one reason why they smoked.

7. Twenty randomly selected billboard ads depicting male and female smokers were shown to 97 college students in a 1985 study. These students, consisting of smokers and non-smokers, generally agreed that the smokers in those ads were "attractive," "well-dressed," "exciting" and "middle to upper class."

8. In New York City a telephone survey revealed that on the average, non-smokers interviewed earn $17,000 a year less than smokers.

9. Surveys conducted in seven Midwestern towns over a two-year period showed no correlation between smoking and religion, smoking and income bracket of smoking and marital status. A correlation was found between smoking and occupation type. Those with desk jobs (secretaries, receptionists, office workers) were found more likely to be smokers than those working outdoors or those more physically active on the job.

10. According to polls taken at Harvard, Yale, and Stanford universities, smoking among the ivy league students has dropped dramatically over the past 20 years.

11. During 1984–1985, celebrities such as Johnny Carson and Mia Farrow have made public statements warning pregnant mothers not to smoke. Sports stars such as Larry Bird and Lynn Swann have also joined the media's no-smoking campaign.

12. In 1981, the Raleigh Tobacco Co. was the first to offer free gifts such as sunglasses and sports wallets with the purchase of its less popular brand cigarettes.

13. Today, nearly 49% of brands sold in the U.S. offer a "light" blend of the original brand.

14. The average smoker today in the U.S. falls in the 20–40 age bracket, is employed, and smokes 18.4 cigarettes per day.

Appendix B: Source Materials—Historical Documents

DOCUMENT GROUP A–E: THE IMPACT OF THE AMERICAN REVOLUTIONARY ERA

Document A

By marriage, the husband and wife are one person in law: that is, the very being or legal existence of the woman is suspended during the marriage, or at least is incorporated and consolidated into that of the husband. . . . For this reason, a man cannot grant any thing to his wife, or enter into covenant with her, for the grant would be to suppose her separate existence. . . .

If the wife be injured in her person or her property, she can bring no action for redress without her husband's concurrence, and in his name, as well as her own, neither can she be sued without making the husband a defendant. . . . (Sir William Blackstone, *Commentaries on the Laws of England* (1765–1769), the work of an English jurist in the decades immediately following the Revolution.)

Document B

I long to hear that you have declared an independancy—and by the way in the new Code of Laws which I suppose it will be necessary for you to make I desire you would Remember the Ladies, and be more generous and favourable to them than your ancestors. Do not put such unlimited power into the hands of the Husbands. Remember all Men would be tyrants if they could. If perticuliar care and attention is not paid to the Ladies we are determined to foment a Rebelion, and will not hold ourselves bound by any Laws in which we have no voice, or Representation.   (Abigail Adams, letter to John Adams, March 31, 1776)

Document C

As to your extraordinary Code of Laws, I cannot but laugh. We have been told that our Struggle has loosened the bands of Government every where. That Children and Apprentices were disobedient—that schools and Colledges were grown turbulent—that Indians slighted their Guardians and Negroes grew insolent to their Master. But your Letter was the first Intimation that another Tribe more numerous and powerfull than all the rest were grown discontented.

Depend upon it, We know better than to repeal our Masculine systems. Altho they are in full Force, you know they are little more than Theory. We dare not exert our Power in its full Latitude. We are obliged to go fair, and softly, and in Practice you know We are the subjects.   (John Adams, letter to Abigail Adams, April 14, 1776)

Document D

He [John Adams] is very sausy to me in return for a List of Female Grievances which I transmitted to him. I think I will get you to join me in a petition to Congress. I thought it was very probable our wise Statesmen would erect a New Government and form a new code of Laws. I ventured to speak a word in behalf of our Sex, who are rather hardly dealt with by the Laws of England which gives such unlimited power to the Husband to use his wife ill.   (Abigail Adams, letter to Mercy Otis Warren, a close friend and frequent correspondent with both John and Abigail Adams, April 27, 1776)

Document E

It is true that there are certain appropriate duties assigned to each sex; and doubtless it is the more peculiar province of masculine strength, not only to repel the bold invader of the rights of his country and of mankind, but in the nervous style of manly eloquence to describe the bloodstained field, and relate the story of slaughtered armies.

Sensible of this . . . [my] trembling heart has recoiled at the magnitude of undertaking [this history]; yet, recollecting that every domestic enjoyment depends on the unimpaired possession of civil and religious liberty, that a concern for the welfare of society ought equally to glow in every human breast, the work was not relinquished.   (Mercy Otis Warren, writing in the preface to Volume One of her three-volume treatise, *History of the Rise, Progress and Termination of the American Revolution*, 1805)

DOCUMENT GROUP F–H:
THE IMPACT OF INDUSTRIALIZATION
Document F

Women carding and spinning in the home, while the man in the family weaves: a typical home scene during the period before the Industrial Revolution, circa 1790.

Document G

Some Major Nonagricultural Occupations
in Which Women Were Employed in 1850
(total free labor force 6,280,000)

	Male	Female
Factory work	990,000	210,000
Teaching	25,000	55,000
Domestic Service	20,000	330,000

Document H

In these olden times . . . the house was a factory on the farm, the farm a grower and producer for the house. There was no affectation of polite living, no languishing airs of delicacy and softness in doors. . . . Harnassed, all together, into the producing process, [were] young and old, male and female, from the boy that rode the plough-horse, to the grandmother knitting under her spectacles. . . .

This transition [from homespun to factory-made clothing] is already so far made that the very terms, *"domestic manufacture"* have quite lost their meaning; being applied to that which is neither domestic, as being made in the house, nor manufacture, as being made by the hands. . . . This transition . . . is a great one . . . one that is to carry with it a complete revolution of domestic life and social manners. (Horace Bushnell, "The Age of Homespun," an address delivered in Litchfield, Connecticut, 1851)

DOCUMENT GROUP I–K: IDEALS OF FEMININITY

Document I

The father, weary with the heat and burden of life's autumn, has forgotten the sympathies of life's joyous springtime. . . . The acquisition of wealth, the advancement of his children in worldly honor—these are his self-imposed tasks. . . . His wife forms the infant mind as yet untainted by contact with evil . . . like wax beneath the plastic hand of the mother.

Document J

Godey's Lady's Book (February, 1852)

Document K

Where lieth woman's sphere? — Not there
Where strife and fierce contentions are,
Not in the wild and angry crowd,
Mid threat'nings high and clamors loud;
Nor in the halls of rude debate
And legislation, is *her* seat.

What then *is* woman's sphere? The sweet
And quiet precincts of her home;
Home! — where the blest affections meet,
Where strife and hatred may not come!
Home! — sweetest word in mother-tongue,
Long since in verse undying sung!
Ladies' Repository (1845)

DOCUMENT GROUP L–N: EDUCATION AND WOMEN

Document L

Another defect in education has arisen from the fact, that teachers have depended too much upon authority, and too little upon the affections, in guiding the objects of their care. . . . For these and other reasons, it seems of great importance that the formation of the female character should be committed to the female hand. It will be long, if ever, before the female mind can boast of the accurate knowledge, the sound judgment, and ready discrimination which the other sex may claim. But if the mind is to be guided chiefly by means of the affections; if the regulation of the disposition, the manners, the social habits and the moral feelings, are to be regarded before the mere acquisition of knowledge, is not woman best fitted to accomplish these important objects[?]   (Catherine E. Beecher, *Suggestions Respecting Improvements in Education*, 1829)

Document M

I am convinced there is an alarming conspiracy formed by fathers and guardians to patronize only such institutions of female learning as are calculated to keep damsels in subordination, in order to prevent them from fulfilling their natural, lofty, destiny — from aspiring to equal power and influence in Church and State.   (Grace Greenwood, a popular author, in *Greenwood Leaves*, 1853)

Document N

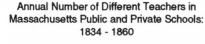

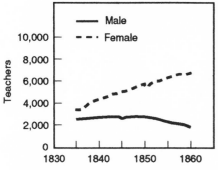

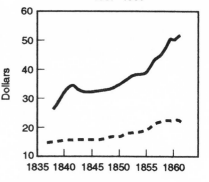

COMPOSITION AND WAGE RATES OF THE TEACHING STAFF IN
MASSACHUSETTS   *Source:* Abstracts of Massachusetts School Returns (1835–1860).

DOCUMENT GROUP O–R:
THE FIRST WOMAN'S RIGHTS MOVEMENT

Document O

We hold these truths to be self-evident: that all men and women are created equal;
that they are endowed by their Creator with certain inalienable rights; that among
these are life, liberty, and the pursuit of happiness; that to secure these rights govern-
ments are instituted, deriving their just powers from the consent of the governed. . . .

The history of mankind is a history of repeated injuries and usurpations on the part
of man toward woman, having in direct object the establishment of an absolute
tyranny over her. To prove this, let facts be submitted to a candid world. . . .

He has made her, if married, in the eye of the law, civilly dead.

He has taken from her all right in property, even to the wages she earns.

He has made her, morally, an irresponsible being, as she can commit many crimes
with impunity, provided they be done in the presence of her husband. In the covenant
of marriage, she is compelled to promise obedience to her husband, he becoming, to
all intents and purposes, her master—the law giving him power to deprive her of her
liberty, and to administer chastisement.   ("Declaration of Sentiments and Resolu-
tions," Seneca Falls, New York, 1848)

Document P

I was disappointed when I came to seek a profession. . . . Every employment was
closed to me, except those of the teacher, the seamstress, and the housekeeper. In
education, in marriage, in religion, in everything, disappointment is the lot of
woman. It shall be the business of my life to deepen this disappointment in every

woman's heart until she bows down to it no longer. I wish that women, instead of being walking showcases, instead of begging of their fathers and brothers the latest and gayest new bonnet, would ask of them their rights. (Lucy Stone, Speech at National Woman's Rights Convention, Cincinnati, October, 1855)

Document Q

. . . I wish I felt the old impulse and power to lecture, . . . but I am afraid and dare not trust Lucy Stone. . . . I went to hear [a] lecture on Joan d'Arc. It was very inspiring and for the hour I felt as though all things were possible to me. But when I came home and looked in [my daughter's] sleeping face and thought of the possible evil that might befall her if my guardian eye was turned away, I shrank like a snail into its shell and saw that for these years I can be only a mother. (Lucy Stone, letter to Antoinette Brown Blackwell, February 20, 1859)

Document R

Of married women and their legal status. What is servitude? "The condition of a slave." What is a slave? "A person who is robbed of the proceeds of his labor; a person who is subject to the will of another. . . ." There is an old saying that "a rose by any other name would smell as sweet," and I submit the deprivation by law of the ownership of one's own person, wages, property, children, the denial of the right as an individual, to sue and be sued, and to testify in the courts, is a condition of servitude most bitter and absolute, though under the sacred name of marriage.

Does any lawyer doubt my statement of the legal status of married women? I will remind him of the fact that the old common law of England prevails in every State in this Union, except where the Legislature has enacted special laws annulling it. And I am ashamed that not one State has yet blotted from its statute books the old common law of marriage, by which Blackstone, summed up in the fewest words possible, is made to say: "Husband and wife are one, and that one is the husband." (Susan B. Anthony, arguing that women should be granted the vote under the provisions of the Fifteenth Amendment to the Constitution, 1873)

6

The Library Revisited:
Exploring Students' Research Processes

JENNIE NELSON

Nothing is more scandalous in schools and colleges than what we call "writing a research paper."

(Ken Macrorie in Olson, 1986, p. 130)

I don't know why I can never bring myself to write research papers until the last minute; it's not a difficult thing to do—in fact, it's rather easy. Maybe it's because it's boring. . . . I can never keep a good train of thought because it's not coming from me or my thoughts; it's coming from some book and all I'm doing is regurgitating information that the teacher already knows.

(Ann, a college freshman, in Nelson & Hayes, 1988, p. 10)

In spite of teachers' misgivings and students' complaints, the research paper remains one of the most common assignments in undergraduate college writing programs across the country (Ford & Perry, 1982). In addition, much of the writing that students are expected to produce in courses across the curriculum requires them to locate and use research material (Bridgeman & Carlson, 1985). Most writing teachers would agree that successful writers must be able to gather, interpret, integrate, and acknowledge material from a variety of sources, but many teachers are disappointed in their students' responses to research paper assignments and disillusioned about their abilities to teach students these critical processes. Surprisingly, in spite of the important role that research plays in academic writing, researchers have only begun to examine how students approach the process of researching a topic for writing (Stotsky, 1990).

In two valuable exploratory studies, Kuhlthau (1983, 1988) used questionnaires, interviews, and journals to examine how advanced high school and college students defined and directed their own searches for information to be used in writing. She found that these students moved through a series of six overlapping stages during the search process, which included developing a personal need for the search, selecting a topic, exploring available sources, developing a focus for the paper, collecting relevant material, and preparing the material for presentation. Most important, students moved through these stages *before* they actually began writing drafts of their papers. This means that a large portion of the critical work required to produce a research paper often takes place during the search process, rather than during the writing process. These findings underscore the vital role that the research process can play in shaping writing and learning and raise important questions for teachers. If we want our students to be able to navigate their own paths effectively when they are researching a topic for writing, we must know more about the factors that influence their choices and approaches.

What Studies Tell Us About the Assumptions and Strategies That Guide Student Researchers

Research reveals that there is a considerable difference between the way many students view the process of research and the way most college instructors and researchers view it. Schwegler and Shamoon (1982) interviewed college students about why they wrote research papers and why they thought teachers assigned them. They found that generally students believe that research writing assignments are intended to test their ability to locate and reproduce information for a teacher who knows more about their topics than they do and who will base their grades on the quantity of information presented and the correctness of documentation. In contrast, they found that teachers believe that the aim of research is to "test a theory, to follow up on previous research, or to explore a problem posed by other research or by events" (p. 819). Perhaps most significant, Schwegler and Shamoon found that "college instructors view the research paper as a means to accomplish one of the primary goals of college instruction: to get students to think in the same critical, analytical, inquiring mode as instructors do—like a literary critic, a sociologist, an art historian, or a chemist" (p. 821). The differences between the students' and teachers' views are striking. Students define the research process as an exercise in information-gathering while teachers see it as a way to extend their knowledge through critical inquiry and analysis.

The differences between these contrasting goals for research writing are even more striking when we examine how students and more experienced academic writers actually go about locating and evaluating sources to be used in writing. John Hayes and I compared the strategies of eight college freshmen and eight advanced academic writers (seniors and graduate students) as they planned and conducted their research on an assigned paper topic. We found that the two groups relied on very different goals and strategies to complete their research task. The majority of the freshmen set out on a fact-finding mission, using "topic-driven" techniques that would allow them to find and assemble information on their topic as quickly as possible. For example, students evaluated possible sources by determining how easily information could be extracted. One student explained her technique for determining this: "Skim the index for your topic; if information is spread out [sprinkled over several distant pages], then reject that book because you would have to read too much . . . you should try to find sources that have pockets or chunks of information that can be read and summarized easily" (Nelson & Hayes, 1988, p. 5).

In contrast, the more advanced writers approached their research very differently. They described their initial purpose for conducting research in various ways: "to make a case; to argue for a position; to find a provocative or new approach" (p. 3). These goals led to "issue-driven" search strategies that allowed students to zero in on issues and to evaluate the relevance and validity of possible sources. For example, three of the advanced students reported that they skimmed periodical indexes, such as *The New York Times* index, in order to get an overview of the major issues surrounding their topic, and they used this information to help them find an "angle" or issue to explore. Unlike the "topic-driven" freshmen, these more advanced students evaluated prospective sources rhetorically, asking "Who wrote this, when, and for what purpose?" They chose sources based on their relevance and reliability, not on how easily material could be extracted and reproduced. What emerges from these studies are very different views of the goals and strategies involved in researching a topic for writing. It appears that some students may interpret the goals of research-based writing in very limited terms and that these limited task interpretations may lead them to choose truncated paths when they are searching for material to be used in writing.

But why do students define and approach their research assignments so differently? There are several possible explanations worth considering. First, perhaps the more experienced writers have particular knowledge about using library resources that the less experienced students lack. The "topic-driven" search strategies we observed may be the inevitable outcome when students don't have the knowledge needed to conduct a thorough search of the library's resources. Other studies of students' search processes suggest that this may be part of the problem. An early study of nearly fifty college freshmen at Bucknell University reported that "the conception of research on the part of many [students] appeared to be limited and unsophisticated—often involving little more than finding a book and checking it out of the library" (Reed, 1974, p. 20). Based on her extensive study of the search processes of advanced English high school seniors, Kuhlthau (1985) has suggested that some students may need to "learn to make a comprehensive search of all sources . . . and to extend their search beyond being satisfied with a few books located through the card catalogue" (p. 39). While college freshmen may need to learn how to take advantage of the range of resources available in university libraries, it seems that unless we change the limited goals that students bring to the research process in the first place, they may continue to be satisfied with a few easily located sources. If their primary goal is to assemble and reproduce what others have written on a topic as efficiently as possible, then long, involved searches are unnecessary. Perhaps this is why students who have attended library tours and received in-depth library skills instruction continue to disappoint their teachers. Such knowledge is largely useless if students are on a fact-finding mission with the sole goal of locating sources with easily plundered pockets of information.

But where do these limited goals come from? We know that writers never work in a vacuum; they write in a specific setting for a particular audience, and the constraints of the writing context will influence how they interpret and approach their tasks. In a second study, John Hayes and I used process logs and interviews to examine the goals and approaches of eight undergraduate students as they completed research paper assignments for a variety of classes. We found that features of the writing situation itself seemed to play a powerful role in determining how students interpreted and responded to research-based writing assignments. When teachers merely assigned a topic and a due date for papers, students were more likely to procrastinate until the last minute and to rely on shortcuts and "topic-driven" search strategies. However, when teachers provided real purposes for conducting research — for example, by asking students to give oral reports before their papers were due in order to share what they had learned with their uninformed classmates — students took a more critical and time-consuming, "high-investment" approach to their research assignments. We speculate that the range and quality of the writing contexts our students are exposed to may be key factors in aiding their development as academic writers (Nelson & Hayes, 1988). If students work in writing situations that actively encourage them to share and interpret research material rather than expecting them to regurgitate it, they may learn to rely on the same "issue-driven" strategies and goals observed in the more experienced academic writers.

Some teachers and researchers have argued that students bring limited goals to research-based writing because of the legacy of their early report-writing experiences in elementary and secondary school. Giacobbe (1986) reports how one first-grader described report-writing: "It's easy to do. I watched my sister Jennifer (who was doing the fifth-grade report on a country because last year she had done the fourth-grade report on a state) and this is what you do. First you copy stuff from a book. . . . And then you draw some pictures and maps" (p. 133). Giacobbe says "we laugh because of the truth we see in this parody of the research paper, [but] if you talk to teachers of children in the upper grades, they are still receiving reports that show no real evidence that the students have learned anything. Instead, reports are frequently copied from encyclopedias and other resource materials" (p. 134). These reports are often read "as though physical appearance was more important than what a student had to say" and graded on how well students followed the outline teachers provided (Giacobbe, p. 132).

Like Giacobbe, Calkins (1986) believes that "something is dreadfully amiss" when students internalize these criteria for report-writing and continue to rely on these limited assumptions and approaches when they encounter research-writing assignments in later classes. According to Calkins, "the irony is that in a field where everyone is saying 'We need to see how real writers go about composing, and to let our students participate in these processes,' few people are suggesting that we also need to study how real researchers go about their work and to use this . . . to begin demythologizing the process of writing content-area reports" (pp. 272–73). In the following section we will do just that by examining in detail how real college freshman researchers go about defining and completing a typical research paper assignment. When comparing these students' descriptions of their research and writing processes, it is interesting to notice the different goals students seemed to set for themselves and the paths they chose to reach them. In each case, we can look for clues that reveal how the students' task interpretations evolved and how these interpretations shaped the choices they made as researchers and as writers.

Observations of Student Researchers

What follows are excerpts from three students' process logs in which they describe how they interpreted and completed a research paper assignment they received in a large introductory psychology class (Nelson, 1992). The students who participated in the study were asked to keep a daily log of their research and writing activities for the research paper and to deliver their confidential log entries to me at least three times a week, even if they had not worked on the paper during that time. They understood that their log entries could include information about the research trail they followed in the library, how they evaluated a prospective source, how they took notes and organized material, any discussions they had with other people, how much time they spent on paper-related activities, and how they actually composed the paper. In addition, students provided copies of all their notes, outlines, and drafts as they were produced. They understood that their goal was to explain in as much detail as possible how their research papers evolved from the first day they began thinking about their assignments until they turned in their final papers.*

All the students enrolled in the freshman level cognitive psychology course chose their paper topics from a list of twenty possible topics prepared by the professor and received a written description of the assignment that included the following guidelines:

> The purpose of this paper is to enrich your knowledge of psychology by encouraging you to explore a psychological topic in-depth. Your paper should be five to eight *typed* pages in length. Your audience should be other undergraduate students who do not know your topic. . . . Your paper should present an integrated point of view; it should be integrated around a purpose; it should *not* be a book review or an unrelated list of facts.

In addition to these general guidelines, students also received a list of criteria for grading that included "knowledge of subject matter, understanding of basic concepts, organization, critical thinking, and clarity for an undergraduate audience." While all the students enrolled in the course received the same general assignment, each of the students discussed below was enrolled in a different recitation section and, in some cases, was required to fulfill certain

---

*These instructions are included in the Appendix, "Conducting Process Research," at the end of this volume.

process requirements—either by turning in a rough draft or giving an oral presentation—while completing the paper.

When comparing these three students' descriptions of their research and writing processes, we might want to ask the following questions:

1. When did each student actually begin to gather and read source material for the paper? How many fruitful trips did she make to the library to locate sources?
2. Are there any clues that reveal how the student interpreted or defined the task for herself?
3. How do the written plans or drafts that the three students produced differ? What do they reveal about how much each student may have interpreted, integrated, and adapted source material rather than simply reproduced it?
4. What kinds of resources did students rely on (i.e., past school-writing experiences, written assignment guidelines, friends, classmates, teachers) to help them to define their assignment and refine their goals and approaches?
5. Overall, what do these students' process logs reveal about the different goals they set for themselves and the paths they chose to reach them? How did the different process requirements students fulfilled (drafts or oral reports) seem to influence their choices as researchers and writers?
6. What kind of paper did each student produce, and how was it evaluated?

Beth—*Topic: Language in Primates Other than Man*
[Note: The final paper was due November 13*]*

October 31: Talked to a friend about the topic of my research paper "language in primates other than man." He told me to look up a man by the name of Kelly. This person has apparently done research in the area. Thought about my research paper. Started getting upset because I have two other research papers due on the same day my psychology one is.

November 1: Went to the library with my roommate. Looked up several categories under "Animal Language" on the Info-trac machine. Decided that it is a wonderful machine. It saved me lots of time as I didn't have to use the card catalogue. Couldn't find anyone named Kelly who had done animal language research. However, I found 8 possible sources; they are all in magazines. I felt good as I had finally started the paper, even though all I did was find sources. [Beth left the library without actually locating the sources.]

November 2: Thought about my paper with a feeling of dread. Decided I had to go to the library that day. Didn't.

November 3: Pushed doing the paper out of my mind. I slept all day.

November 4: Talked about my paper with my roommate (just about doing it). She motivated me to start; said if I would just get going on it, it wouldn't be bad at all. I'm planning, no, I'm *going* to go to the library tonight. Will give you information tomorrow on my progress.

November 7: I went to the library to look up my magazine articles on the machine (view them). I found out that it wasn't working and I got frustrated, so I left.

November 8: Planned to go back—didn't.

November 9: Got sick and didn't feel like going but made a syllabus out for myself for the next four days workwise. Made me feel much better. Don't worry; you will get a lot of work from me on the 10th, 11th, and 12th as I will be doing the entire thing then.

November 11: Went to the library today and found out that it only had 2 of the articles I needed. I photocopied them. I then . . . used the card catalog and looked up approximately 16 books. Then I went and tried to find them. Found 8 I could use . . . I sat down on the floor and leafed through them. I went to the index (and where there wasn't an index I looked in the contents) and looked up page numbers where language was dealt with. I folded down the pages to save me time when I actually got the books home.

November 12: I made an itinerary for my paper (time-wise) as I now only have one day to get it finished. I figure (giving myself extra time) that I can get the thing organized in about five hours. Since it's a research paper, I will barely write anything of my own so it is basically an organization process.

I fell asleep after my classes and slept until 8:00. I still hadn't started the paper yet. At around 8:00 I sat down on my bed and leafed through the books. From the information available I made a small outline. Then I went through the books again and started organizing what they had to say. This took some time—about five hours. I didn't write out any rough draft. What I'm giving you with this last log entry is everything I used for the paper. What I did was footnote the paragraphs out of the books. As you can see from my outline [a portion of which is reproduced below], I wrote down the color of the book (for easy identification at the computer terminal), the number of the paragraph and where it fits chronologically . . . and the page number it's on in the book.

[Excerpts from Beth's outline]

Intro—what is language
  Def. 1
  2nd definition
MAG 1
Plastic dark brown 2—pg. 423
MAG 3 (no new paragraph)
Light green 4—pg. 208
MAG 5
Beige 6—pg. 73
Dark brown canvas 7—pg. 379

When I had finished this (and had written a scanty, sketchy beginning and ending), I went down to the computer terminal with all the books . . . plus my Heath Handbook . . . it shows the correct way to write a term paper (bibliography, spacing, etc.). I started with MAG (magazine) 1 and continued from there conveniently filling in between with my own words. . . . I finished typing [the entire paper] at 7:00 a.m. I don't have another copy of my paper because I erased it to write another one. When (and if) I get my paper back, I will give it to you.

Though Beth released all of her written work to me, she was never interested enough at the end of the semester to go to her professor's office and pick up her graded paper for which she received a C+. From the start, Beth seemed to assume that the research paper assignment was an exercise in assembling and reproducing material, and her last-minute search for sources and color-coded plans reflect this limited task definition. Although Beth visited the library three times, she did not actually locate and begin reading sources until the day before her paper was due. Her clearly articulated (though unexamined) assumption that "since it's a research paper, I will barely write anything of my own" seemed to lead to the last-minute gathering and plundering of sources. Her description of the highly efficient strategies she used to extract and organize material for her paper reveals that she lifted large passages from her source texts and reproduced them verbatim, filling in between these long quotes with her own words. Not surprisingly, she ended up producing a very coherent 1300-word paper in which 1100 words were documented as direct quotes from her sources.

Two features of Beth's research and writing processes are especially interesting. First, she appeared to rely solely on unexamined assumptions (no doubt based on her past experiences with research paper assignments) to help her define her assignment and goals. Second, Beth's streamlined, topic-driven search strategies and the pastiche of direct quotes in her final paper appear to be a logical outgrowth of her own limited task definition. It is interesting to speculate about whether a student like Beth is even aware that there are other paths and goals available for researching a topic for writing than the ones she chose. It appears that if students rely on tacit, unexamined assumptions to interpret research writing assignments, they may unwittingly set themselves up for failure. While her finished paper earned her an average grade from her psychology teaching assistant (who may not have realized that 85% of the paper consisted of direct quotes), it was copied verbatim from her sources and could have led to accusations of plagiarism, even though she acknowledged and documented her borrowed material.

Besides producing a rather unsatisfactory paper, her limited goals and search strategies turned this assignment into a largely unchallenging learning/ writing experience for Beth. Her lack of interest in the project is revealed in her log entries, where she seldom even refers to her paper topic and never discusses the information, authors, or titles from her sources. Furthermore, she reveals that she didn't even save a copy of her paper but erased it from her computer file to write another paper for a different class.

In the following two process logs we not only see students drawing from a much richer set of resources to define their assignments than Beth did, but we see them taking a much more self-conscious, open-ended and critical approach to the entire process of interpreting and defining their research paper assignments.

Lara — *Topic: Biorhythms*
[Note: A rough draft of her paper was due on October 30, two weeks before the final paper was due*]*
    October 17: Began working on paper. Went to the library and looked up topic on the computer file. Had a hard time locating Bio-rhythms. Most information was in the form of magazine articles. Looked up articles. Useless. . . . Not much of a start. Maybe tomorrow.
    October 18: Went to the local public library today. Looked up bio-rhythms in

the card catalog. Found 4 relevant books. Skimmed each book looking for main points, sub-divisions of the topic. Found *Is This Your Day?* extremely interesting — calculating daily biorhythms. Took some notes.

October 19:   Did not work on paper today. Did, however, discuss it with friends over lunch. We are wondering exactly how to approach writing it. What style? The assignment sheet specifies not to write it for a formal audience, i.e., your teacher. Does this mean adapt it for a general audience — fellow students? Be simple? Not technical? We're considering calling our teaching assistants for more specific instructions.

October 20:   I called my TA to clarify the assignment — he said to use my own discretion in narrowing down the topic — choose the information that I feel is relevant, important.

This evening I began to write out a bit of my notes, trying out sentences, seeing how things fit. Gave up after 2 paragraphs. I just wasn't in the mood and didn't feel motivated. Besides, I have lots of time! (Isn't that what I always say, up until the night before the damn things are due!)

October 27:   Too busy with psych test and English homework to think about psych paper. Want to get it done tomorrow night so I don't have to worry about it. . . .

My roommate complains she has to do an oral report with the professor present rather than turn in a rough draft. I think I would rather do the draft because I actually have to sit down and do some work rather than BS my way through an oral. At least I will have a skeleton to flesh out, which will help me a lot in writing the final paper.

October 28:   Well, I did it! I wrote up my rough draft this evening. I think I could have done a better job, but I really just wanted to get it over with. Besides, my teaching assistant says that they will look at the draft in comparison to the final product to determine how much you have changed, adapted, reorganized, restructured the information — so I guess I don't want my draft to be too good — it will make my final product look better!

[Excerpts from Lara's rough draft]

Introduction: What are bio-rhythms?
A biorhythm is defined as the application of mathematics to the biological scheme
  of things (Bio-mathematics)
The principle: nature is ordered, this order can be investigated using mathemat-
  ics — as a probe or tool to understand and explore human activity.
Question: Is there some kind of regularity or rhythm to the fundamental changes
  in man's disposition? Dr. Hermann Swoboda, professor of psychology at the
  University of Vienna, tried to find out — initial research 1897–1902.

October 30:   Draft collected. No big deal.

November 1, 2:   Parents are here. Don't work on paper. They do ask how psych is going, ask about paper — think topic is interesting.

November 3–6:   Didn't do any work on paper. Busy week — papers due, tons of homework.

Roommate panics over oral report — feels intimidated by professor. We talk about doing some serious work on our papers this weekend (Nov. 8, 9). She thinks that the paper is formal, yet informal (?)

We are planning on going to the library and re-evaluating our info. and helping each other structure the papers – look for a unique approach, something to make it stand out from all the others on the same subject.

November 9: I sat down in the library and took a good look at the assignment and the notes I had so far. After a few attempts at starting the final draft, I finally came up with an idea to make the paper interesting and set it apart from everyone else's. By using a character, I thought the paper would be more "personal" and therefore more interesting to read. My rough draft was written in approximately 3 hours, after I got my little "brainstorm."

[Excerpt from the introduction to Lara's revised paper]

Generic Gerald, an average guy from Pittsburgh, Pennsylvania, is a computer technician for the local IBM plant. Every morning he arises at 6:00 a.m. sharp, showers, dresses and grabs a cup of coffee and a bagel with cream cheese on his way to work. . . . So involved is Gerald in his work that when lunch time rolls around, he does not need to consult his clock to know that he's hungry. As he steps out for his lunch break, he notices knockout Noreen, his personal secretary, intently studying the latest issue of *Cosmopolitan*. Peeking over her shoulder, he sees the heading "Bio-rhythms, Superstition or Fact? How to Calculate Your Monthly Cycle." Scoffing quite audibly, Generic Gerald proceeds on his way. Bio-rhythms? Who ever seriously considered bio-rhythms?

Lara's teacher evidently found her paper interesting, as she hoped, for she received high marks in each of the criteria for grading listed on the assignment sheet – in particular for "clarity for an undergraduate audience" – and earned an A as the final grade. Unlike Beth (who was not required to turn in a draft or give a talk), she began searching for and reading from sources two weeks before her preliminary draft was due and nearly a month before her final paper was due.

It is especially intriguing to observe how Lara's task interpretation and goals changed and evolved over time and how she relied on a range of resources – classmates, the assignment guidelines, her teacher – to help her to define her assignment and refine her approaches. Lara reports that she and fellow classmates discussed the assignment over lunch several weeks before the papers were due, trying to define what was expected of them. Interestingly, these early concerns about the audience and style of her paper reappear later as explicit goals to make her paper "unique" and "interesting to read."

In addition to collaborating with her fellow classmates in trying to define her research task, she spoke with her teaching assistant to "clarify the assignment," and learned that the teachers who would be grading the papers would look at the students' rough drafts "in comparison to the final product to determine how much you have changed, adapted, reorganized, restructured the information." Like most astute student writers, she adapted her goals for the draft to meet her understanding of these graders' expectations, and produced a rather sketchy, dry rough draft, explaining "I don't want my draft to be too good – it will make my final product look better!"

Several days after turning in her rough draft, Lara and her roommate discussed plans to return to the library to re-evaluate their information and to help "each other structure the papers – look for a unique approach, something to make it stand out from all the others on the same subject." This high-level goal led to a completely revised paper — one that Lara believed "would be more 'personal' and therefore more interesting to read" — in which she weaves source material in with her own ideas and uses an extended narrative to explain what she has learned about biorhythms.

Lara's process log reveals that students' task interpretations and goals often evolve over time. As Lara gathered information, discussed her plans with classmates and her teacher, and gained more knowledge about her assignment and topic, she developed and expanded her research and writing goals. Her goal to make her paper interesting and find an approach that would "set it apart from everyone else's" appeared after she had written a dry summary of her research notes. The requirement to turn in a rough draft two weeks before the final paper forced Lara to get started early researching her topic, and she used this time to read and accumulate material from sources and to examine and reformulate her goals for the paper. Lara even found the required rough draft useful, explaining that "at least I will have a skeleton to flesh out, which will help me a lot in writing the final paper!" It appears that several factors — including the required draft, feedback from her classmates, friends, and even her parents, and her own personal, high-level goals — combined to make this a valuable and successful research project for Lara.

In the following process log, we see how similar factors shaped another student's goals and approaches. Like Lara's roommate, this student, Shelly, was required to give an oral presentation.

Shelly — *Topic: Biorhythms*
[Note: A brief oral presentation was due one week before the November 13 paper deadline*]*

October 20:   Today I finally began to think about my research paper for psychology because the deadline is approaching a little too rapidly. Since I haven't used the library yet this year I dragged a friend of mine with me to help me get started. We started with the information computer in order to find some books on the topic of Bio-rhythms and unfortunately only located one such book. Then we went over to the computer that lists articles from periodicals where we found a great deal of information and listings, but unfortunately I am not really sure what the topic of Bio-rhythms deals with so it was difficult deciding which articles might be helpful. Eventually, after rejecting articles dealing with plants and cancer, we did come up with a fairly respectable list. As of now it appears that the articles are going to be much more helpful than any books simply because of the amount available.

October 21:   Today I flipped through the two books that I got out of the library. Unfortunately, I am still very confused as to what Bio-rhythms are so I think my next step is to find an encyclopedia and get a feel for Bio-rhythms.

October 23:   I did nothing today.

October 25:   Once again I did nothing today on my paper because all of my other classes have been keeping me so busy.

October 28:   Once again I have done nothing today on my psychology paper because I must write a paper for philosophy first! Maybe tomorrow!

October 29:   I talked to my psychology teaching assistant today about finding more information on biorhythms. He suggested using a reference called psychological aspects [sic] which I think I will try to locate tomorrow.

October 30:   My mind is suddenly at ease because for some reason I had thought this paper was supposed to be 10–15 pages and it only has to be 8–10. Yea! Went to the library and looked through some encyclopedias. I'm still not sure what biorhythms are and if they are different from biologic clocks. I didn't take any notes yet because I'm not sure what I am looking for yet, but the encyclopedias look like possible sources for the basics on biorhythms.

October 31:   No research today. Talked to a classmate who is also writing on biorhythms and he said that biorhythms are very different from biological clocks, so I guess my subject area has been reduced a little bit now.

November 2:   Sick today so I didn't do anything but sleep.

November 4:   *The Encyclopedia Americana* is not a good source as of now anyway because all it mentions are biological clocks. *Collier's Encyclopedia* seems very informative because it is much broader yet more specific on the topic of biorhythms. Took notes.

[Excerpts from Shelly's notes]

Options for the paper so far:
What do I want to center my paper on?
Define — what are biorhythms?
        Is it important to understand them?
Plants, animals, humans?
What type of rhythms? circadian
                        annual
                        lunar
                        short rhythms — NO
Assignment — present an integrated point of view (around a purpose)
                NOT a book review or a list of unrelated facts

November 6:   I am panicking about having to give an oral presentation today in psychology recitation. Got up early to take some last-minute general notes on biorhythms and possibly to copy some articles at the library. Unfortunately, all of the available articles are at the Engineering and Science library and I ran out of time, so I didn't have a chance to get them. Maybe tomorrow.

Because I really don't have much information on biorhythms yet my main goal is just to tell what biorhythms are and then focus on some main points that my paper will probably focus on. As of now the main points that I want to focus on are first, how biorhythms develop in humans and second, how they affect the lives of humans or why they are important for us to understand.

[Excerpts from Shelly's outline for her oral report]

1. What are biorhythms?
2. How do they develop in humans?
3. Why are they important to understand?

November 7:   I used my friend's ID to get books out of the graduate library. They are called *Biological Rhythms in Psychiatry and Medicine, An Introduction to Biological Rhythms,* and *Your Body Clock. An Introduction to Biological Rhythms* looks like it will be helpful for the basic information and it also seems to have an entire chapter on human rhythms. *Your Body Clock* has a lot of information on how biorhythms affect humans as in travel and workshift changes. It also has some information on the development of the biorhythms in humans. . . .

November 8:   Took a few notes from *Your Body Clock.* Began using the introduction to *Biological Rhythms* but wasn't too sure where to begin so I made a list of possible subjects of interest that were listed in the index.

November 10: Took some notes and tried to locate a reference that my psychology TA had recommended to me — psychological abstracts. I actually was able to find them; however, they are set up in such a way that I had no idea how to use them. Basically that was a complete waste of time.

The book that I began taking notes from today proved to be very helpful and seems to contain a great deal of information in the area of human biorhythms. As of now, due to the fact that I really don't understand exactly what biorhythms are and probably couldn't even define them for you if you asked me to, I have decided to deal more with the uses of existing biorhythms and how they are related to humans.

November 11: Took some more notes, wrote a very shallow outline, complained a lot about the existence of the paper but that was about all that I accomplished today. Oh no, time is definitely running out!

November 12: Began writing a paper at 2:00 in the afternoon and literally sat, staring at the paper in front of me and writing a few incoherent pages of nothing. Suddenly at 4:00 I was lucky enough to experience a total wave of thought and I began another totally different paper on biorhythms. The first one seemed to be too precise and scientific which was causing me to just panic at the whole concept of trying to explain this stuff to other people when I hardly understand it myself. The second paper had a much more casual feeling to it and although it does not explain biorhythms very well, it also is not a boring summary about them either. I took one little concept, the effects of biorhythms in relation to humans and are they important to be aware of.

I summed up the majority of my thoughts on this matter on a sheet of paper, then just finished off the body of the paper. . . .

[Shelly's Summary of Uses of Biorhythms]

Summary of Uses

- aged — insight into the extreme sensitivity of the elderly.
- cancer treatment
- understand narcolepsy
- pediatricians can know whether or not a child is developing physiologically at a rate that will allow him to perform with his peers.
- jet lag — takes 2 to 3 days to readjust to a time difference of 6 hours.
- man is more vulnerable and susceptible at night due to body temperature.
- eskimos arctic hysteria
- problems with experimentation

It took me 3 hours to write the second version of my paper, and 5 hours to type it into the computer. Overall, it caused less stress than I had expected.

[Excerpt from Shelly's final paper — opening paragraph]

Now and then you may hear someone stating that he is a morning person or cannot function to his full potential after nine at night and someone else may claim to be a night person who is unable to function very well in the morning. Do these people really know what they are saying when they make these statements? In actuality it all has to do with biological rhythms. Biorhythms are cycles that every living thing experiences, yet very few of us know anything about. Recently there has been much more research on biorhythms, especially concerning their effect on humans. As a result, many practical ways for us to utilize the existence of biorhythms in the medical field have been discovered. We are also beginning to understand how these biorhythms affect the lives of ordinary people such as travelers who experience jet lag, and those people who are forced to adjust to radical work shift changes, thus disrupting their natural rhythms.

As the excerpt from Shelly's paper reveals, she focused her paper around the issue of how biorhythms affect humans and did not produce a "boring summary." She received high marks overall and earned an A− on her final paper. Like Lara, Shelly relied on friends, classmates, her teaching assistant, and the assignment guidelines for help in defining, researching, and planning her paper.

Throughout her log entries, Shelly seems most concerned about understanding her topic and finding a focus, perhaps because she had to give an oral report on her topic several days before her final paper was due. Her search plans reflect this concern. After flipping through the first two books that she located in the library, she reported that she was still confused about the nature of biorhythms and decided to do some background reading in an encyclopedia. In addition, she talked to her teaching assistant about finding more information on her topic, and, though she didn't understand how to use them, did track down the "psychology abstracts" as he suggested. In total, she made seven trips to the library.

A few days before her oral presentation was due, she wrote out her "options for the paper so far"; Shelly's ability to consider "options" for her paper so explicitly differs from Beth's swift, unexamined approach to defining her assignment. In answer to the question "what do I want to center my paper on?" Shelly lists several practical questions about biorhythms that her uninformed classmates might ask and refers to the assignment guidelines, reminding herself that she is supposed to "present an integrated point of view (around a purpose), NOT a book review or a list of unrelated facts." Both Lara and Shelly reveal a concern for meeting their audience's expectations, a concern that Beth does not raise in her logs.

When we compare the various written plans that Shelly produced with Beth's color-coded outline, another striking difference in their goals and approaches becomes apparent. While Beth's color-coded plans are merely instructions for copying passages from source texts in a particular order, Shelly's plans reveal that she was actively selecting and adapting material from her sources to meet her audience-based writing goals. She continues to ask audience-based questions about her topic and paper throughout her research. For example, on the morning before her oral report was due she reviewed her notes and wrote a detailed outline for her in-class presentation which focused around three basic questions concerning the nature of biorhythms, their development in humans, and their importance. These questions became the focus for her final paper as well.

Like Lara, Shelly's goals for her paper evolved over time. As she conducted more research and became more knowledgeable about her topic, her goals for her oral report and final paper were examined and refined. She referred to the assignment guidelines when she was struggling to find a focus for her paper and reports with some satisfaction in her last log entry that her second version of the paper "had a much more casual feeling to it and . . . it also [was] not a boring summary about [biorhythms] either."

Once again, it appears that a number of factors, such as the required oral report, discussions with classmates, and her own goals for writing, combined to make this a satisfying research assignment for Shelly. In fact, in a follow-up interview, she reported that she learned a great deal from this research paper assignment and ranked it as one of her most positive recent school writing experiences.

Helping Students to Become More Critical, Reflective Researchers

What these students' descriptions illustrate in dramatic fashion is the powerful role that writers' self-generated goals and task definitions can play in shaping their research and writing processes. Clearly, each of these students developed very different notions about what their assignment required, and these notions seemed to influence their strategies for completing work at every stage. Most important, these process logs reveal that students actively interpret their research paper assignments, creating their own research and writing goals and formulating the paths they will take to reach these goals. These task interpretations and choices — whether solitary or collaborative, reflective or unexamined — will help to determine whether students' research assignments become valuable opportunities to extend their knowledge through critical inquiry or unchallenging exercises in gathering and reproducing information.

In addition to providing a detailed, behind-the-scenes view of the various assumptions and strategies that guide students when they are researching a topic to be used in writing, these students' process logs also provide concrete ideas for teachers who want to help their students to effectively define and navigate their own research paths. They suggest that we may need to concentrate our efforts in three areas: (1) We need to identify and challenge our students' unexamined assumptions about the goals of research-based writing. (2) We need to share the attitudes and strategies of successful student researchers. (3) We need to provide writing contexts and assignments that call for and support critical, issue-driven research and writing.

As Beth's process log reveals, students may often rely on very limited criteria and goals when they interpret research-writing assignments. These task interpretations are often tacit but can shape students' processes and finished papers in important ways. As teachers, we may need to make our students aware of the important role that task interpretation plays in research and writing and to help them to articulate and, if necessary, revise their interpretations of research-based writing. One way to demonstrate the powerful role of task interpretation in research assignments is to share contrasting descriptions of students' research processes. For example, students could be asked to examine excerpts from Beth's and Lara's logs and to answer the six questions listed at the beginning of the previous section. In addition, students could discuss their own previous experiences with research-based writing assignments, focusing in particular on whether these experiences might lead to the same limited assumptions and strategies that characterize Beth's approaches.

Other factors besides students' tacit assumptions about the goals of research writing assignments can shape students' approaches, as well. These logs reveal that students may rely on a range of resources to help them to interpret and define their research paper assignment, including their past research-writing experiences, written assignment guidelines and feedback from teachers, informal discussions with friends, and collaborative efforts of classmates. Students like Lara and Shelly, who draw from a variety of resources and openly examine, reconsider, and revise their task interpretations, appear to be more successful, effective researchers.

We can help our students to become more aware of the resources and strategies available to them by sharing the goals and approaches of highly successful student researchers. For example, students might be asked to examine Helen's process log, included at the end of this chapter, in which she describes how she completed a research paper assignment for a freshman-level, introductory literature course. Students can study her descriptions and, working in groups, answer these questions:

- What techniques and resources does Helen use to help her to define a topic and goal for her paper?
- What techniques and resources does Helen use to help her locate useful sources?
- What techniques and resources does Helen use to help her plan and compose her paper?
- What techniques and resources does Helen use to help her evaluate her plans and her draft?

In reading Helen's process log, students will see how she struggled to define her research paper assignment and went on to produce a highly successful paper. Her experience illustrates how important and complex the act of interpreting a research-writing task can be. She took advantage of a variety of resources — including her aunt, classmates, friends, and her teacher — to help her to find a topic, locate sources, develop a focus and set goals for her paper (Nelson, 1990).

In addition to examining Helen's story of how her research paper evolved from beginning to end, students might be encouraged to try some of Helen's strategies for locating sources and taking notes when they are writing research papers of their own. They also could be asked to keep their own research process logs, using Helen's technique for organizing log entries into "Goals" and the "Means" for achieving them. Students can share their process logs periodically in small groups, comparing the different goals they developed and the paths they chose to meet them. These discussions should make students more aware of their options and of other methods for interpreting and responding to research paper assignments.

By encouraging our students to articulate and reconsider their interpretations of research-based writing assignments, by sharing the goals and methods
of successful student researchers, and by creating assignments and writing
situations that support issue-driven research and writing, we can help our
students to make critical, reflective choices as they define and navigate their
own research paths.

References

Bridgeman, B. & Carlson, S. (1985). Survey of academic writing tasks. *Written Communication 2*, 247-280.

Calkins, L. M. (1986). *The art of teaching writing*. Portsmouth, NH: Heinemann.

Ford, J. E. & Perry, D. R. (1982). Research paper instruction in the undergraduate writing program. *College English 44* (8), 825-831.

Giacobbe, M. E. (1986). Learning to write and writing to learn in the elementary school. In A. Petrosky and D. Bartholomae, *The teaching of writing*. Chicago: University of Chicago Press.

Kuhlthau, C. (1983). *The library research process: Case studies and interventions with high school seniors in advanced placement English classes using Kelly's Theory of Constructs.* Unpublished doctoral dissertation. Rutgers University.

Kuhlthau, C. (1985). A process approach to library skills instruction. *School Library Media Quarterly 13* (1), 35-40.

Kuhlthau, C. (1988). Longitudinal case studies of the information search process of users in libraries. *Library and Information Science Research 10* (3), 257-304.

Nelson, J. & Hayes, J. R. (1988). *How the writing context shapes students' strategies for writing from sources.* (Tech. Rpt. No. 16). Berkeley, CA: National Center for the Study of Writing and Literacy at University of California, Berkeley, and Carnegie Mellon University.

Nelson, J. (1990). This was an easy assignment: Examining how students interpret academic writing tasks. *Research in the Teaching of English 24* (4), 362-396.

Nelson, J. (1992). *Constructing a research paper: A study of students' goals and approaches.* (Tech. Rpt. No. 59.) Berkeley, CA: National Center for the Study of Writing and Literacy at University of California, Berkeley, and Carnegie Mellon University.

Olson, C. B. (1986). *Practical ideas for teaching writing as a process.* Sacramento: California State Dept. of Education.

Reed, J. G. (1974). Information-seeking behavior of college students using the library to do research: A pilot study (ERIC Document Reproduction Service ED 100 306).

Schwegler, R. A. & Shamoon, L. K. (1982). The aims and process of the research paper. *College English 44* (8), 817-824.

Stotsky, S. (1990). On planning and writing plans—Or beware of borrowed theories. *College Composition and Communication, 41*, 37-57.

Appendix: Excerpts from Helen's Process Log—Writing a Research Paper for a Freshman Literature Course

Here is the research paper assignment that Helen received.

Context: During the second half of the class we will be looking at issues
related to connections between aesthetic form and ideology. We will take up
such questions as: What distinguishes elite from popular forms? Do popular

or elite forms more strongly reflect dominant ideologies? We will ask these questions in the context of reading a series of works from the Victorian period of English literature (roughly 1840–1905) and some works from the 1960s. In order to read these works better, you will want to know more about their repertoire. This assignment will give you the opportunity to investigate the repertoire of Victorian texts and to use this information to interpret one or more of them.

Suggested Length: 5 to 7 pages, typed and double-spaced.

Audience: Other members of your class.

Suggested Topics: Your task in this assignment is to address one of the issues listed above. There are several different approaches you could take. . . . An example would be to emphasize the historical aspect of the paper . . . you might research Victorian bestsellers and show the ideologies these typically reflect.

Remember that a research paper is an argument. It is NOT a report of FACTS, but a careful marshaling of the judgments, opinions, and ideas of others to support your own position.

Special Requirements: This paper must refer to at least three sources. These must be cited according to the system explained in *The Lexington Introduction to Literature.*

Proposal: A written proposal will be due in 3 weeks before the final paper. In the proposal you should indicate the topic of your research, the argument you expect to make, and the work or works you will interpret. You should also include a bibliography of sources you have used so far.

Due date: Finished papers are due April 18.

[Excerpts from Helen's Process Log]

March 8:   My aunt gave me a book she had used in college (*Life in Victorian England* by W. J. Reader) after I told her about my research. The book looks like it may be helpful—the chapters are outlined and include discussions of separate social classes.

March 9:   Goal—to try to establish somewhat of a background on the Victorian Period.

Means—Read first 2 chapters of *Life in Victorian England*: just took some brief notes.

As of yet I'm still clueless as to what I'll do specifically.

March 13:   I planned on spending last night researching, but after speaking with a classmate I realized that I was very confused. My classmate had a totally different idea of the assignment. I decided I had better wait until today and ask the teacher.

I've just come from the class and our teacher has explained our research papers further. I think I have a better understanding of the goal. We are to propose and support an argument that is somewhat new. This argument must deal with the Victorian Era. First, though, I need to choose a topic and create an argument.

March 15:   Goal—to produce a solid topic for my proposal. On the way to the

library I thought of trying to research women and children of the Victorian Era—
like the ideologies about the roles they undertook.

Means—I found lots of information on women of the Victorian Era. I decided to
relate Victorian women to something we had done in class. I thought of Thomas
Hardy's poem "The Ruined Maid" and decided to try to present an argument about
the woman he has portrayed.

Next I began reading through the books I had found and as I was reading I
checked the sources those authors had used and made note of the authors they
mentioned. From there I used the card catalog and found many of these sources.
This method proved the most helpful.

Total time spent—5 hours

March 16:   Wrote a proposal for the paper explaining that I have researched the
actual lives of prostitutes in the Victorian Era and the circumstances surrounding
their "fall." . . . Based on my initial research Thomas Hardy has created a very true
portrait of prostitutes and hopefully this paper will show how. I also listed "Books
examined thus far; Books yet to examine but have; and books wanted."

March 20:   The teacher handed back proposals; He OK'd my idea.

Spring Break

April 3:   I talked with classmates about the teacher's vagueness and we tried to
decide what he wanted for these papers. I think he wants us to use other's arguments
to develop our own. So, in a sense, this isn't a research paper (i.e., telling what's
already been said like high school) but rather an argument that requires research.

Goal—to get most of my research done. To take notes I normally read a chunk of
text and summarize or pull out the main idea and write it in my own words. I only
quote once in a while.

Means—I reread the notes that I had taken and realized that I needed more on
Thomas Hardy. I think I am going to change my proposal where I said that Hardy
shows reality in his poem. I think he may be showing what the public *believes* to be
reality. At night I made a rough tree as to how I'll probably form my paper.

[*Note:*   Helen continued reading and taking notes over several days; her notes consisted of short summaries of ideas from her sources; these summaries were written
in her own words and included the page number and title and author for each source.
In addition, her own ideas and reactions to what she was reading were written in
parentheses throughout her reading notes; for example, next to one quote from
a source she wrote: "This says something about ideologies and prostitution—that
prostitutes had merely lost their moral uprightness. . . . Maybe a good argument
for my paper!"]

April 12:   Goal—finish research and create outline for paper.

Means—I looked over books I had gathered on prostitution and realized that
Finnegan's *Poverty and Prostitution* is really the most useful so I spent 2 hours
reading through her book and taking sparse notes. I really am finished researching
now; I just need to write the paper. I think if I make a detailed outline the writing
will be quite easier. [*Note:*   Helen wrote over 20 pages of sketchy, reflective notes
before finding a focus for her paper and before deciding to write the outline.]

April 13:   Goal—write outline.

I sat upstairs in the grill over lunch and using what ideas I had and the rough
sketch I made earlier, I formed my outline. I usually make an outline before writing

because otherwise I go off on tangents and my papers become hard to follow. I use a tree just to put ideas down.

[Excerpts from Helen's outline]

I. Introduction
   A. Ideal Victorian Woman (*Suffer and Be Still*)
   B. Mathew Arnold—poetry is criticism of life
      1. Thomas Hardy criticizing
      2. Thomas Hardy as meliorist
         a. expose seamier side; discover fall
II. Criticism of Tess of D'Urbervilles
   A. Similarities
      1. Auerbach sees Tess as simple girl to complex woman—"Ruined Maid" is the same: mobility and metamorphosis.
      2. Myth of Fallen Woman's guilt and Sorrow; Tess gains comfort from objects—Ruined Maid revolves around objects (Friedman p. 59). Under similarities—Journey from innocence to experience (quote p. 52). country innocence same in ruined maid.
   B. Differences
      1. Tess experiences disintegration in a single direction—a "fall from poverty to penury" (Friedman p. 57)
Ruined Maid (Auerbach p. 158) falls up "Some polish is gained from one's ruin."

April 15: Goal—get rough draft from which I can work. (Time: 11:20 to 3:00 a.m.)

Worked at the computer; I basically followed my outline and referred back to my sources as I had noted on my outline. I found my condensed notes and placed them right in the paper. This draft turned out better than I had expected. I still do not have a written conclusion but I know where I'm leading.

Just a side note: the class viewed the movie *The French Lieutenant's Woman* last night and afterward we had a discussion of Victorian ideals. I was able to contribute a lot of information to the discussion based on my research. The professor seemed pleased with some of the information I mentioned. I included the ideas he seemed to like in my paper.

April 16: Goal—finish paper

From 9:30 to 11:30 I corrected mistakes in the draft and wrote my conclusion. I had a friend read over my first draft.

[Excerpts from Helen's finished paper for which she received an A; here are the introductory and concluding paragraphs]

Hardy's Conforming Exposure

The ideologies surrounding women of the Victorian age demanded that a woman be sexually ignorant, but also have knowledge of the practice of sexual intimacy. "Knowledge without experience and a marriage-centered home became the twin ideals" (Vicinus xiii) for a Victorian woman. Women were taught that they were morally superior to men because they lacked a sexual drive, but simultaneously were condemned as weaker because of their weaker natures. As such, a woman had to be provided for. Her social status was first determined by her father's economic position and later by her husband's, but each man's moral behavior was in her hands (Vicinus vii–xv). Hypocrisy is an accurate description of the definition of a Victorian woman's role in society.

· · ·

Thomas Hardy, the meliorist, attempted to show his Victorians that prostitution and adultery existed in an age where women were sexually ignorant. They existed precisely because of the hypocrisy with which the role of women was defined. Prostitution was a journey from innocence to experience; however, unless the woman was of very high standing, she was surrounded by 'experience.' The lower class and even middle class girls were not afforded the luxury of sexual ignorance (Finnegan 116). Thomas Hardy has exposed this underworld of girls outcast from their families and condemned by society, but he does not accurately portray their total degradation. If Melia had replied "One's pretty lifeless when ruined" instead of "One's pretty lively," Hardy would not only have exposed the seamier side of Victorian England, but he would have captured the lives of Victorian prostitutes.

II

WRITING IN CLASSROOM CONTEXTS

7

Decision-Making During the Collaborative Planning of Coauthors

REBECCA E. BURNETT

As both a teacher and researcher, I want to understand the nature of the collaborative decision-making process that coauthors use. My interest comes in part from recognizing the benefits of classroom collaboration, which can give students experience and insight into their own thinking and problem solving. Students also gain emotional support, dialectical opportunities, and mutual commitment (Gebhardt, 1980) as well as preparation for academic and workplace collaboration as they work with the conventions and language of a discourse community and receive feedback (Higgins, 1988). My interest is also understandable given the prevalence of collaborative writing activities in classrooms. For example, nearly half of the respondents (46.5%) in a national survey of university and college business communication teachers indicated that they use collaborative writing in their classes (Bosley, 1989). The use of collaboration is increasingly widespread in many other writing courses as well (see detailed review in DiPardo & Freedman, 1988).

The following excerpts show that stripping collaboration of conflict and urging consensus is not necessarily productive. In fact, deferring consensus and engaging in certain kinds of conflict can often have advantages. Let's start by listening to an excerpt from a collaborative planning session between two coauthors, Dean and Sujit, as they consider what recommendations to make for revising a product information sheet for a solar heating/cooling system. In this episode, Dean and Sujit explore one point: revising a paragraph from the product information sheet about a two-speed blower (high speed for winter; low speed for summer).

DEAN   Yeah. What else? Uh, the fact like different temperatures when, uh, you're using the different speeds.

SUJIT   Yeah, okay. I didn't think that was a bad idea where they said that it, uh, it switches for the summer, and uh —

DEAN   Yeah, that was really good, I think. I would say it was good; it just seemed a little wordy.

SUJIT   Yeah.

DEAN   And you can't pick out the information that quick.

SUJIT   So then maybe, uh, perhaps in that paragraph, in the speed paragraph, we want to condense it.

DEAN   Uh-huh. Definitely.

SUJIT   Good idea.

In their *elaboration of a single point*, Dean and Sujit identify one part they want to maintain (switching to a different speed for summer) and two other related aspects they want to change (reducing wordiness and condensing the information). As they elaborate their ideas for revising this paragraph, they consider no alternatives and voice no disagreements. Instead, they reach consensus on each idea quickly as shown by their *immediate agreements* (e.g., "Yeah," "Definitely") that let the other person know an idea has not only been understood but accepted. Can collaborative interaction such as David and Sujit's — characterized by elaboration of single points and immediate agreements, without alternatives or disagreements — lead to a high-quality document?

Before I answer this question, let's look at a contrasting example. Kevin and Neal are dealing with the same task as Dean and Sujit as they consider what recommendations to make about revising the product information sheet; however, their approach is considerably different. In this episode, they focus on the selection and presentation of information for their recommendation report, which they'll write as a memo. They spend a good deal of time in decision-making that involves *considering alternatives* and *voicing explicit disagreement* about content as well as other rhetorical elements, which in this chapter I call *substantive conflict*.

KEVIN   Right. I was thinking that we could say, like, the first thing on the page after the introductory blurb is going to be financial savings, homeowners' financial savings. Then it's going to be, you know, a table and diagram or a table and a chart or a table, and then it's going to say, you know, okay, this table is — at the end and include that table on the memo. So that then they'd have to write out what the figures are. Is that what you're thinking?

NEAL   Oh, no. Um.

KEVIN   What were you thinking? . . .

NEAL   Um. I was thinking, um, all right, we mention financial savings and then we can, since we're talking memo, and we'll say we want to present to each— to actually both groups, the types of financial savings they'd have and then we can just— instead of saying how— exactly in the memo, how much we're going to save, maybe just have little charts, diagrams, or—

KEVIN   In the memo?

NEAL   Example or not? Yeah. I was thinking in the memo or not. Or should we just say that we're going to have a graph? Maybe we'll just say we'll have a graph.

KEVIN   No, I think we should—Well, I don't know. I think that we can. . . . There are two ways. I mean, we could make a little table and the numbers we're going to use, or include it as one of our ex- amples. I think at the end actually, you know, the thing. I don't know—

NEAL   I think the only thing is, um, do we want a graph in the memo or not?

In this episode, Kevin and Neal have a few immediate agreements and elabo- rate single points, both of which serve valuable functions, but they primarily consider alternatives—whether they should use a table, diagram, chart, graph, some combination of graphics, or just text to explain the financial savings. They're not reluctant to disagree with each other; these objections seem to spur consideration of additional ideas. They decide to put numbers in their recommendation memo, but they defer a decision about how to present these numbers. Could they have produced a better document if they had not en- gaged in substantive conflict?

Differences in the interaction of coauthors have led to my questions about the relationship between collaborative decision-making, conflict, and docu- ment quality: Can David and Sujit's elaboration of a single point and immedi- ate agreements lead to a high-quality document? Could Kevin and Neal have produced a better document if they had not engaged in substantive conflict? My research suggests that the answer to both questions is no. In fact, I argue that certain kinds of conflict during decision-making have a positive correla- tion with the quality of documents that coauthors produce. In the study I discuss in this chapter, Kevin and Neal produced a document that was rated far higher than the one produced by Dean and Sujit: Kevin and Neal's recom- mendation report was ranked second out of twenty-four; Dean and Sujit's was ranked eighteenth.

In the remainder of this chapter, I'll review some of the critical information we know about collaboration, discuss results from some of my own research that focuses on coauthoring as a kind of collaboration, and suggest ways teachers can introduce and manage collaboration in their own classrooms so that it is more productive and enjoyable.

Moving Beyond the Theory and Research
in Rhetoric and Composition
to Explain Coauthoring

I see a curious mismatch between what we know about collaboration from theory in a number of disciplines (ranging from small group communication and social psychology to cooperative learning) and what we often observe in coauthoring practices. While researchers in small group theory (see Putnam, 1986) argue that premature consensus can be detrimental and that substantive conflict can be beneficial, a decade of composition practices has urged consensus in collaboration (Bruffee, 1984, 1985, 1986). Specifically, too much classroom collaboration emphasizes consensus without what Trimbur calls "intellectual negotiation" (Wiener, 1986, p. 54) and ignores or suppresses conflict (cf. Ewald & MacCallum, 1990). Simply stated, some elements critical to effective group process and decision-making have until recently been ignored in many writing classes, though some theorists in rhetoric and composition are beginning to address the importance of deferring consensus and dealing with substantive conflict (see Clark & Ede, 1990; Karis, 1989; Lay, 1989; Trimbur, 1989).

In this section, I establish that collaboration functions as scaffolding that can help students learn to be more effective thinkers and writers. Then I describe how collaborative planning works as a specific kind of scaffolding for coauthors. Finally, I explore ways in which conflict can have a positive role in collaborative planning of coauthored documents.

VIEWING COLLABORATION AS A FORM OF SCAFFOLDING

Collaboration in general and coauthoring in particular are based largely on the idea that working together may be more productive than working individually. Why the work may be more productive, though, is a question that intrigues both researchers and teachers. One answer may be to look at collaboration as a kind of scaffolding, which is assistance that enables people to accomplish together what they can't do individually. Using scaffolding, students can often produce better documents than they could have individually, and they can learn heuristics, methods of problem-solving, that will help them approach future rhetorical problems.

The classroom practices in collaborative planning and writing that I'm talking about are based on the notion of a *zone of proximal development*, first proposed by Vygotsky. Specifically, Vygotsky said that, "The discrepancy between a child's actual mental age and the level he reaches in solving problems with assistance indicates the zone of his proximal development. . . . [T]he child with the larger zone of proximal development will do much better in school" (Vygotsky, 1986, p. 187). He suggested that support enables a person to complete tasks that would be too difficult to do individually.

Vygotsky's theory formed the foundation for Bruner's notion of *scaffolding*

(1978), a strategy in which teachers or capable peers help students extend their zone of proximal development by asking them questions and providing appropriate prompts and information. A large body of educational research, primarily in cooperative learning, supports the theory and practice that student collaborators can help each other bridge the zone of proximal development (see especially Forman & Cazden, 1985; Johnson & Johnson, 1987; Sharan, 1980, 1990; Sharan et al., 1984; Slavin, 1980, 1990). While the bulk of this work has been in areas other than composition, such as social studies and math, the interaction that students engage in during problem-solving activities (e.g., acknowledging their classmates' efforts, offering productive ideas, challenging assumptions and practices, and providing direction) tends to result in high-quality decision-making. The question is whether such scaffolding works for writing as well as it does for more easily defined tasks.

Some researchers believe that scaffolding can be a tremendous benefit in writing classrooms. For example, Applebee and Langer use "the notion of instructional scaffolding as a way to describe essential aspects of instruction that are often missing in traditional approaches" to writing. They view learning as "a process of gradual internalization of routines and procedures available to the learner from the social and cultural context in which the learning takes place" (in Applebee, 1986, p. 108). One way to help students gradually internalize the planning practices of experienced writers is to use collaborative planning, which is a pedagogical application of research that has explored differences between experienced and inexperienced writers (Flower & Hayes, 1981; Burtis, Scardamalia, Bereiter, & Tetroe, 1983; Scardamalia & Bereiter, 1987; Flower, Schriver, Carey, Haas, & Hayes, 1989). Writers who use collaborative planning can provide each other with the support necessary to plan and draft more skillfully than they could have done independently. The scaffolding provided by the coauthors' collaborative planning enables them to consider not only content but other rhetorical elements and interrelationships among these elements that might otherwise be ignored in their decision-making.

The support provided by scaffolding sometimes enables students to increase the difficulty of their work and their success in doing it. For example, in scaffolded instruction such as reciprocal teaching, even young students are able to assume the scaffolding role of the teacher when the role has been sufficiently modeled for them (Palincsar, 1986; Brown & Palincsar, 1989). Similarly, the scaffolding of collaborative planning may enable students to complete writing tasks beyond what they would be expected to achieve individually.

However, scaffolding is not a cure-all for writing problems; it does require specific conditions. First, the task needs to be difficult enough to warrant the scaffolding that collaboration can provide. If the task is simple for the students involved, collaboration is unnecessary, perhaps even annoying. For example, Forman reports that pairs of students have demonstrated an ability to work at a faster rate and on more complex combination problems than individual students; in contrast, individuals appear to do better on simple problems (Forman & Cazden, 1985). Next, students' attitudes toward collaboration are important. Some students are predisposed to cooperative activities while others prefer individual ones. If educators respect these differences, collaborative activities (including coauthoring) are one alternative (Sharan & Shaulov, 1990) for teaching writing. Third, student engagement is also important. If the students (either one or both) don't care about the task or the collaboration, the interaction may be perfunctory at best. Fourth, a minimal level of knowledge — of either content or an appropriate problem-solving heuristic — is also essential; otherwise, the collaboration is little more than the blind leading the blind. Finally, scaffolding such as collaborative planning works best if it's a regular part of class rather than an occasional activity. Students' use of scaffolding becomes increasingly productive as their skills as collaborators develop.

This minimal level of knowledge can result in two distinct types of scaffolding for writers. In the first type, one collaborator may be more knowledgeable about the content or task and, thus, provides scaffolding, acting as a guide so that her collaborative partner better understands the process, manages content and other rhetorical elements, and successfully completes the task. In a second type, a collaborator may be a peer who can use a heuristic to remind the writer to consider and reconsider rhetorical elements that are not typically addressed by writers at that particular level of development or experience (Burnett, in press; Flower, Wallace, Norris, & Burnett, in press). This second type of scaffolding is based on the assumption that peers, in this case coauthors, can prompt, contribute, direct, and challenge each other about content and, probably more important, about other rhetorical elements generally considered by experienced writers. I use this second type of scaffolding to explore collaborative decision-making.

Scaffolding, then, works best if the conditions I have just discussed are met: the task is difficult enough to warrant collaboration, the students are predisposed to cooperative activities, and they have at least a minimal level of engagement and a minimal level of knowledge — of either content or an appropriate heuristic. Without these conditions, the coauthors are likely to feel frustrated and lose the benefits that scaffolding can bring to their decision-making.

USING COLLABORATIVE PLANNING

This section takes a close-up look at the scaffolding student writers can provide for each other as they collaboratively plan a coauthored document.* Collaborative planning is a heuristic that makes explicit the consideration of rhetorical elements often explored by individual experienced writers, that is, concerns with purpose and key points, audience, organization and support, and document design (Flower, Burnett et al., 1989; for discussion about the theory and research of collaborative planning, see Flower, Wallace, Norris, &

---

*In other variations of collaborative planning, writers work with supporters who can be temporary collaborators (not responsible for generating any text) or team members rather than with coauthors who form the core of this study.

Burnett, in press). Using the scaffolding of collaborative planning, coauthors can explore, develop, and make decisions about their plans for writing. Assuming, then, that the minimal conditions for scaffolding are met, coauthors typically interact with each other in one or more of these four ways: they prompt each other to clarify, they contribute new ideas as well as modifications and elaborations of their plans, they direct each other to make necessary changes, and they challenge each other's plans for content and rhetorical elements (Burnett, in press). Each coauthor acts as a supporter for the other by prompting, contributing, directing, and challenging.

The most successful collaborative planning sessions occur when coauthors have each thought about and prepared a preliminary plan before meeting together, but are open to an active exchange with their coauthor. While they can ask each other some questions about content, the bulk of their efforts typically focuses on questions dealing with rhetorical elements. I suggest to my students that they consider asking some of the initial questions that are listed here:

Content
> What information might we add or delete? What will our readers expect? need?
> What's the most effective way to say this?

Purpose and key points
> I can't quite see why you've decided to _____. Could you explain why?
> What do we want the readers to do or think? What point do we want to get across in this section?

Audience
> What problems [conflicts, inconsistencies, gaps] might our readers see?
> How will our readers react to this [content, purpose, organization, design]?

Conventions of organization, development, and support
> How will we *organize* [develop, explain] this? What *support* [or evidence] could we use? What *examples* could we use?

Conventions of design
> Why do you like _____ better than _____ as a way to present this information?
> How will this design reinforce our point?

Synthesis/consolidation of plans about content and rhetorical elements
> Why do you think _____ is a good way to explain our key point to this audience?
> Will changing the example clarify or cloud the point we're making here?
> How will the audience be influenced by this approach?

These questions are not meant as a template or checklist but as prompts to help writers consider various content and other rhetorical elements typical of planning used by experienced writers (Flower, Burnett et al., 1989; Flower, Wallace, Norris, & Burnett, in press).

CONSENSUS VERSUS CONFLICT

Theorists and researchers in many disciplines (e.g., decision theory, small group behavior, cooperative learning) recognize that substantive conflict during collaborative interaction can strengthen the decision-making and frequently improve the product. Until recently, though, this view has not been common in rhetoric and composition, where consensus has been encouraged. As theorists and teachers in rhetoric and composition learn more about collaboration — including the value of scaffolding — and feel more comfortable with an interdisciplinary perspective, opinions about what types of interaction and decision-making produce the most effective documents are shifting. Currently, the views of composition theorists reveal tremendous diversity, ranging from those such as Bruffee who sees the goal of collaborative learning and writing as reaching consensus (1984) to Trimbur who argues that consensus in collaborative learning is "inherently dangerous . . . [because it] stifles individual voice and creativity, suppresses differences, and enforces conformity" (1989, p. 602).

Important issues raised by this diversity include the definitions of consensus and the circumstances under which consensus is necessary. The conventional use of the word "consensus" suggests general agreement with a decision and carries the implication that people in the group have reflected on their choices and selected the most appropriate one. However, in working groups that have the pressures of personalities, politics, and time, "consensus" sometimes means acquiescence rather than agreement; it sometimes means settling for unreflective "satisficing" rather than a reflective meeting of the minds about possible alternatives. Consensus — whether by acquiescence or agreement — is necessary for task groups so that the work can be completed; however, when students are urged to prematurely reach consensus, the chances increase of their decisions being the result of acquiescence rather than reflective agreement.

The very nature of groups and the encouragement of premature consensus can lead to several problems. For example, encouraging consensus "may lead to the suppression or exclusion of some ideas and can be an enforcer of conformity, thus subverting the goal of equal contribution and tolerance" (Higgins, 1988, p. 8). Another problem that Higgins identifies with consensus is suppression of "the very conflicts and adversity that might stimulate awareness of group values and conventions" (p. 10). Beyond this concern with students' awareness of themselves as members of a particular community, premature consensus can be a detriment to the kind of conflict that is often essential in fruitful collaboration.

Luckily, the common practice of advocating consensus between collaborators in writing classes has started to give way to a view that encourages substantive conflict. Until very recently, theorists and researchers in rhetoric and composition neglected the role of conflict in collaborative writing. However, interest in the role of conflict in collaborative writing is growing. For example,

Clark and Ede (1990) discuss resistance in collaboration, arguing that "Resistance opens up possibilities for learning for teachers and theorists, as well as for students" (p. 284). Karis (1989) argues that "collaborators (especially students) need to be made more aware of the role and value of *substantive* conflict to the collaborative process" (p. 124).

Writers who are working collaboratively need to be aware of research on work habits (Putnam, 1986) that identifies three categories of conflict — affective, procedural, and substantive. Affective conflict deals with interpersonal disagreements; procedural conflict deals with disagreements about things such as running the meetings. Both can be detrimental to collaboration. However, substantive conflict, which focuses on alternatives and explicit disagreements about content and other rhetorical elements, can be beneficial to decision-making. Thus, students learning to be effective collaborators should discourage affective and procedural conflict while at the same time encouraging substantive conflict about content and other rhetorical elements of the document they're planning. Giving student writers the opportunity to support each other using a scaffolding heuristic such as collaborative planning increases the likelihood of their engaging in substantive conflict, which can have a positive impact on their decision-making and, thus, on the quality of the documents they create.

Substantive conflict is valuable in part because it defers premature consensus (cf. with groupthink, Janis, 1982). Researchers and theorists in a number of allied disciplines — social psychology, decision theory, small group communication, cooperative learning, and computer-supported cooperative work — are unequivocal: urging premature consensus can short-circuit effective decision-making, and neglecting cooperative, substantive conflict can reduce the effectiveness of a group and lower the quality of the decisions (e.g., see Putnam's review of literature, 1986). And the logical corollary argues that certain kinds of conflict are not only normal, but productive. In fact, the collaborative process is beneficial in large part because of the alternatives collaborators generate and their willingness to critically examine these alternatives. In other words, they defer, and in some cases even actively resist, consensus in order to explore alternatives, and they value explicit disagreement that helps them focus on potential problems.

Decision-Making During Coauthors' Collaborative Planning

If we accept the arguments offered in the previous section — that collaborative planning is a form of scaffolding and that substantive conflict during collaborative planning can be beneficial — then we can see the potential advantages of encouraging a heuristic such as collaborative planning that gives writers the opportunity to defer consensus and engage in substantive conflict. In this section, I take a close-up look at the collaborative planning of a coauthored document by pairs of college juniors and seniors in a course in business communications. I examine their decision-making to see whether these coauthors did, in fact, benefit from deferring consensus and engaging instead in cooperative, substantive conflict.

As part of their class work, the students wrote as coauthors in a workplace simulation that asked them to collaboratively plan and prepare a rhetorically complex recommendation report. Collaborative planning provided these students with scaffolding that enabled them to address rhetorical elements that they might have otherwise ignored entirely or probed insufficiently. It also gave them a way to raise questions about rhetorical elements and build a more elaborate plan than if they worked individually (Flower, Burnett et al., 1989; Flower, Wallace, Norris, & Burnett, in press). Their task was to analyze an in-house document about a solar heating/cooling system and recommend ways it could be revised as a product information sheet for customers. Each pair of coauthors met three times outside of class; the analysis and examples I discuss in this chapter are taken from transcripts of audiotapes students made of their second out-of-class planning session.

Although we know a great deal about the writing processes of individuals, we know little about what coauthors do and how their interaction affects their decision-making and the quality of the documents they create. In order to analyze the kind of decision-making coauthors engaged in, I separated the transcripts of their collaborative planning sessions into topical episodes — chunks of conversation that have definable topical boundaries (e.g., a shift from discussing audience to discussing design marks the end of one episode and the beginning of another). Each topical episode that dealt with content or a rhetorical element such as purpose, audience, organization, or design was assessed to determine the kind of decision-making the coauthors used.

My analysis showed that these coauthors used four kinds of decision-making during their collaborative planning sessions: (1) immediate agreement; that is, making an unelaborated decision about a single point, (2) deferring consensus by elaborating a single point, (3) deferring consensus by considering alternatives, which is one kind of substantive conflict, and (4) deferring consensus by voicing explicit disagreement, which is another kind of substantive conflict. There is a strong correlation between the type of decision-making the coauthors used and the quality of the documents they produced. Specifically, coauthors who engaged in more substantive conflict — that is, considering alternatives and voicing explicit disagreement — produced higher quality documents. And the converse was also true: coauthors who engaged in less substantive conflict (and relatively more elaborations of a single point) produced lower quality documents (Burnett, 1991; Burnett, 1992). Since students are often reluctant to engage in rhetorical planning, much less substantive conflict about those plans, the scaffolding provided by collaborative planning gives them a way to consider alternatives and voice disagreements about rhetorical elements. Good students, of course, use these strategies; however, the point is that less experienced and skillful writers can and do learn to use them.

A series of excerpts from transcripts of collaborative planning sessions effectively illustrates the characteristics of these four kinds of decision-making. These excerpts can serve as a starting point for theoretical discussion about the nature of collaboration or they can be used as examples that can be analyzed. The most productive collaborations include all four kinds of decision-making.

IMMEDIATE AGREEMENT

Unelaborated decisions about a single point are immediate agreements, without elaboration or explanation. They usually occur in two conversational turns, although occasionally one of the collaborators will repeat or paraphrase, but not elaborate, what the other person said, thus adding a conversational turn. However, the result is the same: the decision is unelaborated. This kind of decision can also appear as a statement that goes unchallenged and unelaborated by the coauthor, but is clearly accepted because it becomes a basis for other discussion and decisions. The following episode shows Jessica and Margaret as they equally participate in a series of immediate agreements.

MARGARET   — for the memo. In fact, I think this covers most of the memo; this will be, like, 75 percent of the memo just describing the different — how we should organize the facts. Um. Let's see. The main idea we had for organizing the facts were using titles and subtitles?

JESSICA   Yes.

MARGARET   And key point and bullets under the titles and subtitles. Is that correct?

JESSICA   Um. Yeah. Titles — A title for the product name —

MARGARET   Okay.

JESSICA   And subtitles for a specific product component, coupled with a few descriptive sentences stating the benefits.

MARGARET   Okay.

First one of them makes a point, and the other agrees, "Yes." Then one makes another point, and the other agrees, "Yeah" or "Okay." Their typical pattern is point-agreement, point-agreement, and so on, seldom considering alternatives and never disagreeing with each other. Margaret and Jessica wrote a document that was ranked in the bottom quarter, 19.5 out of 24. During their collaborative planning session, 90% of their decision-making was based either on unelaborated or elaborated decisions about a single point; only 10% was based on discussions that involved substantive conflict.

Unelaborated decisions about a single point are an essential part of all collaborative interaction. Frequently, in fact, they are embedded within other episodes. Unelaborated decisions on single points are important because they let collaborators acknowledge each other's statements; such backchanneling is a necessary part of any ongoing conversation, indicating the person has been heard and encouraging her to continue talking. However, unelaborated decisions are a problem if they predominate to the exclusion of other types of decision-making because collaborators do not develop their ideas, consider other possibilities, or disagree with each other.

ELABORATING A SINGLE POINT

Decisions based on an elaboration of a single point extend discussion about one idea or issue, identifying information to be included but not considering this information as alternatives or options. Collaborators can elaborate their own statements if they include three or more separate chunks of information to support their position. The following excerpt shows Ted and Justin discussing what the folder for the product information sheet they're planning might look like. The single point they're pursuing in this episode deals with the appearance of the folder. Embedded within their point about the folder, they also have several immediate agreements, signaled by "Yeah" and "Right."

TED   Okay. yeah, but it's more of a folder now, and you have —
JUSTIN   Yeah.
TED   On the front is, like, the big title.
JUSTIN   Yeah.
TED   And then you open this up. And then inside . . . you have a big diagram.
JUSTIN   Right. On the right-hand side we could have, like, the diagram and the definite talking about the system. And we can still use, you know, a big piece of paper, you know.
TED   Right. And take this part of it to introduce a little bit up here, and then move — maybe have a diagram here and use all this for the description.
JUSTIN   Right.

In this episode, Ted and Justin are similar to Margaret and Jessica in that they don't consider alternatives or disagree with each other; they're different, though, because they do offer a series of details that elaborate the point about the folder's appearance. Ted and Justin wrote a document that was ranked in the bottom quarter, 19.5 out of 24 (tied with the report written by Margaret and Jessica). During their collaborative planning session, 98% of their decision-making was based either on unelaborated or elaborated decisions about a single point; only 2% of their decisions involved substantive conflict.

When elaborations on a single point are productive, they help the collaborators. In fact, Ted and Justin improve their plan as they elaborate their ideas about the design of the folder. However, such elaborations are not always helpful, particularly when the collaborators pursue at great length an idea that is not important or when they offer elaborations that aren't relevant. While elaboration is a necessary part of effective collaboration, if it's the primary kind of decision-making that collaborators use, they won't consider alternatives or criticize existing plans.*

SUBSTANTIVE CONFLICT

As I define it, substantive conflict in coauthoring has four critical characteristics: the approach is cooperative, conflict defers consensus, the focus is on content and other rhetorical elements of the document, and the two types of substantive conflict include considering alternatives and voicing disagreements. Considering an alternative is a kind of substantive conflict because posing an option indicates some level of dissatisfaction with what's already been presented; it's an implied disagreement. Considering alternatives might sound something like this — for example, when one collaborator suggests "Let's do x," the other collaborator might respond, "Yes, x is a possibility, but let's consider y as another way to solve the problem." Voicing explicit disagreements might sound like this — for example, when one collaborator suggests "Let's do z," the other collaborator might respond, "No" or "I disagree" or "I think that's wrong." Encouraging collaborators to voice objections enables them to call attention to potential problems. Explicit disagreements reduce the likelihood that the final document will contain elements unacceptable to either collaborator. They also make clear to collaborators their need to consider alternatives.

Decisions based on consideration of alternatives take place over several conversational turns. Sometimes a suggestion that leads to a decision resulting from an elaboration of alternatives is presented without acknowledging it as an alternative to a previously presented plan. The only way to tell is to examine each topical episode within the context of the entire planning session. At other times, the consideration of alternatives is explicitly signaled, as shown in the next excerpt. Here Mason has proposed a plan that would present each problem and solution as a separate chunk. Greg says, "As an alternative, we could list the problems and then list the solutions under it." Their consideration of alternatives is productive, not only identifying options but discussing whether they'd be effective.

MASON   I think we might be going "Improve—" I mean, uh, "What's wrong with it," and an example showing what's wrong— No, I guess— Well, anyway, "What's wrong with it," "How we're going to change it," and show an example of how we're changing it.
GREG   Combining them?

*At the beginning of this chapter, the episode from a collaborative planning session with Dean and Sujit shows them elaborating a single point with several embedded instances of immediate agreement. Dean and Sujit wrote a document that was ranked 18 out of 24. During their collaborative planning session, 88% of their decision-making was based either on unelaborated or elaborated decisions about a single point; only 12% of their decisions were based on discussions that involved substantive conflict.

MASON   Yeah. Like, make it, like, maybe a "one." Or something— One group of, like, the whole problem and solution. Then the next segment, the problem and solution.

GREG   Okay. As an alternative, we could list the problems and then list the solutions under it.

MASON   Right. Umm. We'd have to find a way— If we did it in just paragraph form, I think it would look . . . it would be hard to follow.

GREG   Yeah.

Episodes in which coauthors consider alternatives sometimes have immediate agreements and elaborations of a single point embedded with them. For example, Greg and Mason acknowledge their agreement (e.g., "Yeah," "Okay," "Right"), which serves as backchanneling. Greg and Mason wrote a document that was ranked in the second quarter, 7 out of 24. During their collaborative planning session, 64% of their decision-making was based either on unelaborated or elaborated decisions about a single point; however, 36% of their decisions were based on discussions that involved substantive conflict. This is a decided contrast to Sujit and David who have 12% substantive conflict, Margaret and Jessica who have 10%, or Ted and Justin who have 2%.

As with unelaborated decisions and elaborations of a single point, decisions based on an elaboration of alternatives can sometimes be productive—and sometimes not. To be productive, an alternative doesn't have to end up in the final plan or be instantiated in the document, but it does need to be offered seriously, have good reasons to support it, and influence the planning. Gratuitous alternatives, those offered just to say something, do little to strengthen the interaction or the document. In the following excerpt, Josh and Pete presents alternatives about fonts, certainly a legitimate concern when designing a document; however, they have few justifications for their alternatives other than an attitude that says, "I like mine better than yours."

JOSH   What font do you think we should use?

PETE   I personally think we should use Geneva 12-point.

JOSH   I kinda like Chicago 12-point. Makes it a little bit more spacious.

PETE   I'll have to see what happens on the computer when I put it on, but I really do like the Geneva 12.

JOSH   Do you? And I prefer the Chicago 12, so—

PETE   Chicago 12 or Chicago 10?

JOSH   Chicago 12. It's more spacious.

PETE   Well, we'll see. Geneva comes up better and bolder.

JOSH   Yeah. Well, we'll see.

In this situation, they have offered alternatives but not considered them. Josh and Pete's question about fonts gets decided when they're drafting their report. They end up using Geneva only because Pete had control of the keyboard. In contrast, the alternatives considered by Mason and Greg end up changing their plan. The report they produced reflects the quality of their decision-making. Josh and Pete wrote a document that was ranked at the bottom, 24 out of 24. During their collaborative planning session, 97.5% of their decision-making was based either on unelaborated or elaborated decisions about a single point. In fact, the episode above is the only instance of substantive conflict in their entire collaborative planning session.

Decisions based on an elaboration involving explicit disagreement are usually signaled by phrases such as "That's wrong," "I don't think that will work," "No," and so on. These elaborations indicate explicit disagreement between the coauthors. The following example presents an excerpt from an episode in which Matthew disagrees with Dorothea about whether the two versions of the information sheets they're redesigning should be "about the same." Several embedded conflicts are included in this excerpt from the episode. For example, Dorothea and Matthew explicitly disagree about both the size and the page design of the document they're designing.

DOROTHEA   Both I think are going to be about the same. They're going to be four pages of text, and there's, like, a front and a back of one and the front and a back of another. Put together and it's almost a little booklet. . . . And as you open it up, have all the information of how it works, the components of it, on two pages that face each other, so we can put all that text right there and then put the diagram on that open page.

MATTHEW   I disagree. I think that the A version should be like a— It should be, like, a not one 8 × 11; it should—

DOROTHEA   No.

MATTHEW   —be perhaps like a thr— you know, a smaller size. With much smaller pages and a lot more pages and larger text. Because I think perhaps, like you mentioned already, that the B version could be just, like, one piece of paper—

DOROTHEA   I don't think it'll fit on one.

MATTHEW   No, because we won't be adding a hell of a lot more information than's already on the information sheet that we have. The information sheet we have, all this information fits on one page.

DOROTHEA   It looks so cluttered. I just think that for the ease of reading—

MATTHEW   But I mean on one, two— both sides of a page.

DOROTHEA   Oh. Oh. Okay.

However, their disagreements led to considering a variety of alternatives, which gave them options for decision-making. Dorothea and Matthew wrote a document that was ranked in the top quarter, 3 out of 24. During their collaborative planning session, 75% of their decision-making was based either on unelaborated or elaborated decisions about a single point; however, 25%

of their decisions were based on discussions that involved substantive conflict.*

These excerpts show coauthors using very different ways of discussing and making decisions about the rhetorical problems that they face. In general, coauthors who reached immediate agreement and elaborated single points without considering alternatives or voicing disagreements produced low-quality documents. However, immediate agreements (i.e., unelaborated decisions about a single point) and elaborations of a single point occur in all collaborative interactions; these types of discussions lead to poor decisions and result in low-quality documents only when they're the only kind of decision-making that occurs. In contrast, high-quality documents were produced by collaborators who also considered more alternatives and voiced more explicit disagreements than those who produced low-quality documents. Considering alternatives and voicing explicit disagreements often seemed to enable the collaborators to make better choices and present these choices more effectively than collaborators who produced low-quality documents. However, merely identifying the kind of decision-making does not account for the complexity of collaborative interaction. For example, students need to understand that making a particular move (for example, considering alternatives) does not automatically lead to a better product. Thus, examining specific moves out of context can misrepresent their value. The excerpt from Josh and Pete as they considered alternatives (Chicago versus Geneva) is a good instance; their conflict is not about a central, substantive issue nor is it typical of their interaction. Learning about decision-making will help students understand their own collaborative interaction, but they should not use this information as a formula; they cannot assume that understanding and using a balance of types of decision-making or a preponderance of substantive conflict will automatically result in higher quality documents.

Introducing and Teaching Collaboration

Students need to learn that the nature of their decision-making can influence the quality of their documents. Learning about the types of the decision-making I have described could help increase students' awareness. But knowing about various types of decision-making—immediate agreement, elaboration, and substantive conflict—and the possible influence of each type is not enough. Students need reasons for these moves and, therefore, benefit from modeling that illustrates these moves. No single category of moves is inherently appropriate or inappropriate; more important is the proportion and

---

*At the beginning of this chapter, the episode from a collaborative planning session with Kevin and Neal shows them considering alternatives and voicing disagreements. Kevin and Neal wrote a document that was ranked in the top quarter, 2 out of 24. During their collaborative planning session, 79% of their decision-making was based either on unelaborated or elaborated decisions about a single point; 21% of their decisions were based on discussions that involved substantive conflict.

interplay of moves as coauthors deal with both content and other rhetorical elements.

A significant body of research (e.g., Flower & Hayes, 1981; Hayes et al., 1987; Scardamalia & Bereiter, 1987) suggests that experienced writers consider more rhetorical elements and consider them more frequently than do inexperienced writers, who tend to focus their attention and energy on content. Students are often intrigued with the notion that working collaboratively with a supporter can provide scaffolding that will help them use behaviors common to many experienced writers. The supporter not only reminds them to consider rhetorical elements that are an intrinsic part of planning by experienced writers but also poses alternatives and voices disagreements.

In this final section of the chapter, I suggest three ways that teachers can introduce and teach collaboration, specifically using collaborative planning that can act as scaffolding.

PROVIDE INFORMATION ABOUT SUCCESSFUL COLLABORATIVE BEHAVIORS

Begin, for example, by giving students general information about cooperative collaborative behaviors. After reading the following list, students quickly recognize that they need to be prepared for a collaborative planning session.

- Have a preliminary plan. Don't go into a collaborative planning session unprepared. Bring notes.
- Actively listen to your coauthor. Show that you're listening. Try to understand this person's opinions and ideas.
- Be receptive to suggestions that may help you improve your own ideas. Be flexible so you can improve the plan.
- Offer comments that help your coauthor think about the plan's strengths and weaknesses. Contribute productive information. Brainstorm. Elaborate.
- Encourage your collaborator to ask you probing, challenging questions. Give thoughtful responses to questions. Be willing to clarify and elaborate.
- Ask your collaborator to explain more, to clarify. Ask probing, challenging questions.
- Be interested, attentive, and engaged.

However, these general behaviors are not sufficient in themselves to help student coauthors become good collaborators. They need to know about specific "verbal moves" that collaborators typically use, and they also appreciate having samples they can use as models for framing their own comments and questions. Suggest to students that they ask questions about content, but that they ask most of their questions about a variety of rhetorical elements: purpose and key points; audience; conventions of organization, development, and support; conventions of design. In addition, they need to ask questions that synthesize or consolidate their plans about both content and other rhetorical elements.

The following verbal moves provide a good repertoire of collaborator behaviors and can be presented as examples for students to use initially as models and later as reinforcement for their own comments and questions. I present these moves to students and then give them the opportunity to identify and discuss the moves when observing collaborative planning sessions in class (see modeling below). Later, they have a chance to use these moves in their own practice planning sessions in class. (For additional discussion about the pedagogical application of this theory and research, see Flower, Wallace, Norris, & Burnett, in press).

Acknowledge Your Collaborator's Views or Work

- That's a convincing argument you're making.
- You've done some really good work so far.

Prompt Your Collaborator to Clarify or Elaborate

- How does what you are planning to do relate to the assignment? It sounds to me like you're writing an argument not a definition.
- That's interesting. Can you tell me more?
- You've said a lot about the content you plan to include. Can you tell me more about what you see as the purpose [or key points, audience reaction, organization]?

Direct Your Collaborator (Infrequently!)

- You should reorganize these three points in order of importance if you want the reader to recognize their relative importance.
- Because the reader might be confused, I think we should try another way of explaining this.

Contribute Information to Your Collaborator

- Let's organize this section by contrasting _____ with _____.
- I think the best example would be _____.

Challenge Your Collaborator

- I think that the audience already knows most of the things that you are planning to say. What will be new and interesting for them?
- I don't think that your decision to leave out an example will work because the audience needs to see what you are saying.

Synthesize/Consolidate Plans About Content and Other Rhetorical Elements

- Why do you think _____ is a good way to appeal to this audience?
- Will using a different example better support the point we're making here?
- Why do you like _____ better than _____ as a way to organize this information?

As with the questions presented earlier in this chapter in the initial discussion of collaborative planning, these comments and questions about verbal moves are not intended as a checklist, but as models students can use as they become collaborative planners. Students generally appreciate such heuristics for managing productive collaborative interactions, specifically cooperative, substantive conflict about both content and other rhetorical elements.

MODEL AND SHOW EXAMPLES
OF SUCCESSFUL AND UNSUCCESSFUL
COLLABORATIVE INTERACTIONS

I've found that nearly every collaborative assignment or project is more enjoyable and productive for students if I spend some class time modeling collaborative interaction—both successful and unsuccessful. I work with a student in front of the class, asking questions that encourage the student writer to consider rhetorical elements and giving the two of us the opportunity to demonstrate different types of decision-making. These opportunities let students observe and analyze collaborative interaction, something they've seldom had the chance to do. They learn techniques they want to acquire and modify as their own—and ones they want to avoid at all costs.

Another way to demonstrate collaborative planning is to invite a colleague to class and work together on a project in front of the students. When I've done this, the two of us decide in advance to work on a real collaborative project, something we need to do for a presentation or article. We don't script the session; it's real. We both prepare as we would for a collaborative session without an audience, coming in with plans and notes and arguments about how we'd like to approach the project. I suggest to students that they listen for particular elements—how we balance attention to content and other rhetorical elements, how we phrase our questions, how we encourage alternatives or express disagreements, what kinds of verbal moves we make.

I also collect examples of students' collaborative planning sessions by using excerpts from videotapes, audiotapes, and/or transcripts from these tapes. Originally, these tapes were from my research, but more recently, I have had students tape their in-class and out-of-class collaborative sessions, which provide a wealth of choices. Examples of unsuccessful collaborative interactions are particularly effective for giving students the opportunity to offer their own analysis and recommend ways to improve the interaction. Nearly always, students have suggestions about how they could have "done it better." And nearly always, different students offer different ways to improve the sessions they listen to.

ENCOURAGE SELF-MONITORING AND REFLECTION

Self-monitoring and reflection are difficult and important elements in being an effective writer, individually or collaboratively (see Higgins, Flower, &

Petraglia, 1992). Students can learn to monitor themselves, but a useful way to learn self-monitoring is to listen to audiotapes of their own collaborative sessions. Students quickly get accustomed to the presence of a tape recorder (which they control). After the session, they listen to their tape in order to assess their contributions and interaction. For example, they can consider the balance they give to content and other rhetorical elements, various kinds of verbal moves, or various kinds of decision-making. Alternatively, students can work in groups of three, with one of the students keeping track of the attention given to these elements.

Listening to their collaborative planning tapes also gives students a way to review their plans as well as providing an evaluative tool that enables them to examine their own process, modify it, and thus, ultimately, improve the resulting products. Specifically, for example, students can determine whether they made effective use of their collaboration by deferring consensus and, instead, considering alternatives and voicing disagreements. They can then assess the influence this behavior seemed to have on their overall interaction and the quality of their decisions and texts.

Conclusion

Many students have difficulty in moving beyond content to focus on rhetorical elements such as purpose, audience, and organization that will affect their writing. Using a scaffolding heuristic such as collaborative planning can help students consider rhetorical elements and ask effective questions about these elements. Collaborative planning is also a useful heuristic for helping students deal with the difficult task of raising and responding to substantive conflict. Becoming an effective collaborator isn't instinctive, so students need guidelines, models, and practice as they acquire a new understanding of what it means to be an effective collaborator. They need encouragement to reflect on their processes; students pay more attention to discoveries they make for themselves. Students also need encouragement to engage in substantive conflict, but they generally are willing once they understand that certain kinds of conflict—considering alternatives and voicing disagreements—can have a positive influence on the quality of decisions they make, their satisfaction with those decisions, and the quality of the documents they write.

Acknowledgment: A note of thanks to my supporters: David Wallace, Kathy Lampert, Lorraine Higgins, and Brenda Daly offered insightful observations and stimulating conversations at critical junctures along the way.

This work is part of the Making Thinking Visible Project at Carnegie Mellon, funded by the Howard Heinz Endowment of the Pittsburgh Foundation and sponsored by the Center for the Study of Writing and Literacy at UCBerkeley and Carnegie Mellon University.

References

Applebee, A. N. (1986). Problems in process approaches: Toward a reconceptualization of process instruction. In A. R. Petrosky & D. Bartholomae (Eds.), *The teaching of writing: Eighty-fifth yearbook of the National Society for the Study of Education, Vol. 2* (pp. 95–113). Chicago: University of Chicago Press.

Bosley, D. S. (1989). *A national study of the uses of collaborative writing in business communication courses among members of the ABC.* Unpublished doctoral dissertation, Illinois State University, Normal, IL.

Brown, A. L. & Palincsar, A. S. (1989). Guided, cooperative learning and individual knowledge acquisition. In L. Resnick (Ed.), *Knowing, learning, and instruction: Essays in honor of Robert Glaser* (pp. 393–451). Hillsdale, NJ: Erlbaum.

Bruffee, K. A. (1984). Collaborative learning and the "conversation of mankind." *College English, 46*, 635–652.

Bruffee, K. A. (1985). *A short course in writing: Practical rhetoric for teaching composition through collaborative learning* (3rd ed.). Boston: Little, Brown.

Bruffee, K. A. (1986). Social construction, language, and the authority of knowledge: A bibliography. *College English, 48*, 773–790.

Bruner, J. (1978). The role of dialogue in language acquisition. In A. Sinclair, R. J. Jarvella, & J. M. Levelt (Eds.), *The child's conception of language* (pp. 241–256). New York: Springer-Verlag.

Burnett, R. E. (1991). *Conflict in the collaborative planning of coauthors: How substantive conflict, representation of task, and dominance relate to high-quality documents.* Unpublished doctoral dissertation, Carnegie Mellon University, Pittsburgh, PA.

Burnett, R. E. (1993). Conflict and consensus in collaborative decision-making. In N. R. Blyler & C. Thralls (Eds.), *Professional communication: The social perspective* (pp. 144–162). Newbury Park, CA: Sage.

Burnett, R. E. (in press). Supporters in effective collaboration. In L. Flower, D. L. Wallace, L. Norris, & R. E. Burnett (Eds.), *Making thinking visible: Collaborative planning and classroom inquiry.* Urbana, IL: National Council of Teachers of English.

Burtis, P., Bereiter, C., Scardamalia, M., & Tetroe, J. (1983). The development of planning in writing. In G. Wells & B. Kroll (Eds.), *Explorations in the development of writing* (pp. 153–174). Chicester, England: John Wiley and Sons.

Clark, S. & Ede, L. (1990). Collaboration, resistance, and the teaching of writing. In A. Lunsford, H. Moglen, & J. Slevin (Eds.), *The right to literacy* (pp. 276–285). New York: MLA.

DiPardo, A. & Freedman, S. W. (1988). Peer response groups in the writing classroom: Theoretical foundations and new directions. *Review of Educational Research, 58*, 119–149.

Ewald, H. R. & MacCallum, V. (1990). Promoting creative tension within collaborative writing groups. *The Bulletin of the Association for Business Communication, 53* (2), 23–26.

Flower, L., Burnett, R., Hajduk, T., Wallace, D., Norris, L., Peck, W., & Spivey, N. (1989). *Classroom inquiry in collaborative planning.* Pittsburgh, PA: Center for the Study of Writing, University of California at Berkeley and Carnegie Mellon.

Flower, L. & Hayes, J. R. (1981). A cognitive process theory of writing. *College Composition and Communication, 32*, 365–387.

Flower, L., Schriver, K., Carey, L., Hayes, J. R., & Haas, C. (1989). *Planning in writing: The cognition of a constructive process* (Tech. Rpt. No. 34). Berkeley, CA: Center for the Study of Writing, University of California at Berkeley and Carnegie Mellon.

Flower, L., Wallace, D. L., Norris, L., & Burnett, R. E. (Eds.) (in press). *Making thinking visible: Collaborative planning and classroom inquiry.* Urbana, IL: NCTE.

Forman, E. A. & Cazden, C. B. (1985). Exploring Vygotskian perspectives in education: The cognitive value of peer interaction. In J. V. Wertsch (Ed.), *Culture, communication, and cognition: Vygotskian perspectives* (pp. 323–347). Cambridge: Cambridge University Press.

Gebhardt, R. (1980). Teamwork and feedback: Broadening the base of collaborative writing. *College English, 42*, 69–74.

Hayes, J. R., Flower, L., Schriver, K., Stratman, J. F., & Carey, L. (1987). Cognitive processes in revision (pp. 176–240). In S. Rosenberg (Ed.), *Advances in applied psycholinguistics*, Vol. 2. Cambridge: Cambridge University Press.

Higgins, L. (1988). *Collaboration in the composition classroom: Theory meets practice.* Unpublished manuscript, Carnegie Mellon, Pittsburgh, PA.

Higgins, L., Flower, L., & Petraglia, J. (1992). Planning text together: The role of critical reflections in student collaboration. *Written Communication, 9*, 48–84.

Janis, I. J. (1982). *Victims of groupthink* (2nd ed.). Boston: Houghton Mifflin.

Johnson, D. W. & Johnson, R. T. (1987). *Learning together and along: Cooperative, competitive, and individualistic learning* (2nd ed.). Englewood Cliffs, NJ: Prentice-Hall.

Karis, B. (1989). Conflict in collaboration: A Burkean perspective. *Rhetoric Review, 8*, 113–126.

Lay, M. M. (1989). Interpersonal conflict in collaborative writing: What we can learn from gender studies. *Journal of Business and Technical Communication, 3*, 5–28.

Palincsar, A. S. (1986). The role of dialogue in providing scaffolded instruction. *Educational Psychologist, 21*, 73–98.

Putnam, L. L. (1986). Conflict in group decision-making. In R. Y. Hirokawa & M. S. Poole (Eds.), *Communication and group decision-making* (pp. 175–196). Beverly Hills, CA: Sage.

Scardamalia, M. & Bereiter, C. (1987). Knowledge telling and knowledge transforming in written composition. In S. Rosenberg (Ed.), *Advances in applied psycholinguistics,* Vol. 2 (pp. 142–175). Cambridge: Cambridge University Press.

Sharan, S. (1980). Cooperative learning in small groups: Recent methods and effects on achievement, attitudes, and ethnic relations. *Review of Educational Research, 50*, 241–271.

Sharan, S. (Ed.). (1990). *Cooperative learning: Theory and research.* New York: Praeger.

Sharan, S. & Shaulov, A. (1990). Cooperative learning, motivation to learn, and academic achievement. In S. Sharan (Ed.), *Cooperative learning: Theory and research* (pp. 173–202). New York: Praeger.

Sharan, S., Kussell, P., Hertz-Lazarowitz, R., Bejarano, Y., Raviv, S., Sharan, Y., Brosh, T., & Peleg, R. (1984). *Cooperative learning in the classroom: Research in desegregated schools.* Hillsdale, NJ: Erlbaum.

Slavin, R. E. (1980). Cooperative learning. *Review of Educational Research, 50*, 315–342.

Slavin, R. E. (1990). *Cooperative learning: Theory, research, and practice.* Englewood Cliffs, NJ: Prentice-Hall.

Trimbur, J. (1989). Consensus and difference in collaborative learning. *College English, 51*, 602–616.

Vygotsky, L. (1986). *Thought and language* (A. Kozulin, Trans.). Cambridge, MA: MIT Press. (Original work published 1934.)

Wiener, H. S. (1986). Collaborative learning in the classroom: A guide to evaluation. *College English, 48*, 52–61.

8

Revising for Readers: Audience Awareness in the Writing Classroom

KAREN A. SCHRIVER

Audience. Revision. These topics resonate for composition teachers and researchers. Over the last two decades, we have seen a burgeoning of work on audience and revision. Although the efforts in these areas have not been fully integrated, we can draw at least one conclusion: We need new research-driven pedagogies for helping students to revise for readers. The ability to revise one's prose for an audience is a valuable asset in school or in the workplace. But up to this point, we have seen few teaching methods developed from what research and experience have shown us. Redefining revision in the classroom cannot occur unless we are able to translate research into action. Just what have we learned that teachers can employ and that writers can use? My aim here is to provide research-driven advice for helping writers to anticipate readers' needs. To do so, I first review the research on audience awareness and revision processes. Then I illustrate how the research can be applied in the classroom by providing a case study of a revision problem. Finally, I offer some ideas for teaching revision.

What We Know About Audience Awareness and Revision Processes

TEACHING AUDIENCE: LESSONS FROM RESEARCH

Rhetoricians have been concerned with the study of audience since antiquity and the impact is readily apparent in the curricula of most writing classrooms.

Some recent composition theorists such as Elbow (1987) have pointed out that our attention to audience borders on overkill. Yet for as much as we have been interested in teaching audience awareness, studies that compare alternative methods for doing so have been rare. Hillocks (1986) points out that the lack of research on audience is particularly surprising in light of the emphasis contemporary rhetorical theory places on the role of audience in the communication process (p. 84). Although there has been less research on audience awareness than we would like, we can still profit by considering the findings that are available. Indeed, some of the findings seem to contradict common assumptions about the teaching of audience awareness in the writing classroom.

Student Writers May Have Difficulty Using Feedback
That They Receive in Collaborative Writing Groups

Although we have enthusiastically embraced "collaborative learning" methods such as peer critiquing and role playing, teachers and researchers are beginning to raise concerns about how well these pedagogies actually work (Berkenkotter, 1985; Freedman, 1987; Newkirk, 1981, 1984). We have been raising questions about the value of students' activities in these groups, particularly with the kind and level of feedback students provide. Developing new approaches for helping student writers to make comments that other writers can actually use has been a goal for many composition teachers and researchers.

But we are finding a mismatch between what we want our students to do, that is, to make "authentic reader comments" and what our methods imply they should do, "make teacherly comments." Research focused on the "talk" of students while engaged in peer critiquing sessions found that students tend to stick closely to the "teacher talk" of peer critiquing checklists. Students' responses were sometimes designed particularly to please the teacher (Freedman, 1987).

We have also been reconceptualizing our role as facilitator of collaborative revising activities. We now more carefully scrutinize the directions we offer students for responding to text. For example, before making up detailed checklists to use during peer editing, we ask ourselves how to encourage students to go beyond the checklists. Our concern is that relying only on the predefined categories of error that we provide may inhibit students from developing their own language for diagnosing text problems. But at the same time, we recognize that without guidance in evaluating text, students may not move beyond general comments about writing such as "this paper stinks." We know that having a language for talking about discourse empowers writers to respond concretely to particular textual features. Through collaborative activities, we want students to cultivate their own language for evaluating writing, a language that will help other students consider their options for revision.

Researchers have been finding that when students receive readers' feedback from audiences other than teachers or peers, they seem more able to use readers' responses. Prentice (1980) examined the role of providing students in grades 3, 5, and 7 with explicit reader feedback on their writing. He asked each student to write two descriptions, one for a first-grader and one for an adult reader. One description was written before students received feedback from the intended readers and the other written after receiving readers' responses. He found that students significantly increased in the information they provided in their descriptions after feedback.

Collaborative Revision and Peer Critiquing Activities
May Benefit Only Some Students

Some teachers and researchers have reported problems associated with collaborative methods, particularly with the social roles individuals sometimes adopt when placed in a group. Students with more assertive personalities seem to benefit more from group activities than others. Personality clashes stemming from poor social interaction strategies occur frequently when small groups function poorly. Teachers have described difficulties with monopolizing or withdrawn students (Weiner, 1986). Some students in collaborative revision teams resent peer feedback, argue that it makes writing frustrating, and are unable to value their team members' advice (Berkenkotter, 1984; Wulff, 1992). George (1984) characterizes three kinds of response groups that can evolve with inexperienced writers: the task-oriented, the leaderless, and the dysfunctional — each of which needs a particular kind of teacher feedback (p. 321). He finds that teachers sometimes have difficulty promoting successful interaction among group members when students just "sit there." Teachers are trying to find ways to enable students to recognize the various types of conflict that may arise during collaboration (see Burnett in this volume).

While conflict about textual decisions can be productive, too often collaborators cannot distinguish between conflict that arises based on personality clashes and problems related to the group's social structure and conflict that may evolve through debating alternative solutions to rhetorical problems. Of course, this problem is not limited to the classroom. People in business have found that the social structure of the group dictates when and if a collaborator will join in what Putnam calls "substantive conflict," that is, conflict over ideas (1986). To encourage more people to engage in arguing over substance, some industries are moving collaborators to a computer instead of to a conference table adorned with coffee and donuts (CNN, 1992). Although making the decision to move ineffective collaborators on-line seems like a premature solution, the research literature offers few concrete alternatives.

Writers Often Have Difficulty Carrying Out
Their Intentions, Even Though They May Have
Considered the Audience Extensively

Although inexperienced writers often analyze the audience as much as experienced professionals, they tend not to act on their ideas for the audience (Flower, Hayes, Carey, Schriver, & Stratman, 1986). Many writers who consider the audience produce papers that seem to ignore the intended readership. Peck (1989), for example, found that inexperienced writers often make elaborate plans for reaching the audience but fall short of executing their intentions.

Peck's "intenders" wanted their messages to be effective for the audience, but they either forgot their plans or could not coordinate their goals. Teachers have been looking for methods to close the gap between planning and performance. To do so, we need more methods that can be used to show students ways to move from intention to textual revisions.

TEACHING REVISION: LESSONS FROM RESEARCH

In 1978 Donald Murray reported that "revision is the least researched, least examined, least understood, and — usually — least taught" of the writing skills (p. 85). Lillian Bridwell added that "little is known about the way revision factors vary or even about the specific nature of the changes writers make" (1980, p. 200). It has been more than a decade since revision was synonymous with cleaning up or polishing. Today most teachers and researchers share the conception of revision as "re-seeing" (Sommers, 1980), "reviewing" (Hayes & Flower, 1980; Nold, 1982), or "reformulating" (Murray, 1978). Moreover, we are beginning to understand the relationship between the processes and the products of revision, between revision and invention. Researchers have raised several issues that may be useful in thinking about revising for readers.

Seeing, Characterizing, and Solving
Text Problems Are Distinct Revising Activities

Although there remains much that we do not know about revision, our experiences have shown that revising calls on: detecting (noticing problems); diagnosing (characterizing detected problems); and solving (fixing problems). Researchers in writing find that an important aspect of these subskills is that they appear to be hierarchically organized and separate (Hayes, Flower, Schriver, Stratman, & Carey, 1987; Scardamalia & Bereiter, 1983). Some student writers do not try to revise certain classes of text problems because they never see them. Others can identify text problems but do not know how to diagnose them (Flower, Carey, & Hayes, 1984; Scardamalia & Bereiter, 1983). Although diagnosis is not obligatory, it is useful because the act of saying what the problem is often suggests solution strategies. But even students who are good at detecting and diagnosing text problems may not be able to fix them. Taken together, these observations may explain why teaching focused primarily on diagnosis seems to have little impact on improving writers' perception of text problems or on their ability to fix them.

Although there have been very few classroom studies designed to explore ways to make writers more sensitive to readers' needs, research is beginning to develop. In a recent study, I evaluated a method — called reader-protocol teaching — designed to improve writers' ability to see problems created for the audience by poorly written text (Schriver, 1992). In particular, I compared five classes of writers taught with the reader-protocol method and five classes of writers taught with a variety of audience-analysis heuristics and collaborative peer-response methods. Through using pretests and posttests, I evaluated how well these methods helped writers to detect and diagnose the kinds of problems that readers may experience with poorly written texts. I found that writers taught with the reader-protocol method, in which they critiqued a set of ten poorly written texts and then carefully analyzed the think-aloud protocol transcripts of readers struggling to comprehend these texts, improved significantly more than did writers taught with the other methods. Although writers taught by using heuristics and peer-response methods did improve in their awareness of the audience, their comments about readers tended to be quite general and were frequently unrelated to text features.

In contrast to the writers taught with heuristics and collaborative methods, writers in the reader-protocol teaching classes improved in their ability to (a) diagnose problems caused by textual omissions, (b) characterize problems from the reader's perspective, and (c) attend to global-text problems. The results of this study showed that students' seeing talents can be improved. Other studies need to explore if improved perceptual abilities actually lead students to make better revisions.

Writers Often Have More Difficulty
Seeing Problems in Their Own Text Than
Seeing Them in Text Created by Someone Else

Why is it so difficult to revise one's own work? Researchers have been trying to understand this phenomenon (Bartlett, 1982; Graves, 1981; Kroll, 1978). Writers tend to view their texts as communicating more effectively than they actually do. Hull (1984) found that while feedback helps both experts and novices to fix problems, even experts have difficulty detecting problems in their own texts.

The most compelling explanation researchers have offered to account for poor detection skills is that topic knowledge may interfere with writers' ability to notice problems. Studies show that the writer who generates a text's main ideas is often the least sensitive reader of that text. Writers reading their own texts can fill in gaps, use their prior knowledge to understand the organizational plan, and generate examples more easily than writers reading another author's text. In a study of government writers revising regulations for the Small Business Administration, researchers observed that seasoned professional writers — who spent most of their time editing texts of the same genre and content — got worse over time, actually deteriorating in their ability to anticipate readers' needs (Bond, Hayes, & Flower, 1980). Too much exposure to the same rhetorical situation made them insensitive to the needs of a lay reader.

Teachers (especially those at the college level) might conclude that it would be useful to help writers recognize that the more specialized knowledge they acquire about the topic and genre, the more they will need to consider the audience's needs. Writers must consider how insider knowledge might make them less able to take the reader's point of view. For example, on the one hand, they may use language that is too technical (such as the sort of terminology found in VCR manuals). On the other, they may lower the level of content so much such that it insults the audience's intelligence (such as the content provided in many political speeches).

Research is showing that the "knowledge effect" can influence writers' sensitivity to readers' problems even minutes after the knowledge is acquired. In one study, participants who read about topics immediately before they were asked to detect problems in poorly written texts on the same topics were worse in detecting problems than participants without topic knowledge (Hayes, Schriver, Blaustein, & Spilka, 1986). High-knowledge writers tended to overestimate the audience and assumed that what they understood would be clear to anyone.

The knowledge effect may be the unseen culprit behind why high-knowledge experts such as lawyers, doctors, computer scientists, engineers, economists, and government representatives frequently produce incomprehensible texts. It may also provide a clue regarding why so many university professors have difficulty in communicating "the basics" to freshmen in introductory college courses. We can conclude that writers who are revising their own texts and who have high topic knowledge may be at a disadvantage in seeing the problems their texts may create for readers.

Classroom experience makes it readily apparent that high knowledge is not the only problem interfering with writers' ability to see problems in text. Writers who have not fully understood the content they are writing about also have difficulty representing the reader's point of view. As Penrose points out earlier in this volume, student writers differ widely in how they read and interpret material about which they will write. This difficult problem of guiding students to see problems in their texts when they are writing about topics about which they know little (e.g., the kind of writing that gets done in most college classrooms) has not yet been well explored by writing researchers.

Writers' Definitions for Revision Influence
What They Attend to and Ignore

Task definition, the writer's mental representation of what a particular task involves, is the starting point of revision. Simply put, a task definition for revision is the writer's conception of what to do and how to do it. It may develop from conscious consideration of the unique rhetorical situation or from habit. Task definition in revision is important because it shapes the writer's overall goals for revision. For example, a writer of a persuasive text might define the task as evaluating the effectiveness of the arguments presented in the text. In so doing, the writer would be likely to focus on the arguments that could be elaborated as well as those that could be modified. Setting such a goal influences what the writer adds and what the writer deletes. Conversely, if the writer defined revision as a word-level activity, the focus of attention would shift from evaluating the text's arguments to scanning the text for misspellings.

Task definition in revision is also consequential because it establishes the writer's criteria for evaluating text. For instance, a writer of a complex scientific text might define her task as revising the text's content for a lay reader. In defining the task in this way, she would spend most of her energy considering those aspects of the text that might confuse a reader without detailed topic knowledge. However, if she instead defined the task as determining whether the scientific content was adequate, she would evaluate the text for technical accuracy rather than for how comprehensible its message would be for a lay reader. The criteria writers invoke for judging their texts have a direct impact on what they ignore during revision. Research and experience shows us that a writer's task definition influences decision-making throughout the revising process.

As teachers, we can teach inexperienced writers to attend to their task definition and recognize how it shapes their revision decisions. While observing writers as they engaged in a complex revision task, Stratman (1984) found marked differences in how experienced and inexperienced writers defined revising:

- Experienced writers read the whole text before they began to revise, frequently creating "an inventory of problems" at the beginning of revision; inexperienced writers tended to begin revision upon reading the initial clause.
- Experienced writers revised by working "in passes," that is, they may have first revised the entire text for tone, then for organization, and finally, for style; inexperienced writers did not.
- Experienced writers frequently extracted the gist of the text, stated its goal or purpose before revision; inexperienced writers did not consider these activities.
- Experienced writers considered the audience's needs before and during revision; inexperienced writers often thought about the audience's needs, but typically in the midst of revision lost track of their goals for the audience.

A Writer's Task Definition for Revision Is
Self Created and Socially Constructed

Graves (1981) provides valuable information about task definition from a teacher's point of view. He argues that many of the reasons why young children do not revise have little to do with cognition. For example, students may not revise if the teacher has the paper supply locked up in a special drawer; they may be intimidated to ask for more paper in front of their peers. Students may not revise if a teacher reads another student's paper in front of the class as an exemplar. Students may ignore revision when teachers simply assign a number or a grade at the end of their papers.

One's ability to take the audience's point of view may shift dramatically depending on who the audience is and on the writer's social role to the audience. Kirsch (1990, 1991) finds that experienced writers foreground different aspects of the rhetorical situation, depending on the author's social status and relation to the audience. Many writers are preoccupied with writing to the boss, to the teacher, or to a powerful discourse community they wish to enter. Bloom (1985) studied graduate students as they struggled to complete their doctoral theses and found that writing for academic audiences is a terrifying and anxiety-producing experience for many young professionals. Elbow (1987) says that people need the ability to "turn off" audience awareness, especially when it confuses thinking or blocks discourse (p. 56). Inexperienced writers may need advice about the kinds of rhetorical situations in which they could benefit from trying to create their first drafts without thinking about audience.

We can also see how revision is socially constructed in the set of currently sanctioned methods for evaluating the quality of revised text. For example, even though there have been many articles pointing to the limitations of readability formulas (Duffy & Waller, 1985), textbook publishers, newspapers, magazines, and even the IRS still revise to the authority of the Flesch, Gunning, or Flesch-Kincaid readability formulas. Why? They are quick. Objective. Require no human input. The absence of other objective ways to index comprehensibility, coupled with a sense of apprehension about using "subjective" methods such as collecting feedback from real readers, have led many organizations to reluctantly but doggedly adhere to readability formulas (Schriver, 1989).

The case study that is presented later in this chapter is designed to help teachers illustrate for students that even mechanically and grammatically correct text can create difficulties for readers. The case study shows just how little guidance readability tests provide for revision. In contrast, it illustrates how useful detailed readers' responses can be.

Writers Can Benefit from Instruction That
Helps Them to Revise by Design Rather Than by Default

Writers generally adopt either a linear sentence-level or a whole-text definition of revision. In its extreme, the sentence-level perspective of revision is one in which the writer:

1. Reads an initial clause or a sentence.
2. Asks, "Is there anything wrong with this clause or sentence?"
3. If "yes," fix it.
4. If "no," go on to the next clause or sentence.
5. After the sentence is fixed or approved of as "OK," he or she continues in this manner, sentence by sentence, to the end of the text.

A major barrier to success in writing lies in students' tendency to revise sentence by sentence, and, for some writers, even word by word (Bridwell, 1980; NAEP, 1977; Sommers, 1980; Witte, 1983). But students do not usually choose to revise linearly; they seem to do so by default. The sentence-level approach to revision creates several kinds of problems for writers. Evaluating sentences one at a time makes it hard to see how individual sentences relate to the whole text. When writers evaluate their texts sentence by sentence, the texts may read very well. But as Scardamalia and Bereiter (1981) pointed out, without attending to the context for the discourse, the writer is not able to judge the adequacy of any given sentence. The linear approach is also problematic because it wastes time. Writers may revise sentences that they later discover should have been deleted. Adopting a linear approach to revision prevents writers from spending time where it is most needed, that is, on the aspects of the text that do not meet the readers' expectations.

The question remains, however, "Do writers adopt a sentence-level approach because they cannot revise more globally?" In a study by Wallace and Hayes (1991), freshmen writers were provided with only eight minutes of instruction in the revision activities that are typically associated with global revision, for example, reading through the entire text to identify major problems. They found that even after such a short period of instruction writers produced better revisions than students simply asked to revise. Similarly, Matsuhashi and Gordon (1985) showed that students asked to "add five things to their essays" to improve it could do so. These studies provide evidence that students are quite able to revise by design; they may just need to be prompted to use their knowledge.

Putting Research into Practice: A Case Study of Revising for Readers

As the research on audience and revision shows, revising for readers is a complex, multiply determined social and cognitive task. One way teachers can help student writers move beyond a notion of "revision as proofreading" is to use texts for class projects that need revision not because they contain surface-level errors, but rather, for example, because they fail to be persuasive, create confusions and misunderstandings, convey an inappropriate rhetorical stance, or project a persona the writer did not intend. This case study is designed to show a student writer's process of (a) evaluating an original text, (b) collecting readers' responses to that text, (c) interpreting readers' feedback, and (d) revising based on readers' responses. The case study shows that collecting readers' feedback can be a useful means of guiding revision. It is based on protocol-aided revision, a method that has been employed effectively in a variety of academic and nonacademic contexts (Swaney, Janik, Bond, & Hayes, 1981; Schriver, 1984, 1991).

This case study evolved from a class project in a "Professional Writing" course. Students in the course were given the task of visiting nonprofit organizations or businesses in their community with the goal of finding a short text that needed to be revised. The idea was that students would revise the texts as long as the organization or business found at least two members of the intended audience who would serve as readers.

The original text, "The Art of Bird Watching" (see Figure 8.1), was part of a short brochure distributed to visitors at a nature conservancy in southeastern Pennsylvania. From the conservancy's point of view, the aim of the brochure was to provide useful information to both newcomers and experienced bird watchers. People who worked at the conservancy were enthusiastic about

The Art of Bird Watching

There are over 800 species of birds representing over 60 families of birds in North America. Bird Watching or birding is becoming very popular in North America. Birding is an art. To become a birder involves developing your own techniques for identifying species of birds. When you go birding, quick and reliable identification of birds species is essential. To identify birds, compare the form of a typical bird in a particular group to birds with similar silhouettes. At first glance, note the invariable features: range, shape, behavior, and voice. Take a journal and make notes that will help you develop your own system for recalling the important species' characteristics. Try to determine a bird's particular features and attributes before you look at a field guide for the answer. In time, you will be able to identify birds by their features and attributes with only a glimpse. The better you get a recognizing patterns related to flight, walking, feeding, courtship, nest-building, and care for the young, the more skilled you will become at identifying species of birds. Spend time studying books and looking at birds in the field. As you become more experienced, you will find the birding technique that works best for you.

Figure 8.1. An Excerpt from the Original Brochure

helping patrons, whether inexperienced or experienced in bird watching, get the most out of their visit. They wanted to make visitors feel part of a growing community of people who love birds. The manager stressed her interest in having visitors form a good impression of the conservancy. Her aim was to create an atmosphere that would make visitors want to come back and perhaps make a donation to help protect endangered species. She felt that one way to help people understand the conservancy's activities was to provide them with clear and persuasive information about the art of bird watching. But after rereading the content of the original brochure, the manager was uncertain about how well it met her goals and the needs of the various visitors.

Ned, a college junior, taking the course in professional writing, chose the conservancy's brochure for his course project. His goal was to determine its effectiveness for newcomers and experienced bird watchers and to provide the conservancy with a revised version of the text. To begin his revision, Ned and his classmates met in peer critiquing groups and shared information about their goals for their revision projects. Ned was not sure what was wrong with conservancy's text and thought that maybe its problems were stylistic. One of Ned's classmates told him it was simple to use a computer to evaluate a text for style, so Ned first ran a popular Macintosh and IBM-based style checker, Grammatik™ 3.0. This software program computes various readability formulas and provides summary statistics on text features such as the number of passive sentences, the average number of words per sentence, and the average number of syllables per word. When he ran the style checker, he received the feedback shown in Figure 8.2.

Except for the negative evaluation of the text regarding paragraph length (the last feature described), the scores Grammatik™ provided are among the highest it offers. Indeed, the feedback regarding the text's readability level ("preferred by most readers"), its sentence length ("most readers could easily understand sentences of this length"), and its word length ("most readers could

Readability Statistics	Interpretation
Readability Level:	
9 (Flesch Kincaid)	Preferred for Most Readers
Reading Ease Score:	
56 (Flesch)	This represents a 6-10 grade level.
Passive Voice:	The amount of passive voice is within a
0%	reasonable range for this writing style.
Average Sentence Length:	Most readers could easily understand
15.4 words	sentences of this length.
Average Word Length:	
1.60 syllables	Most readers could understand the vocabulary used in this document, based on syllables per word.
Average Paragraph Length:	Paragraphs may be too long for most readers to
13 sentences	follow. Try organizing ideas into shorter units.

Figure 8.2. An Analysis of the Bird Watching Brochure by Grammatik™

The Art of Bird Watching

There are over 800 species of birds representing over 60 families of birds in North America. That's a lot. I had no idea there were so many. *Bird Watching or birding* That's a funny word . . . birding . . . are they serious? *is becoming very popular in North America. Birding is an art.* An art of what—just watching birds? *To become a birder* Oh no, a birder? I'm not really into being that . . . sounds a little kinky to me . . . *involves developing your own techniques for identifying species of birds.* Like what? *When you go birding,* When I go birding, hmm . . . this is strange . . . *quick and reliable identification of birds species is essential.* I thought you just looked at the birds. I didn't know you had to figure out species. Sounds hard. Maybe I'll just have my friends show me. *To identify birds, compare the form of a typical bird in a particular group to birds with similar silhouettes.* Well, that would be nice, but how do I know what's typical? What do they mean by silhouettes—heads or beaks? I can't really picture this too good. I could probably recognize pigeons, robins, and maybe bluejays. Oh, and I've seen a lot of seagulls at the Jersey shore. *At first glance, note the invariable features*—Say what? This is getting beyond me you know. *range,* Range . . . is that the length between the beak and the tail? I think I read that somewheres. *shape, behavior, and voice.* Voice, I guess bird song. That part sounds easy. *Take a journal* Where? *and make notes that will help you develop your own system for recalling the important species' characteristics.* They've gotta be kidding, you sposed to take notes. Are you supposed to be like Joe Thoreau? This is too much for a boy from south Philly. *Try to determine a bird's particular features and attributes* What's the difference between a . . . features and attributes? *before you look at a field guide* What field guide? *for the answer. In time, you will be able to identify birds by their features and attributes with only a glimpse.* Yea, sure I will. *The better you get a recognizing patterns related to flight, walking, feeding, courtship, nest-building, and care for the young, the more skilled you will become at identifying species of birds.* I wouldn't know like what patterns to look for. *Spend time studying books* Like what? Are they trying to sell me somethin' here? *and looking at birds in the field. As you become more experienced, you will find the birding technique that works best for you.* And if you're lucky, they'll put you on one of those public TV on one of those nature shows. Sounds like it could be fun . . . for a nerd.

Figure 8.3. A Reading Protocol from an Inexperienced Bird Watcher

understand the vocabulary used in this document") gives the impression that readers would respond favorably to the text. Even with the favorable feedback from Grammatik™, Ned felt that the director was right in believing that the text was inadequate for the people who visited the conservancy. But he needed information about why the text was not working well.

Ned felt that the output from Grammatik™ was not helpful to guide his revision. He felt that although the text appeared to meet word and sentence level standards of readability formulas, there was still something wrong. After several class meetings where he gathered feedback from his classmates, Ned decided to solicit feedback from members of the audience. He collected think-aloud protocols from two members of the intended audience, an inexperienced bird watcher and an experienced "birder" (shown on these two pages).

The inexperienced bird watcher was a twenty-year-old man from Philadelphia, Tony, whose friends had invited him to the nature conservancy. Tony was somewhat skeptical about the idea of going bird watching, but thought he would enjoy getting out of the city, admitting that he might learn something new.

The expert bird watcher, Rosemary, was a thirty-four-year-old woman from Lancaster, Pennsylvania, who had been a member of the Audubon Society for ten years. She was a birding enthusiast and had traveled across the United States and Canada on "birding" camping trips. Figures 8.3 and 8.4, the transcripts of their protocols, provide their response to the brochure. The passage they are reading (Figure 8.1) comes from the beginning of the brochure.

The Art of Bird Watching

There are over 800 species of birds representing over 60 families of birds in North America. That's a recent classification scheme, people actually believed there were many more than that in the 60s. At that time, many species were poorly understood and sometimes males and females of the same family were considered different species. *Bird Watching or birding is becoming very popular in North America.* It's been very popular in the U.S. for at least 40 years. *Birding is an art.* Of course it's an art, but it doesn't say why. Because birding is very sophisticated these days. Birders use all kinds of ways to identify species. Birding was originally associated with the sport of killing birds. *To become a birder involves developing your own techniques for identifying species of birds. When you go birding . . .* This is oddly phrased, it's not like going skiing . . . *quick and reliable identification of birds species is essential.* Obviously. *To identify birds, compare the form of a typical bird in a particular group to birds with similar silhouettes.* This must be for a beginner, it's a much more complex process than that. *At first glance, note the invariable features: range, shape, behavior, and voice.* That's sensible advice although one does not note the range by looking at a bird. It shouldn't say 'at first glance' either . . . they make it sound so easy . . . just take a quick look and note what you see . . . this is misleading. *Take a journal and make notes that will help you develop your own system for recalling the important species' characteristics. Try to determine a bird's particular features and attributes before you look at a field guide for the answer.* The field guide doesn't always match what you see, but that's a good idea for beginners. I agree it's important to develop your own system and style of birding. But birders should also use the well known field marks that anyone can learn. *In time, you will be able to identify birds by their features and attributes with only a glimpse. The better you get a recognizing patterns related to flight, walking, feeding, courtship, nest-building, and care for the young, the more skilled you will become at identifying species of birds . . .* Okay . . . *Spend time studying books and looking at birds in the field.* It doesn't say what kind of books. What about magazines? What about birding in different parts of the country? That's what I like. *As you become more experienced, you will find the birding technique that works best for you.* This brochure is not that useful for me. I find it somewhat misleading and too general. It would be nice to discuss ways to identify similar species of birds . . . that's what birding is all about. But maybe I'm asking too much for a brochure.

Figure 8.4. A Reading Protocol from an Experienced Birder

After collecting the protocols, Ned quickly discovered that the two readers differed in important ways: (a) they paid attention to different parts of the text; (b) they talked differently about how they would use the text; (c) they questioned the text's message in different ways; (d) they brought different knowledge and expectations to bear in understanding the brochure's purpose.

Ned concluded that the brochure was too specialized for the inexperienced bird watcher and too elementary for the expert. He decided that it would be very difficult to satisfy the diverse needs of both audiences in one brochure and requested permission from the director of the conservancy to create two handouts, one for newcomers to birding and one for experienced birders. She agreed.

The reading protocol from the inexperienced bird watcher showed Ned that Tony seemed to trivialize the experience of bird watching by reducing it to just looking at birds. The protocol showed Ned that Tony lacked knowledge about the meanings of "silhouette" and "range." Tony simplified the complexity of identifying bird songs and dismissed the idea that taking notes might be useful. His protocol also revealed that he did not understand the difference between birds' "features" and "attributes." He misinterpreted the conservancy's motive in mentioning that he look at a field guide, characterizing their suggestion as a sales pitch. Another comprehension difficulty the protocol illustrated was that Tony could not act on the advice "to compare the form of a typical bird in a particular group to birds with similar silhouettes" because he did not know what a silhouette was. The reader's feedback led Ned to conclude that the main point of the brochure was not conveyed well for an inexperienced bird watcher.

In response to the Tony's difficulties, Ned supplemented the text with visual examples of typical silhouettes of common bird families (see Figure 8.5). In this way, Ned found a creative way to overcome the brochure's omissions. He decided that the original text included too many references to unexplained bird features such as range, shape, behavior, and voice, and that focusing on a simple feature such as shape would be more informative to a beginner. Ned also felt that more procedural advice was needed regarding how to recognize the general shape of bird families. In contrast to the original brochure, the revised text recommends that the inexperienced bird watcher take a "staged approach" to becoming more experienced.

In the revision, Ned explained more clearly why a journal and field guide are useful, recommending the use of a particular field guide. In concluding the new version, Ned focused on getting newcomers interested in birding as a hobby rather than on developing unique techniques. His decisions for revision were shaped in large part by what Tony said in the protocol. Put differently, the reader helped define Ned's revision task. He was able to make an effective revision because he had detailed knowledge of Tony's misunderstandings and faulty inferences as well as his expectations and assumptions.

In contrast, Rosemary's protocol (Figure 8.3) showed Ned that for an experienced birder, the information in the original brochure was insufficient and, in some places, even questionable. Rosemary found the brochure inadequate

The Art of Bird Watching

It is not surprising with over 800 species of birds representing over 60 families in North America to find that bird watching or "birding" has become very popular in the United States. Birding is the art of observing and studying different species. To identify birds quickly will take considerable practice. Before you go birding for the first time, buy a field guide that provides descriptions, photos, and silhouettes of birds. Beginning "birders" usually identify bird families by comparing birds they see with the illustrations or descriptions in a field guide. Study the silhouettes. Once you are able to recognize the general shape of a family, you will be able to identify a member from its shape alone. The warblers, tanagers, cardinals, sparrows, and finches (shown on the right) make up one of the many families you can learn about in this way.

When you go out in the field, take both a field guide and a journal for making notes about the birds you see. Try to identify the bird's particular features before consulting the field guide. As you become more experienced, you will be able to distinguish families by recognizing distinctive behavior patterns such as flight, walking, feeding, courtship, nest-building, and care of the young.

At first, you will not be able to identify all of the particular characteristics of a species such as an American Goldfinch. Gradually, you will get better at identifying the features that distinguish one species from another—features such as shape, voice, behavior, and color. Spend time studying books and looking at birds in the field. As you become more experienced, you will discover the excitement of identifying a species for the first time and you will realize why so many people have become enthusiastic birders.

Figure 8.5. A Revision for an Inexperienced Bird Watcher

on a number of counts. For example, it had little information about birding as an art, about methods for identifying birds, about field marks and their use in identifying birds, about magazines or books on birds, about birding in various parts of the country, and about ways to identify similar species of birds. In addition, Rosemary felt that the brochure made birding appear much simpler than it is. Her protocol revealed to Ned that she found the information

The Art of Birding

It is not surprising with over 800 species of birds representing over 60 families in North America to find that birding has become very popular in the United States. Birding, the art of using color, pattern, shape, size, voice, habitat, and behavior to identify species has become increasingly sophisticated. Birders are continually finding new ways to distinguish similar species and to identify new species. To become an expert birder will require that you master the fundamental skill of identifying field marks quickly and reliably. Visiting museums and reading books are excellent ways to study field marks before attempting to do so while observing birds in motion or in flight.

To identify birds in the field will demand that you use all clues you know about a species' primary characteristics and features—for example, size, shape, color, pattern, voice, habitat, and range. You will need to consider a number of attributes that together give a species a distinctive personality. At first, you will need to spend considerable time studying the variety of birds within the same species. Next, you will need to study the differences between birds that appear to be similar. For example, even among the closely related species, there may be differences in posture: Yellow-crowned Night-herons often stand in a more upright posture than do Black-crowned Night-herons, and Rough-legged Hawks often perch in a more horizontal posture than do Red-tailed Hawks (shown below).

Rough-legged Hawk   **Red-tailed Hawk**

Expert birders also watch for behavioral patterns of flight, walking, feeding, courtship, nest-building, and care of the young. Some behavior clues are obvious, like the big, splashy dives of Northern Gannets and Ospreys, or the mothlike flight of a Common Poorwill. Others are more subtle, such as the flight mannerisms of kittiwakes or the wing and tail flicks of flycatchers. Time spent studying books such as the Audubon Society's *The Master Guide to Birding* will be well worthwhile. Magazines or journals such as *American Birds* or *Birding* are also informative sources of up-to-date information. Perhaps the best way to sharpen your skills and increase your expertness as a birder is to get plenty of experience in birding in a variety of terrains, ranges, and seasons.

Figure 8.6. A Revision for an Experienced Birder

about how to "note the invariable features" misleading. Her final comment raised the issue that "distinguishing among similar species" is perhaps the central skill in birding—a point the original brochure failed to make clearly.

To solve the problems in the text detected by the expert, Ned focused the revision on ways to develop expert birding skills (see Figure 8.6). In so doing, Ned (who was not an expert bird watcher) consulted the director of the conservancy and the Audubon Society's three-volume set, the *Master Guide to Bird-*

ing (Farrand, 1983) for advice. He chose "posture in hawks" as a means to demonstrate how a feature such as posture can be used to distinguish among species. He selected an example that could be illustrated, adding visual support to the point about using features to discriminate among species. In addition, Ned included details that are missing in the original—details the expert seemed to expect. For example, Ned mentions why birding is becoming sophisticated, why learning field marks is a fundamental skill, how behavior clues vary from obvious to subtle, why birding in different geographical locations is interesting, and why birding during various seasons and different times of year is a way to sharpen skill. Overall, Ned's revision assumes that the reader is an experienced bird watcher who would like to become an expert.

This example shows how audiences may require texts that include different kinds of information. In the revision for the inexperienced birder, Ned provided the silhouettes to help newcomers understand the need to gain skills in recognizing shapes of birds. In the revision for the experienced birder, he included the drawings of the hawks to show the importance of using features to distinguish similar species. Without the think-aloud reading protocols, Ned had no access to the topic knowledge and informational interests of the audience.

The protocols showed Ned that sentence-level correctness was simply not enough. If Ned had only relied on the feedback from Grammatik™, he might not have revised at all. But as he discovered, the problems readers experienced with the brochure were created not so much by poor sentence structure as by inadequate content. The protocols illustrated to Ned how readers respond to various dimensions of the text—content, persona, tone, purpose—and made him recognize that to revise effectively, he needed to find solutions that would take into consideration the problems readers experienced with the whole text as well with the sentences.

Helping Students Revise for Readers

To change the way student writers think about revising, we may need to shift our own perspective. The following suggestions may add to our classroom methods for improving students' sense of audience awareness and their definition of revision.

Develop Classroom Heuristics That Focus Writers' Attention on Specific Aspects of Revising

We have only begun to develop research-driven heuristics for revision. For example, Scardamalia and Bereiter (1983) devised a method called "procedural facilitation" to help student writers in elementary school to detect text problems. By using a set of note cards on which they present statements of an evaluative, diagnostic, or solution-oriented nature, they prompt children to evaluate their texts by using external cues (e.g., "People won't see why this is important" or "I'd better say more"). Presumably, the demands on students' cognitive resources are reduced, thus helping them to carry out their revision

processes. Fitzgerald and Markham (1987), building on Scardamalia and Bereiter's approach, found that using procedural facilitation has beneficial effects with middle school writers. We can imagine creating similar methods for
older writers who have difficulty making certain kinds of textual decisions
during revision.

Another kind of heuristic that might be useful in the classroom is one that
encourages students to delay sentence-level revisions until the whole text has
been considered from the reader's point of view. Students can better manage
their revision activity if they evaluate the global features of the text before the
local ones, such as by considering:

- What the text says to a reader by reading it from a *whole-text perspective*,
  predicting the reader's response to the organization, arguments, content,
  and tone.
- The *sections* and the coherence between main parts of the text, focusing
  on the text's structure and on topical progressions within and between
  sections.
- The *transitions* between and within paragraphs, making certain the logical connections enable rather than inhibit comprehension.
- The *paragraphs*, directing attention to how well each paragraph works in
  relation to the whole text.
- The *sentences*, checking for issues of mechanics, grammar, and style —
  given the reader's knowledge of the topic and expectations for the content.
- The *words*, deciding whether word choices are appropriate for the reader's experience with the topic and the social role of the reader in relation
  to the writer.

Of course, the order in which writers attend to these issues depends on the
rhetorical situation; the point is that if writers begin revision at the level of
words and sentences, they may never evaluate the whole text. This approach
may also have the benefit of reducing the cognitive demands of thinking about
too many revision issues at once. As Scardamalia and Bereiter (1981) point
out, "to pay conscious attention to handwriting, spelling, punctuation, word
choice, syntax, textual connections, purpose, organization, clarity, rhythm,
euphony, and reader characteristics would seemingly overload the information
processing capacity of even the best intellects" (p. 81).

Show Writers the Differences Between Seeing, Characterizing, and Solving Text Problems

Most readers would agree that "not all errors are equal" and that certain
classes of error — organizational problems and errors of omission — are likely
to bother readers more than others (Schriver, 1984; 1992). Students need to
sharpen their sensitivity to the ways texts can mislead readers by being able to
notice the textual cues that create such difficulties. Bracewell's research (1983)
suggests that writers may benefit from a procedure in which they "plant"
errors in their own texts and then exchange papers and search for the "deliber-

ate plants" in their classmates' papers. He posits that students can often recognize and correct errors in others' texts, but, in composing their own, continue to produce the same errors and cannot "plant" those errors (p. 197). Through this method, Bracewell shows students that "seeing" and "fixing" are separate revision activities. One can imagine adapting Bracewell's competitive proofreading activity to teach students to see, characterize, and fix particular types of errors. For example, after providing instruction on "text structure and its relation to readers' expectations," students could practice altering a text's organization.

It seems important that we develop classroom-tested teaching methods that focus students' activities during revision. If students are to develop their ability to revise for audiences (other than themselves, their peers, or their teachers), they need to be taught to detect, diagnose, and fix problems from the reader's perspective.

Structure Writing Assignments
So That Students Collect Feedback from
Readers in Community and Workplace Settings

If we assume that "no one can write better than he [or she] can read, since he [or she] must read his [or her] own text" (Hirsch, 1977, p. 168) then reading is perhaps the most important part of revision. To help increase writers' reading sensitivity, we can challenge our students to discover for themselves how texts are socially constructed, how meaning is a negotiation between reader and writer, and how texts have rich intertextual roots that influence readers' responses. We can do this by structuring writing assignments so that opportunities for making these kinds of discoveries are more likely.

The case study showed how Ned, whose teacher had suggested that he find a text in the community that needed to be revised, discovered that readers of the brochure from the nature conservancy brought different textual experiences to their reading. For example, Tony, the inexperienced birder, drew on his knowledge of Thoreau's *Walden* as well as his experience with television (e.g., public broadcasting's *Nature* show). The experienced birder, Rosemary, displayed her knowledge of Audubon Society publications. Ned also saw that readers who differed in their experience with the topic could also differ in the social knowledge they drew on to interpret the author's motives in creating the text. On the one hand, Tony thought the agenda of the original brochure was to get the reader to buy nature books while Rosemary thought it was to make birding look simple, presumably to get readers to join the conservancy. Differences such as these showed Ned that readers' responses can direct revision decisions.

Not only is the process of collecting readers' feedback useful, but it can be fun. With equipment as limited as a cassette tape recorder, students can conduct their own investigative field work by interviewing and collecting protocols from readers who most represent their intended audiences. If we encourage student writers to get out of the classroom and into community or workplace settings, they are much more likely to find out for themselves that readers construct text in radically divergent ways.

At the beginning of a sequence of assignments, for example, teachers might choose a text for revision that is controversial in subject matter and fails to represent its audience clearly. Teachers could ask students to collect feedback from readers who differ in culture, background, or experience. It may be useful to assign students to work in teams. For example, one team might study how readers construct meaning when they are favorably disposed toward the topic while another team might study readers who are negative. Another team might study the response of experts on the subject matter while another might analyze the responses of a lay audience. Students who collect their own "inside stories" are in a more informed position to hypothesize about the textual features that cue responses from particular audiences. Each team could revise for an audience and then share their revisions and their rationales for textual changes in a presentation to the class. The idea is to create an educational environment that allows students to begin to form their own theories about literate practices and about how readers construct texts.

Another parallel activity for teachers who have access to computers involves having the classroom create a "readers' responses database." Each group could type into a computer file the readers' responses they collect. Then, the teacher can organize the computer files to highlight the differences in readers' responses to the text, either at the sentence, paragraph, or global level. Each student could then use the print-out of the computer file to guide revision of specific text features. Students may discover, for example, that one group of readers respond most specifically to poorly expressed arguments. Students working on revising for that audience might be prompted to focus their revision on the text's argument. Alternatively, another group of readers might call for elaboration. Students revising for that audience might be encouraged to work on building persuasive examples. By using the feedback they collect in this way, students can compare alternative social constructions of the same text and make reader-driven revisions.

Since the 1970s, our understanding of revision has increased and we have changed our definition of its processes and products. Revision is now seen as a recursive activity that calls on representing, evaluating, and modifying text. We now focus not merely on the number of changes writers make to a draft, but on whether the revisions help them in realizing their goals for the reader. But even with the progress that has been made in redefining revision, we are just beginning to turn research into action in the classroom.

References

Bartlett, E. J. (1982). Learning to revise: Some component processes. In M. Nystrand (Ed.), *What writers know: The language, process, and the structure of written discourse* (pp. 345-363). New York: Academic Press.

Berkenkotter, C. (1981). Understanding a writer's awareness of audience. *College Composition and Communication, 32*, 388-399.

Berkenkotter, C. (1983). Decisions and revisions: The planning strategies of a published writer. *College Composition and Communication, 34*, 156-169.

Berkenkotter, C. (1984). Student writers and their sense of authority over texts. *College Composition and Communication, 35*(3), 312–319.

Bloom, L. Z. (1985). Anxious writers in context: Graduate school and beyond. In M. Rose (Ed.), *When a writer can't write: Studies in writers' block and other composing problems* (pp. 116–133). New York: Guilford Press.

Bond, S., Hayes, J. R., & Flower, L. (1980). *Translating the law into common language: A protocol study* (Tech. Rpt. No. 8). Pittsburgh, PA: Carnegie Mellon University, Communications Design Center.

Bracewell, R. (1983). Investigating the control of writing skills. In P. Mosenthal, L. Tamor, & S. Walmsley (Eds.), *Research on writing*. New York: Longman.

Bridwell, L. S. (1980). Revising strategies in twelfth grade students: Transactional writing. *Research in The Teaching of English, 14*, 107–122.

CNN. (1992, February 21). Companies move conferences to the computer. *Science and technology today*. Atlanta, GA: Cable News Network.

Duffy, T. & Waller, R. (1985). Readability formulas: What's the use? In T. M. Duffy & R. Waller (Eds.), *Designing usable texts*. Orlando, FL: Academic Press.

Elbow, P. (1987). Closing my eyes as I speak: An argument for ignoring audience. *College English, 49*(1), 50–69.

Farrand, J., Jr. (Ed.). (1983). *Audubon society: Master guide to birding, Vol. 1: Loons to sandpipers* (pp. 20–22 and pp. 246–248). New York: Alfred A. Knopf.

Fitzgerald, J. & Markham, L. (1987). Teaching children about revision in writing. *Cognition and Instruction, 4*(1), 3–24.

Flower, L., Hayes, J. R., Carey, L., Schriver, K. A., & Stratman, J. (1986). Detection, diagnosis and strategies of revision. *College Composition and Communication, 37*(1), 16–55.

Flower, L., Carey, L., & Hayes, J. R. (1984). *Diagnosis: The expert's option* (Tech. Rpt. No. 27). Pittsburgh, PA: Carnegie Mellon University, Communication Design Center.

Freedman, S. W. (1987). *Peer response groups in two ninth-grade classrooms* (Tech. Rpt. No. 12). Berkeley, CA and Pittsburgh, PA: University of California at Berkeley and Carnegie Mellon University, Center for the Study of Writing and Literacy.

George, D. (1984). Working with peer groups in the composition classroom. *College Composition and Communication, 35*(3), 320–326.

Graves, D. H. (Ed.). (1981). *A case study observing the development of primary children's composing, spelling, and motor behaviors during the writing process*. (Final Report, NIE Grant No. G-78-174). Durham: University of New Hampshire.

Graves, D. H. & Murray, D. M. (1980). Revision: In the writers' workshop and in the classroom. *Journal of Education, 162*, 38–56.

Hayes, J. R., Flower, L., Schriver, K. A., Stratman, J., & Carey, L. (1987). Cognitive processes in revision. In S. Rosenberg (Ed.), *Advances in applied psycholinguistics, Vol. II: Reading, writing, and language processing* (pp. 176–240). Cambridge, England: Cambridge University Press.

Hayes, J. R., Schriver, K. A., Blaustein, A., & Spilka, R. (1986). *If it's clear to me, it must be clear to them—How knowledge makes it difficult to judge*. Paper delivered at the American Educational Research Association Convention, San Francisco, CA.

Hillocks, G. (1986). *Research on written composition: New directions for teaching*. Urbana, IL: ERIC Clearinghouse on Reading and Communication Skills and NCRE.

Hillocks, G. (1982). The interaction of instruction, teacher, comment and revision in the teaching of the composing process. *Research in the Teaching of English, 16*(3), 261–278.

Hirsch, E. D. (1977). *The philosophy of composition*. Chicago: University of Chicago Press.

Hull, G. (1984). A performance study of the editing process in writing. Unpublished doctoral dissertation. Pittsburgh, PA: University of Pittsburgh, Department of English.

Kirsch, G. (1990). Experienced writers' sense of audience and authority: Three case studies. In G. Kirsch & D. H. Roen (Eds.), *A sense of audience in written communication* (pp. 216–230). Newbury Park, CA: Sage.

Kirsch, G. (1991). Writing up and down the social ladder: A study of experienced writers composing for contrasting audiences. *Research in the Teaching of English, 25*, 33–53.

Kroll, B. M. (1978). Cognitive egocentrism and the problem of audience awareness in written discourse. *Research in the Teaching of English, 12,* 269–281.

Kroll, B. M. (1984). Audience adaptation in children's persuasive letters. *Written Communication, 1*(4), 407–427.

Matsuhashi, A. & Gordon, E. (1985). Revision, addition, and the power of the unseen text. In S. Freedman (Ed.), *The acquisition of written language: Response and revision* (pp. 226–249). Norwood, NJ: Ablex.

Murray, D. M. (1978). Internal revision: A process of discovery. In Charles R. Cooper & Lee Odell (Eds.), *Research on composing: Points of departure.* Urbana, IL: National Council of Teachers of English.

National Assessment of Educational Progress (NAEP). (1977). *Write/rewrite: An assessment of revision skills: Selected results from the second national assessment of writing.* (ERIC Document Reproduction Service No. ED 141 826).

Newkirk, T. (1981). Barriers to revision. *Journal of Basic Writing (fall/winter)* 50–61.

Newkirk, T. (1984). Direction and misdirection in peer response. *College Composition and Communication, 3,* 300–319.

Nold, E. (1982). Revising: Intentions and conventions. In R. Sudol (Ed.), *Revising: New essays for teachers of writing* (pp. 13–23). Urbana, IL: ERIC/NCTE.

Peck, W. C. (1989). *The effects of prompts upon revision: A glimpse of the gap between planning and performance* (Tech. Rpt. No. 26). Berkeley, CA and Pittsburgh, PA: Center for the Study of Writing and Literacy.

Prentice, W. (1980). The effects of intended audience and feedback on the writings of middle grade pupils. *DAI, 41:* 934-A.

Putnam, L. L. (1986). Conflict in group decision-making. In R. Y. Hirokawa & M. S. Poole (Eds.), *Communication and group decision-making* (pp. 175–196). Beverly Hills, CA: Sage.

Robbins, C. S., Bruun, B., & Zim, H. S. (1966). *Birds of North America: A field guide identification.* New York: Golden Press.

Scardamalia, M. & Bereiter, C. (1981). How children cope with the cognitive demands of writing. In C. H. Frederiksen, M. F. Whiteman, & J. F. Dominic (Eds.), *Writing: The nature, development and teaching of written communication,* Vol. 2 (pp. 81–103). Hillsdale, NJ: Erlbaum.

Scardamalia, M. & Bereiter, C. (1983). The development of evaluative, diagnostic and remedial capabilities in children's composing. In M. Martlew (Ed.), *The psychology of written language: Developmental and educational perspectives* (pp. 67–95). London: John Wiley and Sons.

Schriver, K. A. (1984). *Revising computer documentation for comprehension: Ten lessons in protocol-aided revision.* (Tech. Rpt. No. 14). Pittsburgh, PA: Carnegie Mellon University, Communication Design Center.

Schriver, K. A. (1989). Evaluating text quality: The continuum from text-focused to reader-focused methods. *IEEE Transactions in Professional Communication, 23*(4), 238–255.

Schriver, K. A. (1991). Plain language through protocol-aided revision. In E. R. Steinberg (Ed.), *Plain language: Principles and practice* (pp. 148–172). Detroit, MI: Wayne State University Press.

Schriver, K. A. (1992). Teaching writers to anticipate readers' needs: A classroom-evaluated pedagogy. *Written Communication, 9*(2), 179–208.

Sommers, N. (1980). Revision strategies of student writers and experienced writers. *College Composition and Communication, 31,* 378–387.

Stratman, J. (1984). *Task definition in revision.* Paper presented at the American Educational Research Association convention, April, New Orleans, LA.

Swaney, J. H., Janik, C. J., Bond, S. J., & Hayes, J. R. (1981). *Editing for comprehension: Improving the process through reading protocols.* (Document Design Project Tech. Rpt. No. 14) Pittsburgh, PA: Carnegie Mellon University. (Reprinted in E. R. Steinberg, Ed., 1991, *Plain language: Principles and practice,* pp. 173–203. Detroit, MI: Wayne State University Press.)

Wallace, D. & Hayes, J. R. (1991). Redefining revision for freshmen. *Research in the Teaching of English, 25*, 54–66.

Weiner, H. S. (1986). Collaborative learning in the classroom: A guide to evaluation. *College English, 48*(1), 52–61.

Witte, S. P. (1983). Topical structure and revision: An exploratory study. *College Composition and Communication, 34*, 313–341.

Wulff, W. (1992). Writer-designer collaboration: A case study of process and product. Unpublished doctoral dissertation. Pittsburgh, PA: Carnegie Mellon University, Department of English.

9

Exploring Feedback: Writers Meet Readers

BARBARA M. SITKO

When writers receive feedback about a text, they are often faced with a series of decisions. The primary decision of whether or not to make changes to their work embeds a cluster of other choices, and if we could listen in on the thought processes of these writers, we would see that they consider more alternatives than they might be aware of. One important alternative concerns how to imagine other ways of seeing their text. In order to imagine ways in which readers might have become confused or lost a point, for example, writers must reproduce a mental version of their texts as seen by the eyes and minds of their readers. Such flexibility in creating alternative representations of words, sentences, and organization is not easy for most writers. Yet this is only the first step. Once writers are able to represent the text from the point of view of their readers, a second cluster of decisions focuses on their strategies for fixing the text (Flower, Hayes, Carey, Stratman, & Schriver, 1986), and a third set of options concerns how they test any changes they decide to make. Thus feedback motivates writers to enter into complex decision making, renegotiating the multiple demands of the writing process (Flower & Hayes, 1981) and reconsidering their original plan (Flower, Schriver, Carey, Haas, & Hayes, in press) in ways they might not have envisioned.

Revising after feedback is somewhat different from revising by oneself (Schriver, this volume) or becoming adept at self-editing (Glover, Ronning, & Bruning, 1990). Working by themselves, writers are continually testing their text against their own internal reader. But by showing their work to others in order to get feedback, they move beyond making guesses about how readers unfamiliar with their work will respond. They test their text, checking to see how it fulfills their intentions and their purposes. Thus experienced writers who get feedback in order to rewrite engage in a powerful strategy. Likewise, students who learn to use feedback intentionally (Bereiter & Scardamalia, 1987a) are adding a critical dimension to their own learning.

This chapter will explore ways in which student writers can get and use a specific type of feedback—interpretive reading—to help them see their texts in new ways, review alternatives, and make decisions about changes. During the course of the chapter I will review research on feedback, revising, and interpretive reading, demonstrate how writers think about feedback and decide whether or not to revise, and illustrate how students can use interpretive reading as a feedback technique. Throughout the chapter, examples will be drawn from my classrooms and those of other teachers whose students have adapted this technique.

What Studies Tell Us About Feedback, Revising, and Interpretive Reading

Processing Feedback Is Important to Learning, Yet Students Have Difficulty Using Feedback About Writing

The literature on feedback in instruction and the ways learners integrate it holds no surprises: learners who seek and use feedback are more successful than learners who do not. An interesting example is an extended classroom study of how students dealt with errors throughout an instructional unit (Gagne et al., 1988). A team of researchers who observed the students in their classroom noted that students who pursued problems actively, asking for clarification about their errors and making notes on their papers during discussions of quizzes, were more successful in a final test than were students who did not appear to be actively seeking feedback.

Research on how students use feedback while writing is more variable, however, perhaps because feedback on writing comes in many forms. Research that looks closely at comments and responses by both teachers and peers, for example, indicates that teacher feedback is highly varied and serves many instructional purposes. For instance, feedback may be intended to help students correct errors, discover more about their topic, see where elaboration might be necessary or interesting to a reader, or ask clarifying questions (Ziv, 1984; Brannon & Knoblach, 1982). Pedagogical practice assumes that when writing is communicative rather than primarily personal or expressive (Britton et al., 1975), the reactions of readers should be important to writers. Teaching practice also assumes that feedback helps writers to fulfill their own purposes. Without feedback, writers have recourse only to imagined or virtual readers; consequently, it is not unreasonable for inexperienced, developing writers to hold the naive theory that their invoked audience (Ede & Lunsford, 1984) interprets their words in the same way as they do. Thus, obtaining feedback would seem to be a necessary part of learning to write and a necessary part of a writing curriculum.

However, studies of how students revise given responses to their writing indicate otherwise, delineating problems that students experience with feedback whether from teachers or peers. Many students, possibly those who most need help (Doyle, 1983; Wittrock, 1986), are unable to use their teachers' responses to their texts. It may be that their teachers' intentions are not clear or that students do not perceive the responses to be explicit enough to be useful (Sommers, 1980; Ziv, 1984). Or it may be that students don't see how comments are connected to classroom instruction and thus miss the reinforcement and practice that personal comments provide (Hillocks, 1982). It may even be that feedback actually distracts writers, presenting them with new problems that direct their attention away from their texts: some simply have difficulty making sense of verbal comments and other marks on their papers (Hayes & Daiker, 1984); some have no practice with substantive comments (Anson, 1989); others are caught up in an affective response (McLeod, 1987).

Studies of the influences of peer response provide equally mixed results. For example, peer groups may so interfere with writers' sense of authority over their texts that they abandon their own purposes in the face of peer criticism (Berkenkotter, 1984). Writers may not value the responses of their peers, regarding the comments as imitations of the commenting practices of teachers rather than as responses from interested readers (Freedman, 1987). Because peers form distinctly different evaluative communities from those of their teachers, students may experience the dissonance of conflicting purposes if they try to write for both audiences (Newkirk, 1978). Although this dissonance is familiar to experienced writers (Geisler, 1992; Sommers, 1992), most students have not yet developed ways of negotiating this lack of harmony.

Part of the difficulty with peer response may be due to the school context in which writing is often produced for a "teacher-examiner" (Britton et al., 1985; Brannon & Knoblach, 1982). Revising in response to the needs of a "real" reader might be quite different from responding to the inspection of a teacher or a peer under a teacher's supervision (Freedman, 1987). Yet students apparently get little practice in writing for readers outside the school context. It should come as no surprise that inexperienced writers have little practice in considering the needs of their readers (Flower & Hayes, 1980).

Readers' Constructive Processes
Can Help Writers Design Successful Text

Because feedback is provided by readers, the more we know about reading processes, the more informed we will be about revision. Readers actively construct an interpretation of a text throughout their reading (Spivey, 1987; see also Greene, Haas, this volume). Text construction is an ongoing process, with readers forming an interpretation of the text and then using that representation to incorporate further elements as they proceed. One specific connection between processes of reading and processes of writing was explored by Meyer (1982), whose research shows that readers who are aware of and actively use the text structure not only are better able to recall individual points but are better able to summarize the whole text. Research designed to specify readers' processes provides clues about why this might be so: readers create a mental version of the text; they summarize points and use those points to predict what they expect to come next (Olson, Duffy, & Mack, 1984; Stauffer, 1969; Vipond & Hunt, 1984).

Experienced writers apparently understand more about how their readers' constructive processes work, and, more aware of readers throughout the writing process, shape texts in ways that they expect will guide the reading processes of their audience. Inexperienced writers, however, need to learn more about how the reading process works. These writers may be able to correct lists of individual sentences, but may not be able to make the crucial move of matching the rules to their own texts, quite possibly because they "see" their own text differently (Bartlett, 1982). Writers may apply a rule, for example, by checking their work for structure, and, because they have a clear mental picture of how the text is woven together, reasonably conclude from their review that the text "seems clear." Without contrary evidence they feel no need to change their original representation of the text. Extended practice in self-editing (Glover, Ronning, & Bruning, 1990), and testing a text for readability (Schriver, this volume) succeed only if writers can achieve sufficient distance to "forget" their mental version of what the text means. Such distancing is difficult even for experienced writers who sometimes must let weeks pass before they can take a fresh look at a piece of their work. Students are not likely to be so patient and persistent, so we need a shorter way to the goal of achieving distance.

If inexperienced writers could somehow get access to the processes of readers, they could make more informed decisions about their texts. Specifically they could use observations of their readers' constructive processes to make the kinds of text-level, global changes characteristic of more experienced writers (Sitko, 1992). While observing reading processes, writers hear for themselves an ongoing record of their readers' attempts to orient themselves within the text. They hear readers try to make sense of the emerging point and speculate about where the text is going. They have specific information about whether the reader understands the text as intended.

What we have seen is that revising after feedback is problem solving with a twist. Writers must make an initial decision to engage in problem solving, to "re-present" the text to their own minds via the understanding or misunderstanding of others. Once they have created space between themselves and their writing, they must be vigilant to detect reader problems, willing to set new goals, and able to devise strategies to reach these goals (Hayes, 1989). Although inexperienced writers may tend to misunderstand the complexity of their readers' processes, may naively represent the text as either "right" or "wrong," and may be unaware of the kinds of decisions they have charge of, they can learn to move beyond these limiting ways of thinking (Ornstein &

Erlich, 1989). Methods for getting useful reader feedback and making decisions about revising are both observable and teachable.

Observing Writers Make Decisions About Revising After Feedback

We can learn more about how writers engage in the problem-solving processes of revision if we listen in on several student writers who are revising their papers. The following excerpts are taken from transcripts of students thinking aloud as they worked with two kinds of feedback. The first cluster of excerpts shows three students responding to the same teacher comment. The second extended excerpt shows a student writer responding to an interpretive reading by an intended reader outside the classroom.

USING TEACHER COMMENTS TO DETECT TEXT PROBLEMS

Three writers think aloud as they review their teacher's marginal notations on their papers. The revision and comments are part of a sequence of lessons on editing. In these excerpts, the teacher's comment focuses the writer's attention on editing for "there is/are." As Hillocks' meta-analysis of writing instruction (1986) suggests, such an integration of classroom instruction and focal commenting should increase the likelihood of students' learning by practice. But, as we will see, the three students whose tapes are excerpted process an explicit directive in markedly different ways, even though each has received the same classroom instruction.

While reading the think-alouds, notice how each writer (1) represents or forms a version of the problem, (2) sets a goal that depends on the representation, and (3) moves toward that goal. Italics indicate original text; underlining indicates the writer's addition to the original text; normal typeface indicates thinking aloud. Ellipses indicate elapsed time rather than elision. No words were omitted.

The first writer, Jan, reads the teacher's comment: "This paragraph has problems with agreement, pronoun agreement errors, expletives and awkward sentence structure."

> Jan: Now this was paragraph 3 . . . I'm going to see what this was . . . well, that's my hardest part, I'm always so bad at revising—let's see now . . . (rereads text) *As I personally know, there are a few benefits*—oh! I get it. That's an expletive. She said that in class . . . (rereads) *As I personally know*, a few benefits one probably would—let's see . . . um . . . let's see . . . *As I personally know* . . . (adds text) a few benefits one probably would experience are . . . learning about oneself . . . settling down of one's environment . . . and additional extras. OK that's one sentence . . . and I can stick it in . . . right there . . . and then just continue with that paragraph.

Chris, the second writer who has received a similar comment, is testing a sentence that he has just rewritten: *No report of physical danger to the residents was reported.*

Chris: Now does that sound more logical than . . . the original sentence says *There was no report of physical danger to the residents* . . . But that has an expletive in it. So I figure . . . *No report of physical danger to the residents* — No . . . No physical danger to the residents was reported. That sounds better. (writes) <u>No physical danger to the residents was reported.</u> That sounds better.

Pat, the third writer, is revising after reading a comment similar to Jan's.

Pat: *In conclusion, the athletic programs* and she crossed out "athletic programs" and put "athletes" . . . yeah — programs don't play on fields — athletes do, that's true. (reads text) *should be able to play upon fields of high quality.* she puts . . . she edits it to say "able to play upon high quality fields" . . . I don't know what that might be — that might be "passive" . . . she doesn't really say . . . let's see . . . let's go back to where she comments on it . . . (rereads comment) "pronoun reference, and ex-plicit — exple-expletives and awkward sentence structure and phrasing" . . . maybe that was . . . maybe that was . . . she said "awkward sentence structure and phras-ing." . . . OK this is where she said "awkward" . . . so maybe expletives? I don't even know what an expletive is so — I don't know . . . It sounds like something describing, so "high quality" — maybe it's adjectives — that's what she must have meant . . . *should be able to play upon high quality fields* . . . fields of high quality . . . maybe that is kind of passive . . . is passive . . . if it is in that sentence . . . I don't know . . . (rereads text) *Because of the bad conditions of the only two fields we have there are increased risks of injuries* . . . maybe I should have put . . . she circled "there" and maybe I should have put "increased risks of injuries exist."

The think-alouds of these writers are interesting for several reasons. First, they illustrate that the teacher's comments function as intended in two impor-tant ways: the comments focus writers' attention on specific classes of editing problems, and they provide important practice reinforcing what students have apparently learned from a lesson in editing — Jan and Chris recognize the problem type — but have not yet applied to their own writing. Second and perhaps less obvious, however, the excerpts illustrate how three students, even though they have different degrees of expertise, engage in essentially the same problem-solving process: they read their teacher's comments, try to match each problem type to the text, devise a way to solve the problem as they see it, and test their revised sentences. Obviously Jan and Chris understand the con-cept of "expletive," search and quickly locate the error in the text, and then call up a strategy to transform the sentence structure. These students have reached the point of being able to diagnose a class of text problems (see Schriver, this volume) with a little help. As they practice applying the concept to their own writing, they give us reason to believe that they have learned to self-edit (Glover, Ronning, & Bruning, 1990) for expletives in future papers for this class. Equally evident is Pat's failure to match the text with the com-ment. We can see that although Pat searches for a fit, she finally detects the problem by using the graphical cue of the circled word rather than the comment about "expletives." But what is striking about Pat's search is how she tries to construct meaning from the meaningless term "expletive" by associating it with the familiar term "adjective," which she can and does match to her text. In fact, what is strikingly similar about all three think-alouds is the consistent pattern of problem solving. As the students work at revising, each represents the problem in some way, fixes it in some way, and tests the solution. All three excerpts, although they show different degrees of knowledge, demonstrate similar cognitive processes at work.

USING INTERPRETIVE READING TO
DETECT TEXT PROBLEMS[1]

The following example illustrates how a writer revises a text given a different kind of feedback, interpretive reading. In this excerpt from a think-aloud session, the writer is reading a transcript of the reader's comments as he revises his first paragraph. Because the reader had paused periodically to summarize main points and to make guesses about what might come next, this interpretive reading gives the writer an opportunity to hear how his text affects readers in ways that he does not intend. We are again listening in at the point where he decides to make some changes. The writer is reading both his text (italics) and his reader's comments (bold) as well as thinking aloud (normal typeface).

Text: *Writing a college essay requires several crucial methods. The most important part of writing a college application essay is to make it stand out to the reader. When an essay asks you to choose a book that has influenced you, the book you choose must be unique. Also, important for writing the essay is that you use good grammar, clear and concise language, and a style that's fun to read.*

Reader (summarizing the point of the text as a whole): **I think the points that came up were too obvious. I mean, you sit through so many English classes in your life and you pick this up after a few.**

Writer: Well, not everybody does.

Reader: **And if you're writing an essay for college, some of this is just—you have to know anyway.**

Writer: Well, but everybody doesn't get in . . . Hm . . . Let's see . . . Maybe I should pull—maybe I'll pull the idea of balancing in first . . . OK, it comes into the third paragraph now . . . Let's see if we can pull it into the first. (rereads text) *The most important part of writing a college application essay is to make it stand out to the reader*—OK, have to bring balance in early—make that the key point. OK. *The most important part of writing a college application essay is to make it stand out to the reader* and have it balance the rest of the application. OK. All right. *You must choose a book.* Back to the first paragraph—You must choose—no . . . (rewrites): The book you choose *must balance the rest of the application* . . . OK . . . (reads text) *Also important for writing the essay is that* . . . OK . . . Let me look at the assignment again, because I don't want to cut out so much that I don't answer the question anymore. OK. (rereads assignment) *In a short paper, describe one problem*

that a 12th grade student might have in writing this essay, and suggest several stra-
tegies that he or she might use to solve the problem. OK, Let's see – to quit boring
this person we could drop the whole grammar and concise language paragraph, and
really shorten this thing down – OK (rereads) *The most important part in the essay –*
Let's read it without those things in it. OK, (rereads) *Writing a college essay requires*
several crucial methods. Which no longer would be my topic sentence . . . Well,
OK, *Writing a college essay* . . . is like a balancing act. Good old analogy . . .
(adds text) is like a balancing act. (rereads) *The most important* – no, that's getting
redundant. *The most important part of writing a college application essay* – how can
I change that to make it more concise and not be redundant . . . the . . . (writes)
The key . . . to writing . . . a . . . good . . . good is a horrible little word . . . the
key to writing . . . a . . . (sigh) . . . (writes) successful . . . college application essay . . . is to make it stand out to the reader.

Like the three writers above, this writer represents a problem, searches for
a strategy, changes his text and tests his solution. But the interpretive reading
influences this writer to diagnose a different kind of problem from those
considered by the students in the previous excerpts. His reader's response
emphasizes not a text problem (such as lack of clear organization or wordy
constructions), but a rhetorical problem, namely, an arrangement of ideas
that appears offensive to his reader. The comment is particularly interesting
because the writer's think-aloud planning session had shown him voicing a
conscious choice to order his points from least important to most important,
a "textbook approach," as the writer had noted. But his reader's reaction to
precisely this choice of arrangement provides him with a very different reading
and induces him to reconsider his previous decision. In a few swift strokes he
reevaluates the shape of his text, reverses the order, eliminates two points that
he agrees are obvious (grammar and concise language), and invents a new
thesis.

This is a striking set of moves for an inexperienced writer. More striking
still is his new rhetorical awareness. Remembering that inexperienced writers
will focus attention almost exclusively on their topic (Bereiter & Scardamalia,
1987b; Flower & Hayes, 1980), and that only more "expert" writers take into
account the effect their text will have on readers, we see that listening to how
his text takes shape in the mind of a reader appears to have altered for the
better this writer's rhetorical awareness.

Teaching Students How to
Use Interpretive Reading to Revise

By the time they reach our classrooms, most students have devised a repertoire
of methods for getting feedback. Many ask family members or older peers to
read a paper to see if it "sounds right." What is missing from most writers'
methods, however, is an important element in intentional learning (Bereiter &
Scardamalia, 1987a), namely, a way to test whether readers understand their
texts as the writers intend. "Sounds good to me" is the typical response of

students who avoid negative comments, who think of peer response as completing questions on teacher-made worksheets, and who have little practice in spontaneously discussing the content of their peers' writing (Freedman, 1992). Such "contentless" responses may make the writer feel good, but don't let the writer know if the reader understands key points, perceives the relationship between main points and examples, or is correctly following the sense of the text. Yet getting interpretive feedback is neither time consuming nor difficult.

In the preceding section, we have seen an example of how interpretive reading can help writers identify text problems for themselves. In the classroom, writers can observe a reader processing a text if the reader follows a few simple rules. The reader must (1) read the text audibly, and (2) pause periodically to "think aloud" about the content by (a) summarizing the point and (b) predicting what he or she expects to come next.

Hearing readers work with a text in this way provides an opportunity for firsthand observation of how the text meets the writer's intentions. As readers simply read through the text, their intonation patterns, pauses, and emphases let writers know how difficult or easy they find the reading. Writers may hear readers, for example, lose the thread of long sentences, return to a previous sentence or paragraph to pick up the sense of the text, and stumble over unfamiliar words. As readers pause to summarize their version of what the text is saying, writers observe the shape of the text: what readers judge to be important, the relationship of ideas and the connections between parts. When readers attempt to predict anticipated text, writers hear how their text cues the readers' interpretations. Readers often look back, for example, quoting or rereading the sentence they are noting as they try to guess what might come next.

I introduced these ideas in a three-part lesson during one class period. First, students can discuss a transcript of an interpretive reading. Next, again reading a transcript, they can listen in on a writer using interpretive feedback to revise. Last, they can work with a partner to get a reading of their own text.

Lesson components are of course modifiable. Rather than read the example of an interpretive reading, for instance, students may watch a teacher and student model a reading (see Burnett, Higgins, this volume, on modeling). Students might discuss their own experiences with revising after feedback, the decision rules they use (such as paying more attention to the comments of their teachers than those of their peers), and the alternatives they face at each decision point. During the interpretive reading, students might audiorecord their partners, using the tape later to review the reading. Once a class has practiced the techniques, students often prefer to get several readings for comparison. They might even ask to use a teacher conference as an opportunity for an interpretive reading, as we will see later in this chapter. With practice, students readily design their own methods and add them to their own repertoire (Sitko & Flower, in press).

I developed the following materials for introductory writing classes; they can be adapted to fit many classroom situations. To focus the lesson on activities that may be unfamiliar even to students accustomed to peer response, I provided a handout summarizing key points. The materials consist of

- An excerpt from a transcript demonstrating an interpretive reading.
- An excerpt from a think-aloud protocol showing the decision-making processes of a student revising after interpretive reading.
- A method describing how students can solicit and use interpretive reading as feedback.

DEMONSTRATION OF INTERPRETIVE READING

In the first part of the lesson, students see an example of how interpretive reading works. The excerpt is taken from a transcript of a classroom session in which students were working in pairs, both having written papers in response to the same assignment. The assignment required that they read an article about discourse communities and apply the concept to a language community familiar to the students. The excerpt shows the reader interpreting the writer's text using the interpretive reading method. During the reading, writers were instructed to simply listen without interrupting or entering into discussion, if possible. If they felt inclined to dialog with the reader, they were encouraged instead to remember what they wanted to say and to add those explanations to the text while revising. We will see an instance of such an interruption; because the writer needs more information, he stops the reading to get it.

This interruption illustrates the need for readers and writers to agree on ground rules. Readers must try to say everything that they are thinking about the text, especially if they are encountering problems understanding. If they hold back, writers may feel cheated of the feedback they expect. In the instance reprinted in this excerpt, for example, when the reader indicates that some of the writer's key words need to be defined, but doesn't specify which ones, his class partner holds up the reading until he gets the specific information he needs.

Reader (reading first paragraph, a quotation defining "discourse community"): **Is this the point of the text — the point of the paper? No, I think he's just defining what a discourse community is. I don't think the point has been brought out into the paper yet.**

Text: *Like any other interest group, the sport of crew has its own discourse community. Crew, usually identified as rowing, is the action of moving a vessel through the water by using bladed sticks called oars. Rowing used to be the only reliable source of propulsion for a boat, but today it is practiced for recreation and has become a highly competitive intercollegiate sport.*

Reader: Do I think this is the point? No, not really. I think he is defining what crew is as a sport.

Text: *Crew is a sport that is catching on, but is still not practiced by all colleges and high schools. Being lucky to attend an institution that promoted crew as a means for physical exercise, I got an early start in the sport. Most rowers don't begin rowing until their college years. It is a sport unlike any other sport because you are confined to a sixty-foot shell with a width of twenty-four inches and you have to be in perfect synchronicity with 7 other team members. Any mistake will not only re- duce speed, but throw off balance and precise swinging motion.*

Reader: I think here he has still not brought his point out clearly, but he's getting locked up in what crew is, and his experience – and not so much the language used in crew.

Text: *Most rowers are usually tall and have somewhat short hair.*

Reader: Um, I think this sentence has nothing to do with the language at all.

Text: *During racing season most of them either get flat-top haircuts or very short army style crops.*

Reader: Um, I don't think this has anything to do with it either. I think he's – he's going off on all these tangents all of a sudden.

Text: *It is a psych factor for the teammates because it not only categorizes them as a group, but makes them look mean by increasing their height and the width of their backs.*

Reader: I think . . . he's got some key words here he needs to define.

Writer (interrupting):   Such as what?

Reader: Well like just bring out what you mean – some could be taken in a couple of meanings.

Writer: What are you talking about? Which ones?

Reader: Like – don't worry about it.

Writer: No, you have to say the words, so I know which ones.

Reader: Like – like psych factor – I think you should go back and try and find something else there.

Text: *Rowers tend to have long arms with big hands full of calluses on the inside of their palm and heavy shoulders with a lean upper body.*

Reader: I think what's happening here is he's going off on this tangent of describing what everybody looks like – and not so much of the language – I think he should go . . . into more detail on their language.

Class discussion of this excerpt can help students see how readers look for and construct a point and how predictions help the writer follow his reader's train of thought. Students can note the importance of readers' providing a full interpretation by saying as much as possible about how they are looking at the text. They can also give themselves permission as writers to make the process work for them, even if it means interrupting.

DEMONSTRATION OF REVISING AFTER FEEDBACK

In the second part of the lesson, students read a transcript, a think-aloud showing how the writer in the previous sample used his partner's interpre- tive reading to test and revise his text. Discussing these excerpts, students can trace how reading feedback influenced the writer's decisions. The excerpts emphasize that the writer is an active problem-solver who needs information about how a text is working in order to evaluate whether the text meets his purpose.

Students can see problem-solving processes at work in each segment if they look first at the writer's decision and then work back through his problem formulation and the search for solutions. Three questions can focus students' attention on the problem-solving and decision-making processes evident in each segment:

1. Is there a decision?
2. What is the problem formulated by the writer?
3. Any search for solutions (strategies? alternatives considered?)

Excerpt 1.   (the writer rereads his opening quotation)   Uh most of the words here are above my head, well at the beginning especially, but it — I mean it's a straight quote — I took it out of them um . . . pamphlet . . . in the library . . . so I'm leaving it in . . . I think it sounds good.

2.   (reads text)   *Like any other interest group, the sport of crew has its own discourse community.* OK I'm beginning to talk about crew after I define discourse community. (adds) In crew rowers not only communicate orally, but they also communicate physically. That I think is my thesis statement right there.

3.   (continues to read text)   *and has become a highly competitive intercollegiate sport.* um those things are kind of irrelevant to the paper but . . . I'm going to leave them in . . . because . . . it's just a little background information to rowing . . . and I'm defining rowing and crew . . . so it — I think it's good.

4.   (new paragraph. reads newly added text)   The rowing community speaks in technical terms during a practice session. I'm relating back to my thesis *The first common word one should familiarize themselves with when speaking of crew is "shell," which describes the boats used in rowing.* That's good because I'm introducing "shell," which is a word I'm going to be using throughout the rest of my paper, and by defining it right at the beginning um I can already clear that — you know — the people that will be reading my paper will already know, so my audience will already be set with the word "shell," so I don't have to define it throughout the rest of the paper.

5.   (new paragraph)   The language used in crew is definitely very technical and precise because it has to be. OK I'm going to explain why. (reads) *When on the water no one can physically demonstrate what the rower is doing wrong, therefore every part of the stroke has a different name . . . a different name . . .* OK — explanation has to follow that . . . you know, a different name of the stroke. And I do that. (reads) *A stroke is the motion* OK, I'm defining a stroke first *A stroke is the motion a rower performs in order to propel the shell . . .*

6.   (reads text)   *When on the water the coxswain (the person assigned to steer and call commands) is very repetitive and loud.* OK, it's in parentheses when I say the person assigned to steer and call commands because I'm defining it right away and I switched it — originally I didn't even have that in there.

7.   (reads text)   *This repetition may seem very frustrating and annoying, but since the oarsmen are only concentrating on their technique and power they subcon-*

sciously do what they are told. Right now I'm not secure with the word "oarsman" because I could say oars—it's used—oarswoman or oarsman, and in the paper I'm writing "he or she" so I'm trying to make it . . . um . . . I'm not trying to make it— I'm trying to make it unbiased . . . well, I'll just—I think I'll just stick with "oars- man" . . . just because in general it is known as an oarsman for both . . . um (con- tinues) *Rowers do not*—I mean rowers is both sexes—so it's all right. *Rowers do not only communicate . . .*

8. (reads text) *Other physical communication can be seen by the way they con- duct—by the way they conduct* no I'll have to say—by the way <u>oarsmen</u> conduct themselves in daily life . . . defines that.

9. (reads text) *Rowers like to convey the idea that they are tough by the way they look and act.* It also goes true for girls I guess. *Most rowers are usually tall and have somewhat short hair. During racing season* no it's—it's also—this is for boys right here I'm talking right now for guys . . . um *Most rowers are usually tall and have somewhat short hair.* it sounds like I'm saying the whole—all the rowers are, but I'm generalizing again . . . I should put something in like "most" . . . because let's see— I'm going to say—OK . . . yeah I did say most rowers, OK . . . *Most rowers are usually tall and have somewhat short hair.*

10. (reads text) *Crew is unlike any other*—OK I'm going to have to close—I am— so I'm OK . . . I like it 'cause I'm talking about a little personal experience . . . I am saying that I'm rowing . . . and you know that the person who wrote this paper has rowed and so they kind of do know what they are talking about . . . I introduced myself very subtly . . . which I think was good . . . (reads) *Crew is unlike any other sport in that there is only one person speaking and eight other people following commands. It is also the only sport in which the athletes travel backwards and in which synchronicity is the essential factor.*

As the above excerpts illustrate, revising after feedback engages a writer in a series of decisions. It is sometimes useful to chart this decision-making process in the form of a tree diagram (Figure 9.1). Representing the decisions as a tree not only displays the complexity of what might appear to students to be simply a single choice of whether or not to revise, but also makes obvi- ous the multiple ways in which a student's progress toward revision can be derailed.

As students discuss the series of options in light of the preceding think-aloud as well as in light of their own experiences, they usually add an alternative, looping back to repeat a step. Omitted from the diagram for simplicity, the third option emerges as an important alternative for learning. When writers don't understand a comment, for example, they can return to it to search for more clues. When they are tempted to take the easy way out by blaming the reader, thereby attributing the problem to a cause that they might feel pow- erless to change (Weiner, 1986), they can instead choose the alternative of searching for the source of a misreading. Locating the problem in the text gives writers the advantage of representing the problem as something they can control.

Using the tree, students see that at each comment the writer's first decision is whether or not a reader's interpretation indicates a problem. If the reader's

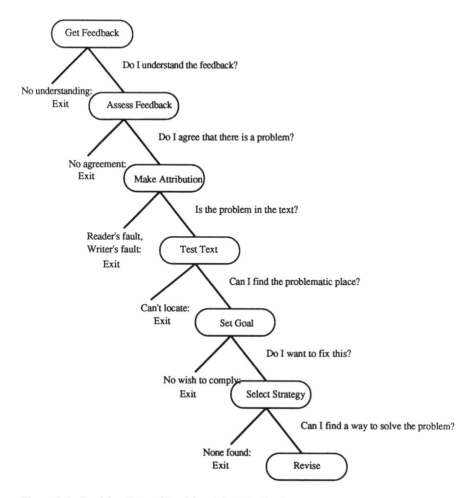

Figure 9.1. Decision Tree of Revising After Feedback

words point to a problem and the writer agrees, the writer must attribute the problem to the text (rather than to the reader's misreading), locate the point in the text that can be altered, decide whether he or she wants to fix the text and then devise a strategy to do so. Whether these choices proceed swiftly or with deliberation, all have to be made to complete revision (Sitko, 1989). Constructing a revision process becomes a complex interplay of writers' own intentions for their text, information from their readers, and their understanding of decision-making.

OBSERVATION OF AN INTERPRETIVE READING

The third part of the instruction can be designed to take advantage of both readers' interpretive process and students' curiosity about how others understand their texts. Building on the first two parts of the lesson in which students have used excerpts of other students' interpretive reading and revising sessions to help them reflect on readers' processes and writers' decisions, in part 3 of the lesson, students work with a partner to get interpretive feedback about a piece of their own writing. I encourage writers to listen and take notes rather than to interrupt or discuss. At this point they concentrate their attention on listening for what their reader's constructive processes can tell them about their text. Later they use the reading to revise.

I summarize this instruction in a handout that focuses discussion on readers' constructive processes, writers' decision processes, and a simple method to get interpretive reading.

INTERPRETIVE READING AS FEEDBACK

Part 1: **Observe a reader summarize and predict, noticing that**
- Readers construct a "point." This "point" influences how they interpret the rest of the text.
- Readers use the point to predict the next move of the text.

Part 2: **Observe a writer use reader feedback, noticing that**
- Writers do not accept feedback uncritically.
- Writers consider alternatives that fit their own goals.
- Writers make decisions: where and what to change.

Part 3: **Observe a partner reading your paper.**
Your reader will use the following plan. If during the reading you feel you need more information, ask for it: "Could you say more about that?"
Paragraph 1:   Read sentence by sentence. At the end of each sentence, ask
Is this the point of the paper?
If no, read next sentence.
If yes, make a gist of the point.
Then predict what will come next in the paper.
Paragraph 2:   Read, stopping at a natural stopping point.
Answer: What is the point of this part?
Then predict what will come next in the paper.
Continue as with paragraph 2.

Students can be guided to experiment with feedback, both in devising ways to get the kind of feedback they need and in deciding how they will use readers' interpretive readings to revise. Such experimentation makes clear to students why they need readers' interpretations and how they can use these different views to reconsider their text and make new decisions. The student whose words will close this chapter describes in her process-tracing paper how in one 50-minute class session of interpretive reading she learned to take charge of her rhetorical choices, take charge of her teacher conference (see Bowen, this volume), and even take charge of her affective response to writing (McLeod, in press).

> On that same day in class, we exchanged papers with our neighbors. This exercise was designed to let us hear our papers read to see if the points which I tried to emphasize sounded as strong coming from another person. Jay read my paper to me first. It was so interesting to hear another person read through my paper. You can see that sometimes the points which you thought were so clearly made were not so clear at all. I could tell from hearing him read my paper that it did not flow together as well as it should have. Listening to this reading proved to be very helpful when it came time to revise my paper. Reading my partner's paper was interesting too. Although the exercise was not supposed to be one for corrections, he often became frustrated with me when I did not clearly emphasize his points. I am sure that we both benefited from listening and reading to one another.
>
> The next day, I went to have a conference with my teacher regarding any revisions that I needed to make. I had her read my paper to me to see if the points which Jay had previously emphasized would be similar. She was very helpful in letting me realize for myself the corrections which needed to be made. I found that I needed more examples to back up my statements. We even made a little adjustment in my thesis statement. Upon leaving the conference, I felt much better about my work and how I was going to revise it.
>
> When the day finally came for me to hand in my three-page final draft, I was ready. I felt that I had learned a lot about how to use the readings assigned in class and incorporate them into a paper. I also felt relieved and accomplished. Those are two of my very favorite feelings.

Throughout this chapter, we have heard students thinking about feedback and making decisions about revising their work. Although the focus of each student's attention is quite different (stylistic awkwardness, statements of purpose and key points, rhetorical arrangement, and whole text reading), their problem-solving and decision-making processes are remarkably similar. Teachers who understand how students represent problems, strategize about their choices, and test the outcomes of their choices can take advantage of these processes by guiding students through comments or in conference. But more important to the purpose of this chapter, students themselves can easily "listen in on" their own processes and, in discussion with teachers and classmates, come to accept not only a broader concept of reading and writing but also a wider representation of the range of their own options. As we see in the last excerpt, some students take the difficult step of pushing beyond their previous limits, construct new ways of testing their texts, celebrate their accomplishments and integrate these new ways of thinking into their own repertoires. Isn't such learning what teaching is all about?

Note

1. Portions of these materials are included in Sitko (1992) and appear with permission. This article describes two studies of revising after feedback.

References

Anson, C. (1989). Introduction: Response to writing and the paradox of uncertainty. In C. Anson (Ed.), *Writing and response: Theory, practice and research*. Urbana, IL: National Council of Teachers of English.

Bartlett, E. J. (1982). Learning to revise: Some component processes. In M. Nystrand (Ed.), *What writers know: The language, process, and structure of written discourse* (pp. 345–363). New York: Academic Press.

Bereiter, C. & Scardamalia, M. (1987a). An attainable version of high literacy: Approaches to teaching higher-order skills in reading and writing. *Curriculum Inquiry, 17*(1), 9–30.

Bereiter, C. & Scardamalia, M. (1987b). *The psychology of written composition*. Hillsdale, NJ: Erlbaum.

Berkenkotter, C. (1984). Student writers and their sense of authority over texts. *College Composition and Communication, 35*, 312–319.

Brannon, L. & Knoblach, C. H. (1982). On students' rights to their own texts: A model of teacher response. *College Composition and Communication, 33*, 157–166.

Britton, J., Burgess, T., Martin, N., McLeod, A., & Rosen, H. (1975). *The development of writing abilities (11–18)*. London: Macmillan.

Doyle, W. (1983). Academic work. *Review of Educational Research, 53*, 159–199.

Ede, L. & Lunsford, A. (1984). Audience addressed/audience invoked: The role of audience in composition theory and pedagogy. *College Composition and Communication, 35*, 155–171.

Flower, L. S. & Hayes, J. R. (1980). The cognition of discovery: Defining a rhetorical problem. *College Composition and Communication, 31*, 21–32.

Flower, L. S. & Hayes, J. R. (1981). A cognitive process of theory writing. *College Composition and Communication, 32*, 365–387.

Flower, L., Hayes, J. R., Carey, L., Schriver, K. A., & Stratman, J. (1986). Detection, diagnosis and the strategies of revision. *College Composition and Communication, 37*, 16–55.

Flower, L., Schriver, K. A., Carey, L., Haas, C., & Hayes, J. R. (in press). *Planning in writing: The cognition of a constructive process*. In S. Witte, N. Nakadate, & R. Cherry (Eds.), *A rhetoric of doing: Essays on written discourse in honor of James L. Kinneavy* (pp. 181–243). Carbondale: Southern Illinois University Press.

Freedman, S. W. (1987). *Response to student writing*. Urbana, IL: National Council of Teachers of English.

Freedman, S. W. (1992). Outside-in and inside-out: Peer response groups in two ninth-grade classes. *Research in the Teaching of English, 26*(1), 71–107.

Gagne, E., Crutcher, R., Anzelc, J., Geisman, C., Hoffman, V., Schutz, P., & Lizcano, L. (1988). The role of student processing of feedback in classroom achievement. *Cognition and Instruction, 4*(3), 167–186.

Geisler, C. (1992). Exploring academic literacy: An experiment in composing. *College Composition and Communication, 43*, 39–54.

Glover, J., Ronning, R., and Bruning, R. (1990). *Cognitive psychology for teachers*. New York; Macmillan.

Hayes, J. R. (1989). *The complete problem solver*. Hillsdale, NJ: Lawrence Erlbaum.

Hayes, M. & Daiker, D. (1984). Using protocol analysis in evaluating responses to student writing. *Freshman English News, 13*, 1–5.

Hillocks, G. (1982). The interaction of instruction, teacher comment, and revision in teaching the composing process. *Research in the Teaching of English, 16*, 261–278.

Hillocks, G. (1986). Research on written composition: New directions for teaching. Urbana, IL: NCTE/ERIC.

McLeod, S. (1987). Some thoughts about feelings: The affective domain and the writing process. *College Composition and Communication, 38*, 426–435.

McLeod, S. (in press). *Notes from the heart: Affect and the writing process.* Carbondale, IL: Southern Illinois University Press.

Meyer, B. (1982). Reading research and the composition teacher: The importance of plans. *College Composition and Communication, 33*, 37–49.

Newkirk, T. (1978). Direction and misdirection in peer response. *College Composition and Communication, 35*, 301–311.

Olson, G. M., Duffy, S. A., & Mack, R. L. (1984). Thinking-out-loud as a method for studying real-time comprehension processes. In D. Kieras & M. Just (Eds.), *New methods in reading comprehension research.* Hillsdale, NJ: Lawrence Erlbaum.

Ornstein, R. & Erlich, P. (1989). *New world, new mind.* New York: Doubleday.

Sitko, B. (1989). Writers' cognitive and decision processes: Revising after feedback. Unpublished doctoral dissertation. Carnegie Mellon University.

Sitko, B. (1992). Writers meet their readers in the classroom: Revising after feedback. In M. Secor & D. Charney (Eds.), *Constructing rhetorical education* (pp. 278–284). Carbondale, IL: Southern Illinois University Press.

Sitko, B. & Flower, L. (in press). Metaknowledge in writing: The fruits of observation-based reflection.

Sommers, N. (1980). Revision strategies of student writers and experienced adult writers. *College Composition and Communication, 31*, 378–388.

Sommers, N. (1992). Between the drafts. *College Composition and Communication, 43*, 23–31.

Spivey, N. N. (1987). Construing constructivism: Reading research in the United States. *Poetics* 16.

Stauffer, R. (1969). *Teaching reading as a thinking process.* New York: Harper and Row.

Vipond, D. & Hunt, R. (1984). Point-driven understanding: Pragmatic and cognitive dimensions of literary reading. *Poetics*, 13.

Weiner, B. (1986). *An attributional theory of motivation and emotion.* New York: Springer-Verlag.

Wittrock, M. (1986). Students' thought processes. In M. Wittrock (Ed.), *Handbook of research on teaching* (pp. 297–314) (3rd ed.). New York: Macmillan.

Ziv, N. (1984). The effect of teacher comments on the writing of four college freshmen. In R. Beach & L. Bridwell (Eds.), *New directions in composition research* (pp. 362–380). Urbana, IL: National Council of Teachers of English.

10

Using Conferences to Support the Writing Process

BETSY A. BOWEN

Conversations between students and teachers about writing are not new, but in the past twenty years they have gained considerable attention as an effective tool in teaching writing. Researchers and theorists, such as Murray, Moffett, and Graves, have argued that students need to talk about drafts in progress with skilled, attentive readers. Recently, research on cognitive processes has begun to consider writing conferences as sites where writers may reveal something about the goals and decisions that influenced their writing. As a result, writing conferences, with teachers or with peers, have become a prominent part of new approaches to teaching writing.

Enthusiasm for writing conferences has not been limited to theorists. Teachers and students—the people who matter most—have found that writing conferences can profoundly change the teaching of writing. At the University of New Hampshire, where weekly writing conferences have been part of the freshman composition program for more than fifteen years, Carnicelli (1980) examined student evaluations of their effectiveness. He found students almost unanimous in their support for conferences, even students who were otherwise unenthusiastic about writing. In fact, in the more than 1800 evaluations he analyzed, no student reported learning more from class than from the writing conference.

Teachers who have used writing conferences have found them equally productive. In a study sponsored by the National Institute of Education, Freedman and colleagues (1985) surveyed 500 teachers nationwide who had been identified as outstanding by their principals or department heads. When asked to select the most effective means of responding to student writing, these teachers overwhelmingly chose writing conferences. (Perhaps equally significant is that these teachers rated written comments on final drafts – the traditional response to student writing – as the *least* effective means of response.)

Other potential benefits of conferences are more difficult to discern but at least as important. Some researchers believe that conferences can encourage metacognitive awareness. Studies by Flower (1988), Flower and Hayes (1984; Hayes et al., 1987), Scardamalia and Bereiter (1982, 1985), and others have uncovered some of the complex cognitive processes writers employ as they write and revise. Writers search and organize their prior knowledge; they set goals for their texts and test their developing draft against their goals. While the connection between a writer's cognitive processes and the conference dialog needs to be examined further, conferences clearly give teachers a special opportunity to talk about the thinking students do as they write.

Conferences also provide opportunities for modeling language different from most classroom discourse. Initial research (Freedman et al., 1985; Cazden, 1983) suggests that teachers may engage in different kinds of talk in conferences than in whole-class discussions. Students, too, may have the chance to talk differently, with longer conversational turns and more sustained development of a topic. Students who do not have the linguistic abilities that full participation in the classroom demands may benefit particularly from the enriched talk in the conference.

Wertsch (1985) suggests that the talk that goes on in conferences may have an additional benefit. Using Vygotsky's (1978) concept of the social origin of higher order skills, he argues that learners first develop new skills in interpersonal relationships and then internalize those skills in new forms. If so, the talking and thinking a student shares in the conference may enable her later to carry out these same skills independently. This intriguing speculation, however, remains to be tested.

In a more straightforward way, writing conferences do seem to help writers transfer skills to new contexts. Sowers (1982) offers anecdotal evidence of this. Freedman and Greenleaf (1984) provide more extensive evidence of transfer and discuss the conditions required to bring it about.

These and other studies of conferences have only begun to exploit the potential of conferences for revealing something about the cognitive processes of writers. They suggest further questions that we might ask about the relationship between what happens in the writing conference and what we know about the intellectual activities employed in writing. How well, for instance, can writers articulate the intentions they had for the draft or the constraints they felt were imposed by the audience or genre? What comments in the conference suggest that the writer's goals for the text were more sophisticated than the text itself indicates?

This chapter will examine some of what we have learned about writing conferences in the past two decades and consider what conferences may reveal about the assumptions, strategies, and decisions that shape writing.

What We Know About Writing Conferences

Most simply, the writing conference is a conversation between writer and reader about a text in progress. In the conference, the student talks about the piece, the decisions she made as she wrote it, the problems she sees in it, and what she plans to do next. The teacher listens, follows, offers suggestions. Above all, the teacher asks questions — questions that push the writer to talk about what she intended her draft to say, what she knows about her topic, the decisions she made while planning and writing, and the options she sees now for her writing. Donald Graves (1983) maintains that this "simple, yet highly complex act of helping someone to speak can't be left to chance" (p. 97). The principles that underlie good conferences have begun to be revealed by the research of the past two decades.

This research has been rich and varied. Our initial understanding of conferences came from the reflections and anecdotal reports of Murray and others. By the mid-1970s, their work was supplemented by descriptive studies of writing conferences in a variety of contexts. Studies by Graves and his colleagues, in particular, added to our understanding of the ways teachers use writing conferences to help young students develop as writers. (See, for example, Calkins, 1986; Graves, 1983; and Sowers, 1982.) Recently, Freedman and colleagues at the Center for the Study of Writing-Berkeley (1982, 1984, & 1985), Walker and Elias (1987), and other researchers have undertaken more fine-grained analyses of what happens during writing conferences.

At the same time, research on metacognition, by Flower, Hayes, and colleagues (1984, 1988; Hayes et al., 1987), Scardamalia and Bereiter (1982, 1985, & 1986), Palincsar (1986), and others, has illuminated some of the generally covert processes involved in planning and writing. This research, reviewed in Chapter 1 and throughout this volume, has revealed ways in which writers understand the rhetorical context in which they work, develop plans and goals, employ strategies for realizing those goals, and develop mental representations of their emerging drafts. While these two strands of research — naturalistic observation of classroom practices and process tracing research on writing — have sometimes been seen as incompatible, more recent work suggests that they can inform each other to provide a rich understanding of what happens as we write. Certainly that seems to be so in studying writing conferences. As writers in a conference discuss their intentions for a text or evaluate that text and its problems, they provide information about the possibilities they perceive in their texts and the information they have available to them.

Obviously conference transcripts are not straightforward records of participants' thoughts during the conference. The conversation is constrained by factors such as time, the limits of the writer's recollection and his or her desire for privacy, and by such social factors as participants' respective positions within the institution. Nevertheless, we should expect conferences to offer us some information about the processes of writing and revising that have been the focus of much process tracing research.

These two strands of research have highlighted four critical characteristics of effective conferences. *First, effective conferences are characterized by reversible role relationships* (Cazden, 1983; Graves, 1983; Freedman, 1982; Jacobs & Karliner, 1977; Meier, 1985; Sperling, 1990). Unlike most classroom activities, conferences allow both student and teacher to take the lead in discussion. Either speaker may introduce topics, ask questions, make hypotheses. Linguists, such as Cazden (1983) and Ninio and Bruner (1978), have observed that these reversible role relationships characterize fundamental learning between parents and infants and enable learners to take on an increasingly active role in the exchange as their abilities develop. Reversible role relationships may likewise help students develop advanced competence as speakers.

Second, these conferences provide the opportunity to discuss both process and product (Calkins, 1986; Graves, 1983; Murray, 1979, 1982; Scardamalia & Bereiter, 1986; Sowers, 1982). While written comments on student drafts tend to deal with the text alone, writing conferences ask the student to consider both the draft and the process by which she brought it about. The teacher or peer may, for instance, encourage the writer to reflect on her implicit definition of the writing task or her perception of the needs and goals of her intended audience. Students who are aware of their writing process have additional resources when they encounter new problems in writing.

Third, conferences offer writers carefully attuned support (Calkins, 1986; Graves, 1983; Freedman, 1982; Freedman & Sperling, 1985; Meier, 1985). This support may enable students to do with assistance what they could not yet do on their own. As the student's ability increases, the conference partner's assistance decreases until the student is able to take over the activity on her own. Vygotsky's (1978) concept of the "zone of proximal development" — or the range of activities a child can currently do with assistance and will soon be able to do independently — seems to be at the foundation of the teachers' and researchers' interest in this carefully regulated collaboration.

Finally, conferences provide a predictable structure for writers (Graves, 1983; Sowers, 1982). Graves and Sowers both maintain that a predictable structure in the conference frees students to concentrate on what is most important and makes it easier for them to internalize the principles of the conference. Students, Graves argues, should know that when they have a conference they will be expected to speak first, they will be asked to talk about what they wrote and how they wrote it, and that at the end of the conference they will be expected to have a plan for what to do next with the draft.

As we incorporate conferences into the classroom, we may need to reexamine other classroom practices in order to create an environment in which conferences can be effective. That may mean changing other ways in which we teach writing that, tacitly or explicitly, keep students dependent on us as writers. Otherwise, Meier (1985) warns us, we will "reduce a highly complex process to an overly prescriptive and simplistic technique." When that happens, Michaels, Ulichny, and Watson-Gego (1986) and Jacobs and Karliner (1977) point out, the conference becomes little more than a charade from which neither teacher nor student really benefits.

This research on conferences suggests a number of guidelines for using them effectively in the classroom.

1. *Expect the writer to speak first.*   When students begin to take responsibility for their own writing and are encouraged to speak as experts about it, they grow as writers. In addition, students who know they will be expected to initiate the conversation learn to review their own writing as they prepare for a conference.

2. *Ask questions about what is essential in the draft.*   Graves (1983) suggests that teachers begin by "receiving" the piece, restating in their own words what they understood from the draft. This response helps students see how well what they intended to say in the draft comes across to a reader. It also encourages student and teacher to begin with the meaning of the text and the writer's intentions, rather than being distracted by surface-level errors.

Sowers (1982) recommends questions that help writers reflect on what they have done in the draft, expand their ideas or plans, and select appropriate material or strategies for developing the text. In the end, however, there are no "magic questions" (Sowers, 1982), only an attentive, informed listener and a writer working on a text.

3. *Ask questions to develop students' metacognitive awareness.*   The purpose of conferences is to develop better writers as well as better writing. Conferences provide unique opportunities for revealing and reflecting on the decisions that underlie writing. In fact, writers often experience a developmental lag in which their intentions exceed their performance. They may form sophisticated intentions for their text long before they can execute those intentions skillfully. As a result, students' written work on its own gives an incomplete picture of their writing ability. Conferences supplement that picture by enabling us to see more about the knowledge and decisions involved in writing.

We can help students become more self-aware as writers by asking them to think about what they do as they write. We might ask, How did you decide to start the piece this way? How do you think this section works to support the point you're making? We can also help students consider new strategies and become sensitive to constraints and possibilities that they have not yet discovered on their own. Teachers use questions such as, What other relationship could you establish with your readers? How would that affect their reaction to your text? What if you had wanted to reconcile the two sources that you considered – how could you have done that? Questions like these push students to think about their thinking.

4. *Keep conferences focused.*   It is tempting to "overteach" in a conference, to try to resolve all the problems in a draft. Instead, by discussing in depth even a single problem in the text you may provide the writer with a model for solving problems on her own.

Looking Closely at Conferences

We can learn more about the work that goes on in conferences by looking at sections of several conferences drawn from a study of collaborative revision

(Bowen, 1989). The study examined a series of conferences between students and peer tutors using the cognitive model of revision developed by Hayes and colleagues (1987). That model depicts revision as an interaction between cognitive processes—such as evaluating the draft or selecting strategies to remedy problems—and the knowledge that these processes both depend upon and generate. Writers, Hayes et al. maintain, draw on a variety of skills and kinds of knowledge in revising, including their perception of the writing task, their implicit definitions of revision, their sense of the rhetorical situation, their subject-matter knowledge, and their ability as readers.

The study was designed to determine, first, the extent to which a cognitive process model of revision could account for what happened in conferences and, second, what such a model might reveal about the ways in which speakers collaborated on revision in the conference. The results of this analysis help us answer a variety of questions such as whether tutors help students develop more fully elaborated definitions of their task and what criteria participants relied on as they evaluated the draft or plans.

Two features of the conferences are noteworthy. First, each conference involved college students and writing tutors, not teachers. We can expect student-tutor conferences to differ from student-teacher conferences in several, possibly contradictory, ways. Clearly tutors are closer to students than teachers in age, experience, and social status. As a result, Bruffee (1984) points out, discussions between peers—or in this case, near-peers—may be more truly collaborative than discussions between students and teachers and, as such, a better introduction to the process by which knowledge within disciplines is socially constructed and maintained. If Bruffee's assessments are accurate, we might expect to see relative parity between the participants, with each introducing new topics, evaluating the draft or plans, and speaking roughly the same amount during the conference.

At the same time, however, student tutors are generally less experienced than writing teachers at responding to other students' drafts and may lack confidence. Tutors may, as a result, be timid in offering a response or, at other times, overly prescriptive, relying on inadequate or inappropriate models of response from their previous experience. It may be particularly difficult for tutors to help students reconsider the decisions they made while writing or the assumptions they made about the writing task. We may expect, then, to see relatively little discussion of writers' decisions and strategies in these conferences and, possibly, greater attention to the surface features of the drafts.

A second notable feature of the conferences examined here is that they occurred as part of a university's "writing across the curriculum" effort. Students were writing for courses in art, history, psychology, and mathematics. While not "experts" in those fields, the tutors all had previous experience with the conventions and expectations of those disciplines.

We can learn about these conferences most easily by looking at one that the student, at least, considered unsuccessful. In an interview after the conference, this student reported that she felt her needs were not met in the conference and that she felt "misled" by the tutor's comments at their previous meeting. The tutor herself said that she was unhappy with her conferences overall.

In examining the small section that follows, consider why both participants felt unsatisfied by their collaboration in the conference. The excerpts are taken from the second half of the conference; the last two lines occurred a bit later, at the end of the session. (Throughout the transcripts, punctuation has been added and "place fillers" such as "um" and "ah" have been deleted to make the dialog easier to follow. Square brackets indicate overlapping speech, with both participants speaking at the same time. "T1" designates the tutor; "S1" designates the student.)

```
T1   You have to just clarify the introduction a little bit more so that I
     can
S1      okay [so that you know what I'm talking
T1           [so that we know what you're going to talk about. And other
     than that I thought it was good. And change these topic sentences so
     that you're not breaking it up by the tables.   You're breaking it up by
     the different [variables
S1              [variables
T1                      that you're looking at
S1                                   okay
T1                                         make sure that you
     keep referring in parentheses to the tables
S1                                     alrighty


                             . . .


T1   And that's really it unless you have any questions
S1                                     no nothing
```

In this section, as throughout this conference, the tutor's and student's roles differ sharply. The tutor does most of the intellectual work—evaluating the draft, detecting and diagnosing problems, suggesting alternative goals for the piece. The student is left merely to agree with the tutor's assessment. The only time the student offers an extended remark, the tutor overlaps it with her own comment. Throughout the conference, the student finds little opportunity to participate and is offered very limited advice about how she might revise her goals for the piece or develop the strategies needed to realize them. It is not surprising that by the end of the conference, the student is so disengaged that she declines the tutor's late invitation to participate.

Several productive kinds of discussion are missing from this episode. The tutor does not push the student to reflect on the choices she made—or could have made—as she wrote. She does not, for instance, ask the student to·talk about what she had intended in the introduction, nor does she help her consider other ways of defining the task at that point. Moreover, the tutor does not involve the student in the assessment of the draft; instead, she detects problems and identifies solutions by herself.

The difficulties in this conference may have a variety of causes: participants' narrow or incompatible senses of their roles; the tutor's lack of sophistication about the writing process and writers' needs; an unwillingness to take on the difficult work that a productive conference may require. Whatever the causes, the effects are clear: dissatisfied participants and little likelihood that the writer will learn skills she can transfer to other contexts.

Contrast this first conference with the excerpts that follow from another student-tutor conference. The student and tutor in this conference are discussing a draft written in response to the same assignment as in the first conference. The tutors in both conferences had comparable training and tutoring experience, but the interaction in the two conferences is markedly different.

The first episode occurs at the start of this conference, after some greetings and preliminary comments. Here, the student begins by talking about his plans for a paper that examines relationships between economic variables and the public's reactions to the Great Depression.

s2   I just tried to make a few points you know from what I could see in the data
     without like really caring that much for style 'cause, like, I really didn't do an
     introduction or a conclusion or anything
T2   exactly
s2   or anything like that
T2   What's your thesis though? I didn't really seem to get a hold of
s2   of [well I
T2   [What's your
     thesis for this book? Did you find the question really broad?   Did [you
s2   [yeah it is, it
     is but I think I could probably tie it together better
T2   um huh
s2   if I just gave it a little
     more thought
T2   Did you have a general thesis when you went into this? Like, how
     did you want to approach this?
s2   Oh I was just, well I was just looking at the
     drafts to see the different trends between the variables and then I just thought
     of reasons
T2   um huh
s2   to explain why these things happened.

Several features of this conference dialog are worth noting. The episode begins with the student explaining his intentions in the draft. The tutor then asks about the thesis, making an implicit but clear judgment that the writer's thesis needs work. However, instead of merely detecting this problem or supplying a solution of her own, the tutor inquires about the sources of the problem ("Did you find the question really broad?"). Four turns later she probes again, asking the student how he had wanted to approach the task. While it may be impossible for a writer to reconstruct precisely his intentions while composing, these questions invite the student to recall, and possibly reconsider, some of the decisions he made while writing. The student's explanation continues at length and eventually reveals what the student and tutor interpret as a source of his problems in the draft.

In the brief excerpt that follows, we can see this tutor checking the accuracy of her interpretation of one point in the draft. The cognitive process model of revision suggests that, for individual writers, such text representation is an essential part of revision, since it enables writers periodically to update their sense of the text. In the conference, this not only allows the tutor to test her understanding but also prompts the student to explain his intentions in the passage.

T2   What you're trying to say is that — you're saying that the majority of the people under $1000
S2   um huh
T2   were comfortable?
S2   Right, right, although this one's kind of harsh because there's a, there's a — it seems to have a — I would look for this to — there's like a general — see this whole area? (pointing to a chart in the draft)
T2   um huh
S2   It seems to be pretty heavy
T2   okay

The student's hesitation and twisted syntax in his last two turns suggest that he still finds it difficult to explain the point he intended to make in that section. As the dialog continues, the tutor and student try to figure out together how to make sense of the economic data that had confused him.

A final episode from the conference shows the tutor helping the student recognize and remedy a problem in his draft. The tutor and student have been working on the issue raised in the preceding episode — what the student meant to claim about people who earned less than $1000. Now they turn to a particular sentence. (Italicized text indicates material being read aloud from the student's draft.)

T2   Actually read it just from here
S2   Read it from here?
T2   Yeah, *One note*
S2   *One note of int/* Got it. Well, you want me to read it?
T2   Yeah, [you can
S2   [Okay. *One note of interest* I, I, when I read that sentence again I realized that it was a pretty, pretty hard one to handle. *One note of interest is the fact that a number of observations in the "Very Comfortable" and the "Very Uncomfortable" categories* That, um . . . *range from low to higher and higher to low respectively from right to left with increased income.* Ah, that's really bizarre!
T2   [laughs]
S2   I was kind of tired when I was writing this and I guess I was going for the idea rather than the syntax or message.
T2   Well, tell me what's going on there.

At the start of the excerpt, the student seems to recognize that the tutor's request that he read a sentence aloud indicates that she feels there is a problem in the sentence. He demurs initially, then reads and identifies a problem himself. After finishing the sentence, the student continues his assessment. The tutor agrees, pressing him at the end to sort out what he meant to say himself.

This analysis of the two conferences is not meant to suggest that there is a single "good" or "bad" pattern to which conferences may conform. Numerous observers of conferences have pointed out the ways in which conferences vary depending on the needs of the student and the ability of the tutor or teacher. (See, for example, Graves, 1983; Sperling, 1990.) Instead, this analysis suggests some of the ways that a cognitive process model can help "unpack" what is going on in conferences. The model helps us consider the kinds of decisions participants make in the conference and the knowledge or assumptions that shaped those decisions. It helps us to determine how planning and revision done in a conference differ from those same activities carried out by writers working individually. Such information enables us to make better informed decisions about the ways we use conferences and what we expect to accomplish in them.

Learning from Conferences in Your Classroom

Teachers and students can benefit from examining the talk that goes on in writing conferences and the implications that talk has for learning. The final section of this chapter discusses ways in which we and our students can begin to understand how writing conferences function in our classrooms.

EXAMINING CONFERENCES YOURSELF

The best way to begin is simply to tape some of your conferences and listen to them. What do you hear? What seems to be going on? You may feel pulled to determine if the conference is "successful," but resist that temptation initially if you can. If you begin by trying to judge—rather than describe—the conferences, you are likely to overlook the particulars of what is going on. It is in those particulars—the negotiations about meaning or intentions—that you can see most about students' learning.

After you have listened to a few of your conferences, you may want to find a small section that intrigues you and transcribe it. You do not need to transcribe everything you record; if fact, trying to do so is probably counterproductive. Transcribing a section so that you can see how your remarks and the student's interact makes it easier to get a sense of the conversation. As you look at sections you transcribe, ask yourself some of the following questions:

- Who is talking? For what proportion of the time? Does that proportion differ from student to student, or with one student over the semester?
- What sorts of remarks do students make? Do they introduce topics of

their own in the conference? Do they ask questions? Disagree? Make hypotheses of their own?

- Do the participants help the writer, or one another, develop a more fully elaborated representation of the writing task? Do they work toward better articulated diagnoses of problems in the text or plans?
- When does the teacher or tutor check his impression, or mental representation, of the draft against the writer's intentions? How close a match is there between the two?
- How do you negotiate differences? When and how do students' intentions for their pieces prevail? When do yours prevail? How do you accommodate the tension between guiding students to see new possibilities and encouraging their independence as writers?
- To what extent does the conversation focus on global issues, such as the writer's sense of audience or purpose? To what extent on local issues, such as an unclear sentence?
- How frequently are exchanges genuinely collaborative, with both participants contributing substantively to the dialog? How often are exchanges managed independently, with one participant talking and the other silent or nearly so?

Research on writing offers some guidance about what characterizes an effective writing process. Sommers (1980) and Bridwell (1980) found, for instance, that skillful revision is characterized by the ability to make changes at the global level. Scardamalia and Bereiter (1982, 1985) have found that young students see writing as "knowledge telling," while older or more sophisticated writers have a broader and more rhetorically based sense of their task.

Nevertheless, writers' needs and the role of conferences vary so much that it would be naive to expect conferences to follow a particular pattern. Sometimes the student benefits from the chance to talk at length about her topic; sometimes she needs you to talk and help her see options she did not know she had. Sometimes it is appropriate to talk about surface-level problems; at other times students need to work on reconceptualizing the content of their drafts. The understanding you develop from looking carefully at your conferences helps you make these decisions more effectively. Examining conferences in this way can also help tutors or graduate students learn what to look for in their dialogs with students.

HELPING STUDENTS EXAMINE THEIR OWN LEARNING

Students benefit too from looking at the interaction in conferences. While students are generally accustomed to analyzing literature or other students' writing, most are unaccustomed to analyzing talk. You may want to have students listen to tapes of conferences in groups of three or four. Ask the group to listen to the tapes and use the questions listed above to guide their analysis of the interaction. Have them pick out a section that seems especially interesting and try to figure out what is going on.

Doing this analysis teaches students to recognize and describe the strategies writers use. In addition to helping students develop the metacognitive awareness necessary for critical reflection on their own work, such activities can provide the basis for discussion of students' roles as peer readers and make students better able to support other writers in the classroom.

References

Bowen, B. (1989). Talking about writing: Collaborative revision in peer writing conferences. Doctoral dissertation. Carnegie Mellon University.

Bridwell, L. (1980). Revising strategies in twelfth-grade students' transactional writing. *Research in the Teaching of English, 14* (3), 197–222.

Bruffee, K. (1984). Collaborative learning and the "conversation of mankind." *College English, 46*(7), 635–652.

Calkins, L. (1986). *The art of teaching writing*. Portsmouth, NH: Heinemann.

Carnicelli, T. A. (1980). The writing conference: A one-to-one conversation. In P. Donovan & B. McClelland (Eds.), *Eight approaches to teaching composition* (pp. 101–132). Urbana, IL: NCTE.

Cazden, C. B. (1983). Peekaboo as an instructional model: Discourse development at home and at school. In B. Bain (Ed.), *The sociogenesis of language and human conduct* (pp. 33–58). New York: Plenum.

Flower, L. (1988). The construction of purpose in writing and reading. *College English, 50*, 5: 528–550.

Flower, L. & Hayes, J. R. (1984). Images, plans, and prose: The representation of meaning in writing. *Written Communications, 1*: 120–160.

Freedman, S. W. (1982). Student-teacher conversations about writing: Shifting topics in the writing conference. Paper presented at the annual meeting of the Conference on College Composition and Communication, San Francisco.

Freedman, S. (1985). The role of response in the acquisition of written language. Final Report to the NIE; NIE-G-083-0065.

Freedman, S. W. & Greenleaf, S. (1984). The acquisition of skill: Intuition and conscious knowledge during instruction. Paper presented at the annual meeting of the American Educational Research Association, New Orleans.

Freedman, S. W. & Sperling, M. (1985). Written language acquisition: The role of response and the writing conference. In S. W. Freedman (Ed.), *The acquisition of written language: Revision and response*. Norwood, NJ: Ablex.

Graves, D. (1983). *Writing: Teachers and children at work*. Exeter, NH: Heinemann Educational Books.

Hayes, J. R., Flower, L., Schriver, K., Stratman, J., & Carey, L. (1987). Cognitive processes in revision. In S. Rosenberg (Ed.), *Advances in applied psycholinguistics*, Vol. II (pp. 176–240). Cambridge: Cambridge University Press.

Jacobs, S. & Karliner, A. (1977). Helping writers to think: The effect of speech rate in individual conferences on the quality of thought in student writing. *College English, 38*, 489–505.

Meier, T. (1985). The social dynamics of writing development: An ethnographic study of writing development and classroom dialogue in a Basic Writing classroom. Doctoral dissertation. Harvard University Graduate School of Education.

Michaels, S., Ulichny, P., & Watson-Gego, K. (1986). Writing conferences: Innovation or familiar routine? Paper presented at the annual meeting of the American Educational Research Association, San Francisco.

Murray, D. M. (1979). The listening eye. *College English, 41*, 1: 13–18.

Murray, D. M. (1982). Teaching the other self: The writer's first reader. *College Composition and Communication, 33*, 2: 140–147.

Ninio, A. & Bruner, J. (1978). The achievement and antecedents of labelling. *Journal of Child Language*, 5: 1–15.

Palincsar, A. (1986). The role of dialogue in providing scaffolded instruction. *Educational Psychology, 21* (1 & 2), 73–98.

Sommers, N. (1980). Responding to student writing. *College Composition and Communication, 31* (4) 378–88.

Scardamalia, M. & Bereiter, C. (1982). Assimilative processes in composition planning. *Educational Psychology, 17*, (3), 165–171.

Scardamalia, M. & Bereiter, C. (1985). Fostering the development of self-regulation in children's knowledge-processing. In S. Chipman, J. Segal, & R. Glaser (Eds.), *Thinking and learning skills*, Vol. 2. Hillsdale, NJ: Erlbaum.

Scardamalia, M. & Bereiter, C. (1986). Research on written composition. In M. Wittrock (Ed.), *Handbook of research on teaching* (pp. 778–803). New York: Macmillan.

Sowers, S. (1982). Three responses in the writing conference: Reflect, expand, select. In T. Newkirk & N. Atwell (Eds.), *Understanding writing*. Exeter, NH: Heinemann.

Sperling, M. (1990). I want to talk to each of you: Collaboration and the teacher-student writing conference. *Research in the Teaching of English, 24*, 3: 279–321.

Walker, C. & Elias, D. (1987). Writing conference talk: Factors associated with high- and low-rated writing conferences. *RTE, 21*, 3: 266–285.

Wertsch, J. (1985). *Vygotsky and the social formation of mind*. Cambridge, MA: Harvard University Press.

Vygotsky, L. (1978). *Mind in society*. Cambridge, MA: Harvard University Press.

APPENDIX

Conducting Process Research

If we could actually hear ourselves think, studying reading and writing processes would be an easy and straightforward task. Of course we can't—we can only listen for individual notes and sequences and try to pick up the melody. The process-tracing methodologies described in this volume share two important features: they aim to describe processes rather than products, and, in doing so, they do not tell the whole story or catch the whole tune. Working with process data, as with any other type of data, is an interpretive act: we make inferences about writers' goals, strategies, and understandings based on clues gathered from their notes, drafts, process logs, interview responses, protocol comments. To use the Hayes and Flower (1980) visual metaphor, we see the porpoise only when it breaks the surface of the water; from these glimpses we infer the path it follows below.

In the classroom and in other research settings, we enhance our chances of gathering rich and telling data by carefully controlling the circumstances under which we conduct our research and by being aware of the nature of those circumstances. We are careful not to generalize too far, for example, from studies in the lab or in the classroom, where particular sets of constraints (on time, audience, motivation) apply. And we are careful to clearly articulate the nature of our interest to the writers and readers we study. For example, when we collect "think-aloud" protocols, we want writers to verbalize their thoughts, plans, and strategies as they work, but we don't want them to step back and narrate those processes for us or to reflect on or interpret their actions. We just want to catch them in the act of reading or writing. In this volume, Haas (Chapter 2) asked students to think aloud while reading in order to determine whether they noticed text features or speculated about the context of the passage they read. Penrose (Chapter 4) used the protocol technique to trace the way students transformed source text material into their own drafts. In both cases, protocol transcripts provided a running account of what readers and writers attended to as they worked. Students were asked to report, not to analyze their processes.

On the other hand, when we ask students to keep a process log or to write other sorts of retrospective reports, we want the benefit of their hindsight: we want them to reflect on their actions, their motivations, and the contextual influences they perceive. When Nelson (Chapter 6) asked students to use process logs to describe their steps in the research process, she was interested not just in when they went to the library, but also in why they chose the topics and strategies they did and in how they evaluated the sources they found. The logs provided rich information about students' attitudes and concerns as well. When Greene's students (Chapter 3) commented retrospectively on their writing processes, they were encouraged to explain their strategy choices and to reflect on alternative approaches. Retrospective reports can provide valuable information about writers' choices and the reasons behind them.

When we ask students to provide verbal reports, we need to be sure they understand the specific purpose of the research technique. We can do this easily by providing explicit instructions and by demonstrating the technique for them. For example, the students in the protocol study Penrose describes in Chapter 4 received instructions like those in Figure A.1.

It's also useful to have students do a quick practice protocol, perhaps on a different type of task. Greene's students, who gave think-aloud protocols in addition to the retrospective reports mentioned above, practiced thinking aloud first with a math problem and then with a summary task. Any of these warm-up activities help students become comfortable with thinking aloud and help them understand the nonreflective nature of the task. In contrast, Nelson used the directions in Figure A.2 to help students in her process log study understand that reflection is an expected and necessary component of retrospective reporting.

Many dimensions of reading and writing processes have been studied via verbal reports. Think-aloud protocols have been used to study planning strategies (Perl, 1979; Flower & Hayes, 1981; Berkenkotter, 1983), revision (Flower et al., 1986), the influence of prior knowledge on writing (Ackerman, 1991), monitoring processes (Durst, 1989), and the cognitive demands of writing tasks (Durst, 1987; Langer & Applebee, 1987). Retrospective reports have provided insights into writers' attitudes, interpretations of academic tasks (Sternglass & Pugh, 1986), search strategies (Nelson & Hayes, 1988), summary strategies (Garner, 1982), and reading processes (cf. Afflerbach & Johnston, 1984).

The value and validity of verbal report techniques have been much debated. Some observers worry that thinking aloud may interfere with natural processes, that retrospective reports may be unintentionally distorted, that both

Thinking Aloud

In this writing study I am interested in two things, your products and your processes. The "products" of your work, your notes and drafts, will be pretty easy for me to examine. However, examining the process you went through in developing those products is a bit more difficult. Psychologists have developed a technique called the "think-aloud protocol" to help them look at the processes people go through as they work on different kinds of tasks. For example, researchers have had people think aloud while solving arithmetic problems, while playing chess, and while working out arguments in writing. I'll be asking you to use this technique as you work on your writing and studying tasks.

The technique is very simple. Basically, your job is to speak out loud as you work. We'll tape the sessions, and later I'll have transcripts made of the tapes. Then I'll be able to look at the transcripts and see just what you were doing as you worked.

The only rule to remember in giving a protocol is *keep talking*. Say whatever comes to mind as you read, as you jot notes, as you write, as you sit & think, etc. Don't describe or analyze what you're doing, just keep verbalizing your thoughts. Don't worry about speaking eloquently or using complete sentences. Just say what you're thinking. Do try to speak clearly and audibly. The procedure will seem a little awkward at first, but after a few minutes most writers seem to forget about the tape. Just concentrate on your writing.

The following is a brief excerpt from a protocol. As this excerpt begins, I am reading a passage about asteroids and meteorites. The reading material is in italics in the transcript; the words I'm writing are underlined. Follow along with the transcript as you listen to the protocol.

> . . . *the orbit of this asteroid will take it past the Earth's orbit at perhaps ten times the moon's distance. Planeta—* . . . wait a second . . . wait . . . so that means its orbit is ten times . . . wider than . . . the moon's orbit? . . . hmm . . . okay . . . wait a sec . . . wait . . . let me just jot this stuff down . . . so the <u>orbit</u> . . . the orbit seems to be . . . is <u>10 ×</u> the <u>moon's</u> . . . *Planetary astronomers who have been using spectroscopy to determine the composition of thousands* . . . *of already catalogued asteroids turn their equipment on this new* . . . *object* . . . okay so they want to find out the <u>composition of the</u> the composition of the <u>asteroid</u> . . . and <u>we know its orbit</u> . . . okay . . . um . . . what else have I got here? . . .

As this example illustrates, sometimes you will just be reading parts of the article out loud. Sometimes you'll be reading some notes or sentences as you write them. And sometimes you'll just be thinking out loud. Remember, the primary rule is *keep talking*.

Figure A.1. Think-Aloud Protocols: Sample Instructions for Students

techniques provide incomplete and unreliable information, that interpretation of verbal data is necessarily subjective. In formal studies, researchers employ rigorous coding procedures and reliability checks in order to minimize interpretive bias or inconsistencies. For further discussion of the conduct and validity of protocol methodology, see Hayes and Flower, 1983; Cooper and Holzman, 1983; Ericsson and Simon, 1984; Dobrin, 1986; Steinberg, 1986; Smagorinsky, forthcoming. On the use of retrospective reports, see Garner, 1984; Afflerbach and Johnston, 1984; Tomlinson, 1984; Sternglass and Pugh, 1986; Greene and Higgins, forthcoming.

Why Keep a Process Log?

We are interested in finding out how people go about completing particular kinds of writing assignments, in this case, a research paper. Above all, we are interested in your natural way of doing things and do not want to interfere with your natural processes. Your job is to keep a record in a log of all the work you do on this paper, from daydreaming to writing. Don't think that any part of this process is irrelevant; just jot down a log entry every time you ponder, talk, read, write, or do any kind of work on your paper.

We also want you to keep copies of all notes (even very informal scribblings), drafts (even material you end up not using), and of course, the final paper. Clearly we want to trace the entire process you go through to create your research paper. Once you begin thinking seriously about your paper, start making regular entries in your log, even if all you have to report is that you didn't work on the paper that day. Don't worry if you have to report "no work" many times; we know that everyone works at their own pace.

The following kinds of information *might* appear in your log entries:

- Conversations with other people or conferences with teachers.
- Decisions about the topic or focus of your paper.
- Names of books or other sources you find useful or reject.
- Your comments on how to evaluate the usefulness of an idea or source.
- Copies of notes you take, including library jottings or notes while writing the paper.
- Insights that come to you while taking a shower or walking to school.
- The research trail you follow in the library.

Figure A.2. Process Logs: Sample Directions for Students

In classroom use, we usually interpret verbal reports less formally, examining transcripts and logs impressionistically to determine, for example, whether readers notice an author's moves or attend to context (Greene, Haas), to observe how different writers approach a given task (cf., Penrose, Nelson, Higgins), or to see where readers have trouble with our texts (Schriver, Sitko). However, in these settings it is equally important that student researchers maintain an objective perspective on the research task. If they are to provide accurate accounts of their processes and concerns, they must understand not only the nature of the research task (e.g., to report only or to report and reflect) but also the consequences of the activity. If students suspect these tasks will be graded, for example, they may assume there is a "right answer" or a right approach and try to produce it, thereby defeating the exploratory purpose of the activity. Even when we are recording naturally occurring verbal activities such as collaborative work sessions (cf. Burnett, Chapter 7) or writing conferences (Bowen, Chapter 10), we need to be sure that students understand the descriptive goal of such research. Process observations provide a means for developing rather than testing knowledge about writing and reading. The value of the classroom activities described in this volume depends on students' appreciation of the exploratory nature of these inquiries: students must truly see themselves as researchers, aiming to learn more about the processes of writing and reading.

References

Ackerman, J. (1991). Reading, writing, and knowing: The role of disciplinary knowledge in comprehension and composing. *Research in the Teaching of English, 25,* 133–178.

Afflerbach, P. & Johnston, P. (1984). On the use of verbal reports in reading research. *Journal of Reading Behavior, 16,* 307–322.

Berkenkotter, C. (1983). Decisions and revisions: The planning strategies of a publishing writer. *College Composition and Communication, 34,* 156–169.

Cooper, M. & Holzman, M. (1983). Talking about protocols. *College Composition and Communication, 34,* 284–293.

Dobrin, D. (1986). Protocols once more. *College English, 48,* 713–725.

Durst, R. (1987). Cognitive and linguistic demands of analytic writing. *Research in the Teaching of English, 21,* 347–376.

Durst, R. (1989). Monitoring processes in analytic and summary writing. *Written Communication, 6,* 340–363.

Ericsson, K. A. & Simon, H. A. (1984). *Protocol analysis: Verbal reports as data.* Cambridge, MA: The MIT Press.

Flower, L. & Hayes, J. R. (1981). Plans that guide the composing process. In C. H. Frederiksen & J. F. Dominic (Eds.), *Writing: The nature, development, and teaching of written communication,* Vol. 2 (pp. 39–58). Hillsdale, NJ: Erlbaum.

Flower, L., Hayes, J. R., Carey, L., Schriver, K., & Stratman, J. (1986). Detection, diagnosis, and the strategies of revision. *College Composition and Communication, 37*(1), 16–55.

Garner, R. (1982). Verbal-report data on reading strategies. *Journal of Reading Behavior, 14,* 159–167.

Greene, S. & Higgins, L. (in press). "Once upon a time": The use of retrospective accounts in building theory in composition. In P. Smagorinsky (Ed.), *Verbal reports and the study of writing.* Newbury Park, CA: Sage Press.

Hayes, J. R. & Flower, L. (1980). Identifying the organization of writing processes. In L. N. Gregg & E. R. Steinberg (Eds.), *Cognitive processes in writing.* Hillsdale, NJ: Erlbaum.

Hayes, J. R. & Flower, L. (1983). Uncovering cognitive processes in writing: An introduction to protocol analysis. In P. Mosenthal, L. Tamor, & S. S. Walmsley (Eds.), *Research on writing: Principles and methods.* New York: Longman.

Langer, J. A. & Applebee, A. N. (1987). *How writing shapes thinking: A study of teaching and learning* (Research Rep. No. 22). Urbana, IL: National Council of Teachers of English.

Nelson, J. & Hayes, J. R. (1988). *How the writing context shapes students' strategies for writing from sources* (Tech. Rept. No. 16). Berkeley: Center for the Study of Writing.

Perl, S. (1979). The composing processes of unskilled college writers. *Research in the Teaching of English, 13,* 317–336.

Smagorinsky, P. (in press). Think-aloud protocol analysis: Beyond the black box. In P. Smagorinsky (Ed.), *Verbal reports and the study of writing.* Newbury Park, CA: Sage Publications.

Steinberg, E. R. (1986). Protocols, retrospective reports, and the stream of consciousness. *College English, 48,* 697–712.

Sternglass, M. S. & Pugh, S. L. (1986). Retrospective accounts of language and learning processes. *Written Communication, 3,* 297–323.

Tomlinson, B. (1984). Talking about the composing process: The limitations of retrospective accounts. *Written Communication, 1,* 429–445.

Index